INFLATION ACCOUNTING

INFLATION ACCOUNTING

Elwood L. Miller, Ph.D., CPA

Saint Louis University

VNR VAN NOSTRAND REINHOLD COMPANY
NEW YORK   CINCINNATI   ATLANTA   DALLAS   SAN FRANCISCO
LONDON   TORONTO   MELBOURNE

Van Nostrand Reinhold Company Regional Offices:
New York Cincinnati Atlanta Dallas San Francisco

Van Nostrand Reinhold Company International Offices:
London Toronto Melbourne

Copyright © 1980 by Litton Educational Publishing, Inc.

Library of Congress Catalog Card Number: 79-22065
ISBN: 0-442-21909-1

Manufactured in the United States of America

Published by Van Nostrand Reinhold Company
135 West 50th Street, New York, N.Y. 10020

Published simultaneously in Canada by Van Nostrand Reinhold Ltd.

15 14 13 12 11 10 9 8 7 6 5 4 3 2 1

Library of Congress Cataloging in Publication Data

Miller, Elwood L
  Inflation accounting.

  Bibliography: p. 207.
  Includes index.
  1. Accounting—Effect of inflation on. 2. Account-
ing and price fluctuations. I. Title.
HF 5657.M53   657'.48   79-22065
ISBN 0-442-21909-1

To my teammate,
Virginia

Preface

In 1920, John Maynard Keynes warned in *The Economic Consequences of the Peace* that:

There is no subtler, no surer means of overturning the existing basis of society than to debauch the currency. The process engages all the hidden forces of economic law on the side of destruction, . . . All permanent relations between debtors and creditors, which form the ultimate foundation of capitalism, become so utterly disordered as to be almost meaningless; and the process of wealth-getting degenerates into a gamble and a lottery.

Now, 60 years later, businessmen have yet to appreciate the warning that inflation represents the only *real* threat to capitalism and free enterprise. This book may help businessmen to recognize that any short-term benefits that accrue to some sectors as a result of our inflation psychology are not worth the long-term risk. An aroused business community *has* the influence to bring the government inflation machine to a halt.

The credibility of accounting—the language of business—has also been challenged by inflation. In response, the accounting profession has not evidenced much of the pragmatism (or common sense) with which it has been credited. Accounting students learn, early on, that the ability *to interpret* separates the accountant from the book-keeper. Yet, members of the accounting profession have evidenced precious little willingness to call for and review the fairness (or common sense) of interpretations of financial reports on the part of the business community, much less make any interpretations themselves. Instead, they have sought out and clung to normative (simplex) methods that can make economic sense only by accident when applied to situational (complex) problems. This book attempts to encourage some rethinking by accountants.

Until inflation is arrested, businessmen and accountants have been furnished with the perfect vehicle for returning credibility to financial reports—FASB *Statement No. 33.* This book sets the stage for and examines the *Statement.* Businessmen are perceived to have two choices: restore credibility to financial reports by using *candor* and *reasoned explanations,* or, permit we accountants to further garble the language of business with more normative approaches that produce economic nonsense.

Elwood L. Miller

Acknowledgments

All works are built upon the ideas of others. This book is no exception.

The thoughts and suggestions of the many pioneers and contemporary writers concerning inflation accounting have been appropriately acknowledged. However, the seeds of ideas implanted by countless teachers and associates—many whose names have been forgotten—have been woven into the weft and the warp of this book, unacknowledged but not unappreciated.

Each person is held to be a debtor to his or her profession. Accountancy has been good to me. Inflation accounting has been smoldering for some time and represents the first real challenge to the retention of accounting standards in the private sector. I have been convinced that the effects of changing prices can only be explained, in words and supporting numbers, by managements, primarily, and by accountants, secondarily. A consensus exists just below the surface of most discussions. The means exist, we have but to put them to use. Recognition and implementation would serve the best interests of the business community, the accounting profession, and the many publics they serve. Perhaps this book will help.

Particular gratitude is owed to many. My wife, Virginia, typed each word many times, provided constructive criticism, and served as a willing (and demanding) taskmaster. Special appreciation is due the editors and publishers of *Harvard Business Review* for their permission to use portions of my article, which appeared in the November–December 1978 issue. Special thanks must also go to the editors at Van Nostrand Reinhold for their interest and efficiency.

Errors of omission or commission are mine.

Suggestions and comments are invited and would be appreciated.

LIST OF FIGURES

LIST OF TABLES

Contents

INFLATION ACCOUNTING

1
The Malady — Inflation

It is by no means coincidental that inflation is consistently described as a disease. What does seem unusual, at least on the surface, is that the virulence of the disease has not been recognized by those who are in a position to do something about it.

As a pestilence, inflation is much more insidious than any plague the world has experienced to date. A plague infests openly, destroying the physical substance of mankind. There is usually a single cause, or very few causes, to combat. Few persons, if any, can be said to benefit and, therefore, few act to impede efforts toward discovering and administering a cure. Inflation, on the other hand, is much more treacherous. It attacks the economic and social substance of mankind in myriad ways not readily apparent. Inflation has many causes, each feeding upon the other. Some individuals, companies, and governments benefit from inflation—at least in terms of the present or the near future. These benefits, whether real or illusory, serve to inhibit curative measures. Symptoms are treated superficially at times, while the disease is permitted to run its course virtually unabated. These conditions will persist until accountants, economists, business people, and elected officials finally recognize that the disease of inflation represents the only *real* threat to capitalism and free enterprise.

This chapter will examine the nature of the international disease known as inflation—its symptoms, its effects, and the medications suggested by prominent economists.

In the process, accountants may well benefit from recall and reconsideration of the economic phenomena they propose to account for. More often than not, inflation will be recognized as a complex malady that does not affect all parts of an economy (or a complex enterprise) in the same way. Medications and accounting treatments that have been suggested often reflect different perspectives and interests.

CAUSES OF INFLATION

Inflation has several meanings. In the context of price levels, inflation represents a persistent, upward trend in the level of general or average prices. Conversely, from the standpoint of money, inflation means a general downward movement over time in the purchasing power of money.

Much like the proverbial accountant's stool, inflation has been around for a long time. Other than serving as another issue for economists to ponder, inflation was not of widespread concern in the United States (since it averaged slightly less than 2% per year) until the late 1960s. Then, conditions and events transformed inflation into a household word—as well as a global disease. Movements of the consumer price index in the United States since 1935, together with related events, are shown in Figure 1–1.

Economic Theories

Among economists, there does not appear to be any more of a consensus regarding causes of inflation than there is among accountants concerning how to account for inflation. Stones are not being cast at either group. The observation simply indicates the nature of the organism known as inflation. It is a persistent and ever-increasing evil, much like the mythical Hydra—lop off one of its heads and it grows two others. Simplified versions of the more familiar theories of inflation are presented in order to illustrate the complexities that exist.

Too Much Demand. The seeds of the demand-pull theory were planted by John Maynard Keynes' work, *General Theory of Employment, Interest and Money,* published in 1936. Keynes' interest

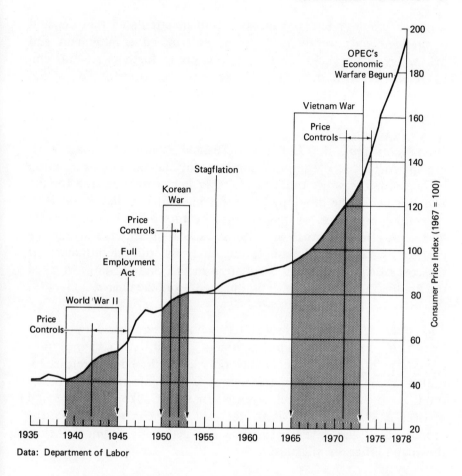

FIGURE 1-1. CONSUMER PRICES AND RELATED EVENTS, 1935-1978.

was in unemployment, not inflation, but he stipulated that demand determined output which, in turn, determined employment and prices. Sir John Hicks carried the reasoning further. At full employment of men and capital, excessive demand for goods and services drives up the general level of prices. This concept is often translated as too much demand chasing too few goods and services.

Overemployment. In 1958, a New Zealand economist, Alban W. H. Phillips correlated the level of employment and the rate of inflation in England. His work today is probably better remembered for the "Phillips curve" he developed than for his evidence that, as the level of employment rose or fell, so did the rate of inflation. Governments, in effect, were faced with a tradeoff—price stability at the cost of some unemployment, or, relatively full employment at the cost of some inflation. Stagflation in the United States wrecked the Phillips curve; recent inflation pushed it off the charts.

Too Much Money. The monetarist school, exemplified by Milton Friedman, makes the simple argument that inflation cannot proceed very far without the money on which to feed. Therefore, inflation results when too much money is available to bid up prices on the existing goods and services. In effect, like the goods and services it chases, money is treated as a *stock concept.* Reduce the money stock and, given a lag time, the economic engine will slow down and inflation will subside.

The Velocity of Money. The neo-Keynesians agree that money matters but it is not all-important. They consider money a *flow concept.* Money has a velocity, or rate at which it circulates and multiplies itself. Recipients of money have liquidity preferences, or reasons to spend or store money in various ways. This group argues that outputs of goods and services, as well as the prices charged for them are determined exogenously; that is, without dependence upon money supply. The money stock and the velocity at which it circulates are reactive; they adjust to the demand. In effect, inflation is considered to be primarily a political phenomenon.

The two preceding views of the roles of money can be illustrated by the following equation of exchange:

$$M \cdot V = P \cdot Q$$

where

M = money supply
V = velocity of money
P = price level
Q = quantity of ouput

The monetarists consider V as a constant. If M increases faster than Q can respond, then P must increase. The neo-Keynesians stipulate that P and Q are set by producers; both M and V merely respond to the needs of the goods markets.

Cost-Push. Sir John Hicks and others blamed rising costs for rising prices. Today, such escalations are aided and abetted by market imperfections. Oligopolists are charged with setting prices between those which keep the least efficient member content (the floor), and those which invite government intervention (the ceiling). Monopolists, by definition, charge what they please. Labor also is accused of cost-push tactics (wage-push or union-push). Strong industrial unions, able to negotiate wage increases greater than productivity increases, better their position at the expense of other sectors of the economy. Even worse culprits yet are said to be those workers in the service sector who receive wage increases that can be offset little, if any, by greater productivity.

Bottlenecks. For a variety of reasons, a strong demand for goods within a single industry will occur although aggregate demand remains stable. Increases result in wages, prices, and profits in the industry affected and, directly or indirectly, influence other sectors of the economy. Where the products are intermediate goods, the higher prices flow through to all users resulting in cost-push. Indirectly, other sectors often press for increases since, like people, they wish to keep up with the Joneses. This process, known as structural or sectoral inflation, is possible in industrial countries since prices of manufactures are notorious for their upward flexibility and downward rigidity. Prices of raw materials tend to fall as well as rise since most are susceptible to substitution. (Petroleum has been a unique exception, at least to date, yet its technological displacement will come about eventually.)

Bail-out Inflation. By means of the Employment Act of 1946, the U.S. Government accepted responsibility for promoting full employment, as well as preventing both depression and inflation. Bail-out inflation is said to result when the government primes the pump to increase lagging demand and avoid unemployment. Two results have been cited. First, increases in both wages and prices occur but real income remains unchanged. Second, the business cycle is flattened since the normal bottoming is either prevented or diminished. Price and wage levels are shored up artificially thereby banking the fires of inflation.

Markup Inflation. A relative of cost-push, markup inflation results from the application of a constant rate of markup by producers and sellers. As the input costs of goods and services increase, the addition of a constant markup rate results in larger absolute increases in output prices as well as profits. This is a common ailment of free-enterprise economies and persists in virtually all sectors, except those in serious decline. The impact of markup inflation is most significant on those products passing through many intermediate hands in the process of manufacture and distribution.

Economic Realities

Much like theories of accounting, economic theories that appear neat on the surface become untidy when confronted by economic realities. Two reasons appear to be plausible. First, inflation has been considered a national phenomenon and has been examined in that framework by many economists. Second, inflation has been regarded as a temporary infection of industrial countries that could be cured by application of selected patent medicines, and the passage of time.

An International Disease. Hindsight indicates that, in the United States, the germs of a new, virulent strain of inflation were ingested during the 1956–1958 period. The military-industrial complex emerged with sabers rattling, since society paid little attention to the earlier warnings of President Eisenhower.[1] Economists coined a new word, "stagflation," to describe the simultaneous occurrence of significant inflation and unemployment during a business recession. Textbook theories of free market mechanisms became the first victims of the new disease.

From 1965 through 1972, the remaining economic theories didn't have an opportunity to test their mettle because of political skull-duggery. The Johnson administration, during 1965–1968, attempted to supply both guns and butter during the Vietnam conflict—while concealing the real cost of the guns. The Nixon group was also less than honest during the 1969–1972 epidemic of inflation—Phases I and II of the price-control program were allegedly disemboweled by generous boosts in money supplies to stimulate growth and assure re-election.

By 1973, economic wounds were festering in the United States and elsewhere. Most developed nations reached peak industrial capacities at about the same time; shortages resulted in many basic materials. Demands for armaments began to strain economies. New nation-states emerged, each an eager consumer attempting to develop overnight. The world population exploded. Disastrous weather conditions created short supplies of many foodstuffs. Prices of commodities were further inflated by widespread speculation. The telling blow, of course, was struck in 1973 by the Organization of Petroleum Exporting Countries (OPEC) as oil prices were increased from about $2.50 to more than $11 a barrel.

OPEC did not create inflation, but it exacerbated it in every nation that imported oil. In effect, OPEC declared economic warfare on the rest of the world and, in one stroke, transformed inflation into an international disease, respecting neither national boundaries nor economic systems. In addition, because of the other economic pressures existing at the time, inflation became extremely pervasive. The contagion was transmitted among countries by means of trade linkages. This spill-over effect left few nations untouched by the malady. Once considered the bane of developing countries, double-digit inflation infected the industrial world. (Figure 1-2.)

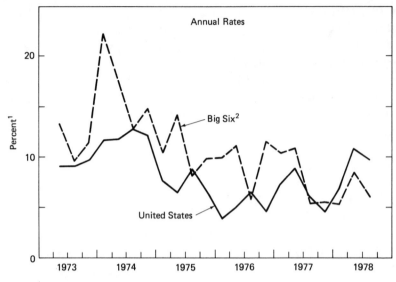

[1] Percent change from preceding quarter at annual rate

[2] Japan, Germany, France, United Kingdom, Canada, and Italy data based on 1977 GNP/GDP weights and exchange rates

Source: *Economic Report of the President,* transmitted to the congress January 1979, p. 138.

FIGURE 1-2. CONSUMER PRICE INFLATION RATE IN THE U.S. AND SIX MAJOR INDUSTRIAL COUNTRIES.

A Persistent Malady. Prior to the OPEC debacle, most economists attempted to diagnose and treat inflation not only as if it were a national ailment but a temporary one as well. Stagflation rudely dispelled naive beliefs that free markets and unemployment would reduce inflation, given time. Free markets became hard to find, if in truth many existed at all after the Industrial Revolution. Also, unemployment rates in excess of 9% were not capable of dampening prices in 1975. Economic realities transformed inflation from a temporary illness to a persistent malady.

Government myopia. The government, it seemed, could (or would) do little right. It tried to satisfy the insatiable needs of people, business, and the military-industrial complex without much concern over the wherewithal needed.

It increased minimum wages, indexed social security benefits, and created welfare programs that made it more profitable to loaf rather than work. It raised social security taxes and promulgated environmental, health, and safety regulations that escalated costs and prices.

The government meddled with markets and prices. It boosted farm price-supports and paid farmers not to produce. It attempted to defend endangered industries that had permitted themselves to become fossilized (steel, textiles, railroads, and shipping are examples). It had the gall to suggest that U.S. domestic oil prices be decontrolled and determined by the whims of the most infamous cartel in history. On the other hand, it rebuked Mexico for offering the United States natural gas at reasonable, negotiated prices and for volunteering to bear the construction costs of the pipelines necessary.

The government acceded to pressures of the military-industrial complex until the aggregate annual costs of the Department of Defense (including military fringe benefits, pensions, and a pro-rata share of the interest costs of the national debt) exceeded the total income taxes collected in 1975 and 1976 from every individual taxpayer in the United States! (See Table 1-1.) During 1977, defense consumed only 90 cents of every individual's tax dollar primarily because inflation boosted individual tax revenues by 19%. For the 3-year period, 1975-1977, defense expenses consumed 99 cents of every individual's income tax dollar.

The armed forces have been retained at high levels because Congress bases personnel strengths upon the top-heavy number of officers—and this is permitted in a technological age in which it would be difficult to justify the continued garrisoning of troops.

The cumulative effects of continued deficit spending earned the government the dubious title of "the great government inflation machine."[2]

Business greed. Business moaned about inflation yet didn't hesitate to spread the infection. Free competition was cheered, so long as it affected another's industry and market. Big business grew even bigger by means of mergers and acquisitions that provided both vertical and conglomerate integration. Prices in more and more industries became established by fewer and fewer industrial leaders. Prices were increased in spite of lagging demand and excess capacity; steel is an excellent example.

Table 1-1. U.S. Individual Income Tax Revenues and National Defense Expenses, 1975-1977.[a] (Amounts in billions.)

	U.S. GOVERNMENT FISCAL YEARS		
	1975	1976	1977
Individual income tax revenues	$122.4	$131.6	$156.7
Defense expenses:			
National defense	$ 73.3	$ 83.1	$ 90.8
Income security:			
Military personnel	23.1	28.1	17.8
Veterans compensation	14.2	4.7	12.5
Veterans benefits	9.4	9.0	7.7
Subtotal	120.0	124.9	128.8
Pro-rata share of net interest expense	10.2[b]	10.7[b]	11.5[b]
Total defense expenses	$130.2	$135.6	$140.3
Defense expenses over (under) individual income taxes	$ 7.8	$ 4.0	$ (16.4)
Defense expenses as a percentage of individual income taxes:			
Per Year	106%	103%	90%
For the 3-year period		99%	

Notes:
(a) For prior years, details on income security are not available.
(b) Interest calculations:

	1975	1976	1977
1. Defense subtotal	$120.0	$124.9	$128.8
2. Total government expenses	$385.2	$433.9	$470.3
3. Line 1 ÷ line 2	31.15%	28.79%	27.39%
4. Total interest expenses	$ 32.7	$ 37.1	$ 41.9
5. Line 3 × line 4	$ 10.2	$ 10.7	$ 11.5

Sources of data: Consolidated Financial Statements of the United States Government, Fiscal Years 1976, 1977.

As the dollar declined overseas and the costs of imports rose, U.S. auto manufacturers also boosted their prices and reaped windfall benefits. Steel producers screamed to the government for help even as exchange rates and ocean freight costs raised the landed costs of steel imports in the United States. Business offset rising interest rates by creating an interest-futures market. Brakes on money supplies, when they were imposed, were sidestepped by tapping foreign financial markets. Prices for most goods were established at what the traffic would bear, plus—to protect against possible price controls, rebates and money-off coupons were widely used.

With the exception of a very small number of products for which prices were reduced by technology and foreign competition, manufacturers had little difficulty in passing inflation through in their scramble for advantage.

Labor pressure. Labor unions joined in the scramble. The more powerful unions were able to keep abreast of inflation, if not acquire additional real income and fringe benefits. Power, not productivity, became the negotiating basis. Business resisted to a point, then passed the increases along together with an added markup. Regional and national agreements tended to lessen the resistance of business since all members of an industry would be similarly affected; no particular firm or group of firms would be placed at a disadvantage. Three-year contracts with built-in cost-of-living adjustments reduced the pains of bargaining and inflation—and reinforced the downward inflexibility of wages and prices.

Salaries of government employees were raised to the levels of their so-called civilian counterparts (although similarities of function and risk rarely existed), regional differences in costs-of-living were not reflected, and escalator clauses were instituted.

Even military salaries were increased to conform with their mythical civilian counterparts, but retirement benefits, based upon the more meager salary scales, were not revised downward. Military personnel can, without contributing a dime "retire" at a ridiculously low age (41 for the average enlisted man, 46 for the average officer); collect more in retirement pay than earned while in uniform (132% and 144% for enlisted and officer personnel, respectively); and enjoy no restrictions on the amount or source of earnings after "retirement." Many military retirees with narrow skills simply doffed the uniform for civilian clothes and acquired similar positions in the Civil Service—a practice known as "double dipping." Costs of military pensions have been called awesome. They rose from $1 billion annually in 1964, to $10 billions today, more than $30 billions in 20 years, and, unless revised, could reach $100 billions per year for those now in uniform. (A commission studied the pension program and submitted recommendations for change to the President in April 1978.)[3]

Political self-interest. Politicians must share criticism for showing evidence of more concern over votes than economic sense. Spend now, pay later became a practicable ploy. Future interest costs on the national debt (now larger than the annual sales of General Motors) were hidden by the government's cash-basis accounting systems, could be passed on to future generations, and never came up for a vote. The concerns of business, people, and inflation rose and fell in ascendancy. As inflation filled the tax coffers to overflowing, tax cuts were doled out from time to time to assuage outcries, yet provided rough justice, at very best. Efforts to reduce money supplies increased unemployment and led to expansionary responses. Unemployment became feared more than inflation. These chameleonlike actions to restrict, expand, then restrict again produced a form of "roller-coaster inflation ranging from 4% to 10% per year."[4]

Inflation in the United States has become a persistent malady having many causes, each feeding upon the other. Attempts to identify a single cause—or a few causes—to treat in isolation are fruitless endeavors. People cause inflation, not inanimate things like money or goods. People institutionalize inflation by building its effects into their future expectations, whether the people represent consumers, businesses, or governments. These expectations become a significant and intractable cause, as well as an effect, of the disease.

EFFECTS OF INFLATION

Inflation has been described as a complex malady. As such, it affects some, but not all, and in various ways and degrees. It afflicts the poor and the weak more readily than the rich and powerful, whether individuals or nations. The short-term effects are obvious. Less obvious, and therefore more insidious, are the medium- and longer-term effects.

Short-Run Effects

Inflation represents the cruelest tax on those with fixed incomes. It impoverishes the aged. While the Consumer Price Index increased

40% over the last six years, the prices of necessities soared more than 66%. Food consumed at home increased over 50%. Utility costs have more than doubled since 1968, rising at an average rate twice that of the Consumer Price Index. Costs of medical care have soared more than 300% since 1970. Poor persons on fixed incomes are often faced with the choice of paying for food, or rent, or utilities.

Industries are confronted with steadily rising costs and, like consumers, find that some critical commodities are more volatile than others. The indices of producer prices (shown in Table 1-2) indicate clearly that inflation does not affect the prices of all industrial goods to the same extent.

Economic growth is curtailed. Business reduces investment as uncertainty makes otherwise desirable ventures too risky. Productivity diminishes as long-term investments are sidelined in favor of temporary ones. Industrial capacity becomes inadequate to provide the jobs needed, unemployment rises, and bail-out measures are used as temporary balms.

Table 1-2. Selected Producer Price Indexes, Seasonally Adjusted, December 1978 (1967 = 100).

CATEGORY	GROUP	PRODUCER PRICE INDEX
Crude materials		252.4
	Foodstuffs	224.7
	Fuel	494.9
	Other	249.5
Finished goods		202.1
	Consumer foods	215.4
	Consumer durables	171.9
	Capital equipment	206.6
Industrial commodities		217.0
	Textiles	163.5
	Fuels	334.1
	Chemicals	202.2
	Rubber	179.6
	Furniture	163.7
	Lumber	288.7
	Metals	236.6

Source of data: Department of Labor, Bureau of Labor Statistics.

Wage earners adopt inflation psychology (resort to escalator clauses, cost-of-living adjustments, long-term contracts) and confuse rising money wages with real income.

Medium-Term Effects

There is a trend from savings to consumption—if not consumerism. Consumers dip into savings in order to buy now in advance of expected higher prices. The ratchet effect on prices lowers the standard of living of the middle class and ruins retirement hopes.

Savings and capital move from soft to hard or stable currencies. Those nations struggling to emerge, and having the greatest needs for new capital infusions, find few providers. Traditional financial markets are virtually wrecked. Debt becomes more readily available and attractive than equity capital. Business is faced with a capital crunch and strained liquidity while seeming to enjoy an earnings glut. Business complaints merely create a credibility gap in the minds of the public. New financial markets spring up to capitalize on opportunities—the new market in interest-rate futures is an example.

The period of significant inflation in the United States has, in the author's opinion, evidenced effects of the medium term.

Longer-Term Effects

Economists argue that the long run is a myth that never materializes. Economic organisms exist, or cease to exist, only in the short run. Were such the case, inflation would not pose such a threat. Unfortunately, the long-term effects of rampant inflation, left unchecked, are all too evident in many countries.

A crisis of confidence in money occurs. Small investors desert the stock markets. Money is either spent as it is received or stored in more tangible forms: land, gems, gold, Krugerrands, and the like. The adequacy of the funding of pension programs becomes threatened as present costs become impossible for firms and employees alike. Reported money-levels of wages and profits distort the decisions of businesses, governments, and unions.

A significant redistribution of purchasing power is brought about since not everyone or every nation is worse off as a result of inflation. Debtors gain, while creditors tend to lose. (In the U.S. economy, financial institutions and households traditionally have been net creditors.) Governments grow fat on confiscatory taxes levied on businesses and individuals. Cheating the tax collector becomes the national pastime. The priority of government expenditures increasingly becomes determined by the "squeaky-wheel" technique—the sector screaming loudest receives the oil.

The distinctions between economic classes become more apparent as the gulfs between the strata widen perceptibly. Class unrest ensues. The traditional social frameworks and institutions are questioned and, often, are discarded without the presence of something of value to replace them. The government, as a social institution, also becomes threatened and, as a defensive measure, resorts to the use of widespread controls.

In the author's opinion, barring a depression of global scale, inflation in the United States can only lead to government controls. Politicians have little at risk. Accountants, economists, and business people must recognize that the disease of inflation represents the only real threat to capitalism and free enterprise. *Curing inflation* must be accepted as the goal. Problems of reporting the effects of inflation are miniscule in comparison.

ECONOMIC REMEDIES

While accountants have argued over how to account for inflation, economists have concerned themselves with seeking cures for the disease. Many medications have been suggested. This should not be surprising given the nature of the illness described. Space permits only abbreviated versions of the remedies proposed by some of the eminent, contemporary economists.

Patent Medicines

Historically, the presence of some inflation has been considered an unwelcome but necessary symptom of economic growth in industrial countries. Growth and unemployment were considered opposites; encouraging the former ameliorated the latter. However, expansionary and inflationary forces moved in the same direction.

Remedies suggested were usually admixtures of fiscal and monetary policies, together with fine tuning as needed. Although the remedies sounded easy, much depended upon guess and chance. Timings of the medications were fraught with problems of lead and lag times, as well as dependence upon individuals to respond collectively in the same fashion to a particular stimulus. For example, tax cuts may be used by consumers to reduce outstanding indebtedness first before serving to stimulate demand. Also economic advisers deal in aggregates. Dysfunctions in selected sectors of the economy can nullify the intended effects of a given action. Finally, fine tuning represents an educated guess, at best, where aggregate data in complex economies are concerned.

Indexation

Milton Friedman, and others (including the author), are convinced that contemporary inflation in the United States is largely a political phenomenon. Consequently, political remedies must be administered before economic medications can be effective.[5]

Indexation of government taxes and borrowings is the first, essential step. Only one congressional decision would be required as opposed to continuous hagglings for comparative tax advantages. Indexation of federal taxes would become automatic as individual tax brackets (not rates) would be adjusted based upon movements of a selected inflation gauge, such as the Consumer Price Index. Corporate incomes would also be adjusted by the same (or a similar) index in order to determine the taxable base. Income taxes would then be levied upon a reasonable approximation of real income (at least to the extent that the incomes to be taxed moved with the index applied). Thereafter, refinements could be introduced in pursuit of greater equity. For example, geographical indexation might be considered. Similarly, the continued desirability of many of the anomalies existing in corporate taxation might be reconsidered— LIFO costing and accelerated depreciation are two examples. Inequities would continue to surface but, on balance, the indexation proposal mentioned would certainly represent an improvement over the rough equity resulting from the indirect indexation methods used by Congress in the recent past.

The indexation of government borrowings and interest payments would close the loop. Those holding government securities would be assured of the maintenance of the purchasing power of their principal invested as well as the real interest expected. The arbitrary confiscation of the wealth of the small saver by the U.S. Government is a particular disgrace. The current rate of nominal interest on U.S. savings bonds is approximately 6%, well below the rate of inflation since 1972. Adding insult to injury, the government also taxes the alleged interest earned—savers have no benefit such as the dividend exclusion afforded those who play the stock market. In sum, the government extracts a portion of the real wealth of small savers while deluding them with promises of a return on their investments in their country. In aggregate terms, the deception is significant. With current holdings of savings bonds at $80 billion, inflation of 10% permits the government to absorb nearly $4 billion per year from bondholders. Moreover, if any real return due the bondholder is considered, the loss becomes greater—as does the disgrace perpetrated upon the small saver. Indexation would correct this transgression. Also, government securities would become more attractive to others and, in the process, would return a measure of real control over the effective money supply to the government.

Advocates point out that indexation would not, by itself, eliminate inflation. Rather, it represents a necessary initial step that would accomplish several desirable things. First, it would place the government in the same position as individuals and businesses adversely affected by inflation, rather than permitting it to benefit and remain aloof. Second, as inflation reduced revenues and increased the costs of financing deficits, government would be faced with paring expenditures down to means or increasing tax rates. Less reliance would need to be placed upon politicians, individually and collectively, to apply the brakes to the government inflation machine. Third, as the government's purse became thinner, priorities would be re-examined and, as a defensive measure, expenditures in the more inflationary sectors would tend to be curtailed.

Tax-Based Incomes Policies

A relatively new economic sobriquet, tax-based incomes policy or TIP, has been proposed by Henry C. Wallich and Sidney Weintraub.[6] In its basic form, TIP would levy a corporate income tax surcharge upon those companies granting wage increases that exceed a standard established by the government. Conversely, those firms holding wage increases below the established standard would receive a tax reduction. Proponents stress that TIP is designed to reduce the inflationary pressures of wages on costs and prices by using market mechanisms rather than controls. TIP is not intended as a revenue-raising device. In fact, proponents argue, if tax surcharges exceed the reductions granted then TIP isn't working.

A refinement of TIP, suggested by Lawrence Seidman, would provide an incentive to wage earners by applying similar tax penalties/rewards for violation/compliance with the wage guideline.[7]

Space does not permit more than a cursory review of what TIP is, and is not, as well as indicate some of the assumptions upon which it is based. TIP is a relatively new and innovative remedy. It is not without controls—a standard set by the government, applicable to the entire economy, and buttressed by surveillance of the Internal Revenue Service is a control indeed.

The assumptions supporting TIP proposals are many and controversial. As with analysis of any model, if one cannot accept the underlying assumptions, then the mechanism has little merit. The assumptions are listed in order of their perceived importance:

- Inflation is a disease generated primarily by the private sector, not the government.
- Within the private sector, inflation is the product of a wage-price spiral.
- Implementation is practicable; it is feasible, equitable, and worth the costs involved.
- Most of the work force is unionized; wages are established by collective bargaining.
- Unit labor costs (to which prices have been correlated) are influenced more by wages than productivity; or, that lower levels of wages (and profits) will not lower productivity even more.
- A uniform wage standard can eliminate distorted wage differentials that exist among unions, and not adversely impact the progress of programs to upgrade earnings of women and other minorities.

The validity of the first assumption, it seems, places TIP on shaky ground. The second topples the structure. The third should (but probably will not) put the subject to rest—for practical implementation requires a vivid imagination. (Accountants and tax attorneys would get gray hair, but also richer as a result of it.) The remaining assumptions are moot, but do not seem to be logical on the surface.

Indicative Planning

This inflation remedy is considered by many to be the horror-of-horrors—a cure to be feared more than the disease of inflation itself. National economic planning or, to be more precise, indicative planning is viewed in some sectors as equivalent to surrender of the free enterprise system.

Wassily Leontief is the most widely recognized and staunchest advocate of national economic planning. His approach employs complex economic models supported by input-output relationships.[8] Recently, Professor Leontief expanded his model to encompass the international economy in a study for the United Nations. Leontief does not wish to surrender the profit motive or the free enterprise system. Instead, he wishes to "civilize" them as, in his analogy, man has tamed rivers by recognizing and using the force of gravity, rather than by attempting do do away with it. He is convinced that the macro approaches followed by economic advisers are tools that are much too blunt to guide complex economies. Macrodata, much like consolidated financial statements, tend to conceal more than they reveal. Attention must focus upon microdata, some of which is not yet collected routinely, in order to foresee problem areas, whether inputs or outputs, before they arise. Crisis management would be minimized. Professor Leontief has illustrated his idea of national economic planning by comparing it with a sailing ship: the profit motive is the wind propelling it; national economic planning is the rudder keeping the ship on course and off the rocks.[9]

Other prominent economists have recommended that indicative planning be used to enhance the market system and manage exhaustible resources. Kenneth Arrow pointed out that capitalism functions best in a market system that is relatively stable and free of unexpected crises. As a result, Arrow argued that indicative planning can improve the market system by anticipating problems, reducing uncertainties, and enhancing stability.[10] Rober Solow recommended that economic planning be focused upon exhaustible resources, such as oil, in order to anticipate and minimize imbalances of critical materials. Forward thinking and early warning would permit co-ordination of exploitation, storage, and use, as well as provide the incentive and the time to develop alternative sources and/or technologies.[11]

Irving S. Friedman also stressed indicative planning, based upon an avowed goal of zero-rate inflation, and augmented by international cooperation. First, bottlenecks and shortages of resources should be identified and addressed. Second, since inflation has become institutionalized, efforts should be directed toward changing the *composition* of consumption by tax incentives (such as not taxing savings or interest earned) and tax sanctions (high levies on luxuries). Third, greater emphasis should be placed upon the economics of resource allocations rather than political motivations. Last, but equally important, the need for international cooperation must be awakened. Inflation is now a global disease. The actions of any single nation, no matter how favorable and decisive, can lead only so far and no further.[12]

SUMMARY

Inflation is an international disease. It is virulent. It is pervasive and pernicious, afflicting not only the living but also generations yet unborn.

Inflation is an extremely complex malady, affecting some, though not all, and in various ways and degrees. While the contagion is general, it does not affect all parts of an economy (or a diversified enterprise) in the same way. Some parts benefit from the effects and continuation of inflation. Redistributions of wealth occur without due cause or consideration among classes and nations. The poor, whether individuals or nations, have little recourse and few champions.

The persistence of inflation has transformed the malady from an economic to a political disease. The transformation made diagnosis and cure less elusive but also less tractable. The following *St. Louis Post-Dispatch* editorial sums it up rather well:

For the first time in 20 years, the report of the Joint Economic Committee has been endorsed by both Democratic and Republican members, largely because it generally reflects the prevailing mood in Congress of caution and restraint. The report argues that the twin evils of inflation and unemployment can best be dealt with by promoting savings and investment so as to improve worker productivity. Thus the emphasis is more on stimulating supply than demand, and to this end the committee recommended budgetary restraint, moderate monetary growth, tax breaks for business, and less government regulation.

The budgetary restraint and the moderate monetary growth the committee called for are already well underway, though there may be considerable disagreement over the most appropriate degree of each. As for the plea for more tax relief for business, it hardly seems justified in view of the Commerce Department's report that after-tax corporate profits rose 15.8 percent last year from 1977, seemingly enough to permit the investment the committee wants to encourage. Finally, no one can disagree with the need to establish "cost effectiveness" in government regulations, but too often that turns out to mean that any environmental, health or safety regulation adding to the cost of a product is unneeded, unproductive and inflationary. Nevertheless, as a generalized expression of goals the recommendations are acceptable enough.

But concealed by the talk about budgetary restraint, cost effective regulations and improved productivity is the most important single component of America's economic problems: energy. The report deals with the problem almost incidentally, suggesting more spending to develop secure nuclear waste storage systems and less costly pollution abatement systems for coal-burning installations. To its credit, though, the committee recommended greater use of Canadian and Mexican energy.

But the inflationary-recessionary effects of the deregulation of natural gas that Congress approved last year go unmentioned, so of course there is no proposal advanced for dealing with them. Nor does the report examine the impact of the impending deregulation of domestic oil or discuss the desirability of a rebatable gasoline tax to restrain demand without harming consumer purchasing power.

Perhaps the major unaddressed issue is the part played by the international oil companies. Though most of the global oil companies are American, there is nothing necessarily pro-American about their policies; yet the most powerful government on the face of the earth allows them to operate in ways that are at times inimical to America's national interest. By changing the tax laws that have encouraged the oil industry to invest overseas, by entering world oil markets itself instead of letting the oil companies decide how much petroleum will enter this country and from where, by requiring the oil companies to obtain federal charters, the government could transfer control over this country's economic future from Houston to Washington.

The Joint Economic Committee, however, confined itself to the stock economic palliatives. It is not so much that they are wrong as they are pathetically inadequate. That Sen. Bentsen of Texas, who is chairman, was able to secure a consensus from the members is more a commentary on the innocuousness of the report than its perceptiveness.[13]

Results in the political arena depend upon the coexistence of determination, common sense, and confidence—qualities not often found there in combination. In lieu of these qualities, indexations of government taxes and borrowings appear to be necessary to replace political rhetoric with motivation. A second essential step is adoption of indicative planning, often called "political economics." Given the inherent imperfections in national and international market systems, further debate concerning whether or not indicative planning is logical seems unnecessary. Attention should focus upon when and how. Now, only the naive would believe that politicians would suddenly change; they are going to have to be convinced. The job of convincing can only be accomplished by the collective political pressures of business and labor, once they awaken to the fact that they have the most to lose by inaction.

In the international sphere, the disease of inflation can only be cured by nations acting in an economic consortium, supported by international institutions, such as the World Bank, and the International Monetary Fund. No nation is self-sufficient. The OPEC members have oil, but they also have significant needs that other nations possess. An economic consortium would go far toward recognition that nations which create economic upheavals do so only at their own eventual peril.

CHAPTER 1 NOTES

1. *Public Papers of the Presidents of the United States* (Washington, D.C.: Office of the *Federal Register,* National Archives and Records Service, 1953–), Dwight D. Eisenhower, 1953, p. 182.

2. Special Report, "The Great Government Inflation Machine," *Business Week,* May 22, 1978, pp. 106–109, 113 passim.

3. William K. Wyant, Jr., "Military Forces: Mortgaged to Pension System?", *St. Louis Post-Dispatch,* April 25, 1978, p. 3c.

4. Richard F. Vancil, "Inflation Accounting—the Great Controversy," *Harvard Business Review,* March–April 1976, p.58.

5. Milton Friedman, "Monetary Correction," in Herbert Giersch, et al. *Essays on Inflation and Indexation* (Washington, D.C.: American Enterprise Institute for Public Policy Research, 1974), pp. 25–61.

6. "Another Weapon Against Inflation: Tax Policy," *Business Week*, October 3, 1977, pp. 94, 96.

7. Lawrence S. Seidman, "TIP: A Handle on Inflation?", *Wall Street Journal*, March 30, 1978.

8. Interview with Wassily W. Leontief, "What an Economic Planning Board Should Do," *Challenge*, July–August 1974, pp. 35–40.

9. Wassily Leontief, "National Economic Planning," *The Second Annual Distinguished Guest Lecture Program*, Saint Louis University School of Business and Administration, April 23, 1976, 40 pp.

10. Kenneth J. Arrow's presidential address to the American Economic Association, "Limited Knowledge and Economic Analysis," *American Economic Review*, March 1974, pp. 1–10.

11. Robert M. Solow, "The Economics of Resources or the Resources of Economics," *American Economic Review*, May 1974, pp. 1–14.

12. Irving S. Friedman, *Inflation: A World-Wide Disaster* (Boston: Houghton Mifflin, 1973).

13. "A Set of Economic Palliatives," editorial, *St. Louis Post-Dispatch*, March 22, 1979, p. 2B. Reprinted by permission.

2
Accounting Frameworks

Accounting frameworks are simply ways of thinking. Serious consideration of any complex accounting issue—such as inflation—can benefit from an examination of the various frameworks upon which accounting has been (or could be) constructed.

The major benefit, of course, is a better understanding of the issues. Understanding often requires both distance and proximity. Sometimes, we must stand back to see from whence we have come in order to appreciate where we are and in which direction we might proceed.

In addition, the perspective created is not limited arbitrarily. Unlike contemporary model-building (which is forced to restrict and simplify the parameters of the real world), analysis of accounting frameworks can expand the horizons of thought while providing a useful context.

Finally, such reflections benefit so-called theorists and practitioners alike—although there can be no such dichotomy where accountants are concerned. Accounting theorists cannot divorce themselves from the needs and practices of the real world—if they wish to make useful contributions. Similarly, practitioners cannot divest themselves of concepts since they must continuously explain why one accounting or reporting alternative was selected over others.

THE BASIC FRAMEWORK

The basic framework of accounting—double-entry bookkeeping—has remained virtually unchanged over six and one-half centuries. There is general agreement that bookkeeping was neither a revelation of science nor a phenomenon of chance. It was invented in response to the needs of commerce.

As the language of business, accounting grew in complexity along with business. Accounting ways of thinking were adapted to serve evolving needs. The ability to adapt enabled accounting to grow and prosper. However, this very adaptability also generated charges that accounting and reporting practices were developed in the absence of any cohesive or definitive framework at all.

Today, financial statements are criticized for failing to reflect "economic reality." Consequently, there is a clamor for ever-increasing management disclosures in order to restore common sense in external reporting. Standard-setting bodies in the United States have perennially been charged with brush-fire approaches to accounting and reporting problems. For these reasons (among others), the Financial Accounting Standards Board (FASB) is scurrying about in search of a new conceptual framework for accounting.[1]

ENVIRONMENTAL STRUCTURES

Business, and accounting (as the language of business) are influenced by the legal, political, and socioeconomic environments in which they function. The environmental frameworks reflect societal attitudes toward business and the extent of governmental direction or intervention. These structures also influence responses to inflation, as well as how the effects of changing price-levels are to be reported, if at all.

Although there is a considerable amount of interaction and overlay among the environments, they will be examined separately as a matter of convenience.

The Legal Environment

Most contemporary Western societies operate within legal frameworks based upon either:

- Civil law—derived from Roman Law or the Napoleonic Code, or
- Common law—developed by the judicial process over time.

Civil law serves as the framework for most continental European countries. Civil laws tend to be *prescriptive*—they stipulate what shall be done. There is a tendency toward inflexibility, if not rigidity, and the maintenance of the status quo. Accounting and reporting systems in civil law countries lean toward uniformity by prescription in many respects. The uniformity offers certain potential advantages: increased comparability; the relative ease of development and transfer of accounting skills; and the enhancement of government planning, oversight, and control. On the other hand, uniformity tends to restrict the ability of financial reports to serve the needs of diverse users or changing times. No useful generalization can be made with respect to accounting or reporting for inflation. The methods in use, if any, would depend upon the nature of the economy, the structure of business, and the degree of governmental control.

Common law frameworks are *proscriptive* in that they attempt to stipulate what actions are prohibited. England and the United States are examples of countries that function under common law. Accountancy has flourished in common law environs. The wider latitude of behavior under the law places more reliance upon judgment in social and business matters, and allows for the flexibility needed to cope with change. Accounting systems tend to stress fairness, however defined, and usually permit selection of recording and reporting practices from more than one generally accepted alternative. Disclosures are emphasized because of the presence of choice and to enable financial reports to serve the needs of various users without becoming misleading. Conversely, social and business abuses of the behavior latitudes that exist lead to their restriction by legislation, regulation, and additional disclosure. In general, accounting systems in common law environments are essentially reactive. As problems arise, trial and error are typically employed in search of solutions. Reflecting the impacts of inflation or changing price-levels would not be an exception.

One final observation holds for all legal frameworks of accounting. They specify only the minimum standards that must be maintained. Rarely will firms or accounting bodies be restrained from supplying more information than the minimums called for.

The Political Structure

A thin and very arbitrary line separates politics (or government) and the law. Much of the business of politics is reflected ultimately in the law. Yet, those who govern determine what will become regulation or law. Therefore, the frameworks of accounting would be incomplete without at least a cursory overview of the political sector.

All economies need some government direction. There is no such thing as laissez-faire. The relative stability of governments and their policies furnish the confidence necessary for business operations, and the basis for such accounting assumptions as the going concern. Governments, in turn, extract the wherewithal needed to operate from those who are governed, usually in the form of taxes. Tax structures are politically determined and affect the behavior of businesses and individuals. The relative importance of corporate, individual, and other taxes (such as the Value Added Tax) directly affect, if not determine, accounting and reporting practices in some countries.

The foundation for government regulation of a society—and the functioning of the professions within a given society—is the public interest. Although this fact should be self-evident, it is often ignored or forgotten.

Governments use as well as affect accounting information. In the United States, governments represent the largest accountable entities, yet attempt to operate with accounting systems no more sophisticated than those used by a housewife to maintain her checking account. These systems, collectively called governmental or fund (and sometimes "cookie-jar") accounting, focus upon compliance and cash-basis methods. With the assistance and urging of prominent accountants and business executives, the Federal government and four states (Colorado, Michigan, New York, and North Dakota) have begun to use accrual methods and consolidated reportings, at least in prototype statements.[2]

There now appears to be a growing, albeit belated, recognition that the use of generally accepted commerical accounting principles provides government officials (and interested private citizens) with more realistic and useful information regarding financial position and operating results. For example, accrual methods disclose the future costs of present and past decisions heretofore ignored by cash-basis reportings. (The burgeoning costs of interest on the national debt and the magnitudes of pension programs are cases in point.)

Governments impact financial accounting and reporting in the private sector directly and indirectly. In some countries, such as France, the national government prescribes what accounting will be—uniform methods of accounting and reporting by all firms. In other countries, such as Sweden, the government influences business decisions and the accounting for them by means of fiscal and tax policies—investment incentives and tax benefits are allowable only if officially booked.

In the United States, government interventions into accounting and reporting have represented attempts at tax relief and responses to illegal business conduct. With the exception of the myths introduced into financial reports by tax provisos, most governmental requirements have been met by supplementary disclosures. Although businessmen grumble over the costs involved, accountants generally agree that disclosures have largely prevented political, social, and tax considerations from being woven into the fabric of accounting practices to the extent that they overshadow responsible financial reporting to investors.

Some peers of accounting warn against the increasing politicization of accounting standards,[3] and the growing possibility of confusing rules of measurement (accounting activities) with rules of conduct (political activities).[4] Others criticize accountants for doing much too little political marketing of their ideas.[5] On balance, however, most accountants resent the fact that political compromises between conflicting interests often result in irrational reportings of economic events.

Political considerations will determine how the disease of inflation will be treated in the United States. In the process, the credibility of business—and the language of business—may be damaged unless reason prevails.

The Economic Framework

The economic milieu impacts accounting directly and significantly. In some countries, such as Germany, a university degree in accounting is not available; one in business economics is offered instead. In all countries, the number of public companies, the extent of public shareholdings, and the composition of those shareholdings (whether by individuals, families, or banks), usually determine the importance attached to financial reporting as well as the extent of the disclosures presented.

In the United States, economists and accountants deal with the same raw material—economic data—but different ends and means are involved. Economists strive to *explain* economic events, primarily on the *theoretical* plane. Accountants attempt to *measure* these events, generally from a *practical* standpoint.

Both disciplines are charged with deviating from economic reality. In the pursuit of the aura of science, economists allegedly have overemphasized the mathematical assertions and manipulations of models to the extent that their abstractions have created a wide gap between economic theory and reality. While the charge is moot, the evidence indicates that economists have forgotten that the vagaries of human behavior are intractible to model-building. Accountants, on the other hand, have been criticized for: adhering to their assumption of the stable dollar in an era of significant inflation; for permitting tax legislation to prostitute financial reports; and for piecemeal approaches to reporting problems that encourage uneconomic actions by managements and investors. Each of these criticisms has substance.

Although economic and accounting concepts of income differ in the United States (and rightly so), economics has provided the framework for a general understanding of the focal points of accounting systems. (These concepts will be beneficial when the approaches to price-level accounting in other countries are examined in subsequent chapters.) Gerhard Mueller, for example, classified national accounting practices as: (1) macroeconomic; (2) microeconomic; (3) uniform; and (4) independent-discipline systems.[6]

Macroeconomic and *uniform* systems differ only in the degree of specificity in accounting practices. Both are founded upon government direction of the economy (in the public interest) through influence or regulation of the actions of firms. Each system relies upon prudent reactions of firms to tax and other economic incentives made available to accomplish national goals. In such environs, financial and tax accounting are identical and public accountants serve dual roles of auditor and tax agent. Accounting practices have no foundation in theory, only in government policy. Among industrial nations, Sweden typifies the macro framework. Many developing countries employ, or should consider, similar approaches to encourage and monitor growth. Uniform systems are used by France (by choice) and by controlled economies (by necessity). In all instances, accounting serves the nation first, the firm second, and the stockholder (if any) last.

The *microeconomic* framework, according to Mueller, is exemplified by the Netherlands. The nucleus of the microeconomic framework is the firm, supported by concepts of private property and the profit motive. The purpose of accounting is to assure survival of the firm. The primary approach is maintenance of the economic susbstance (physical capital or productive capacity) of the firm. Accounting procedures follow "sound business practices," not the least of which is replacement-value accounting. In fact, the valuation concept is so overriding that other accounting procedures are of limited importance. Actually, the microeconomic framework represents a very sophisticated *managerial* accounting system. Tax accounting, which serves a different (macro) purpose, is completely separated from financial reporting. Accountancy serves the firm first, the stockholders second, and the nation last.

Mueller's last framework—the *independent discipline*—is not an economic ordering but will be mentioned here for continuity and convenience. There is no such thing as an independent discipline in the social realm. Social ways of thinking cannot exist as separate entities. A more appropriate name tag (and probably Mueller's real intention) would be that of an independent profession. The foundation of the profession would rest upon the public interest, defined as that of the investing public. Financial reports and the supportive accounting practices would be guided by the single criterion of fairness, however defined, but basically as opposed to misleading to investors. Auxiliary guidelines would emphasize accountability (or stewardship) of management (consequently the use of historical costs) and the separation of financial, managerial, and tax accounting, since each would serve different purposes. As business conditions and stockholder interests changed, so would the accounting for them. Firms as well as accountants would often devise more than one accounting and reporting alternative to reflect the same economic event. As professionals, accountants would often have to choose which alternative represented the fairest presentation *to the investor.* (This choice could not reside with managements who would have vested interests, although not necessarily in presenting the most favorable picture.) The presence of alternatives would mandate full and fair disclosures. Accountancy would serve the investor first, the firm second, and the nation last.

Until the recent past, accountancy in the United States could best be described as an independent profession. There now seems to be a shift toward the microeconomic framework. How much of a shift will occur remains to be seen.

FRAMEWORKS OF THEORY

In this section, theory will be examined in the context of accounting as an independent profession. The notion of theory has little relevance in the macroeconomic or uniform frameworks since accounting will be whatever the governments decide—good social accounting is good accounting for any purpose. Theory is also of lesser importance in the microeconomic framework since accounting assumes an *active* role in assuring survival of the firm. Whatever methods enhance the survival of the firm—or sound business practices— determine accounting and reporting. Accounting is not only the language of business but acts as its conservator as well.

In the framework of an independent profession, theory is expected to serve as part of the general reference (or conceptual framework) and the common body of knowledge. The Financial Accounting Standards Board will be involved with its conceptual framework project for some time to come. The profession's attempt (cosponsored by the Carnegie Corporation) to define the common body of knowledge in 1967 was ineffective, to say the least.[7]

Approaches to Theory

Of the half-dozen or more approaches to accounting theory that have evolved, the four most common forms will be examined: deduction, induction, pragmatism, and ethics.

Deduction. The deductive method, the standard approach of the natural sciences, reasons from the general to the particular. The process begins with the stipulation of objectives against which premises may be tested by research. Deduction is favored by many because it produces a cohesive or integrated framework.

Deductive approaches are well suited for the natural sciences since, in most cases, the search is for existing laws or principles awaiting discovery. When applied to accounting, deduction is fraught with all the problems common to the social sciences, together with those peculiar to the discipline itself.

Social science premises generally deal with nonobservables incapable of direct measurement. The fiat or bridge-assumptions used instead can increase the level of confidence but cannot prove the premises. To make social research efforts operable, many are pared or fragmented to the extent that the results usually are of little interest or relevance.[8]

In addition to the above general problems, the accounting profession in the United States has yet to construct and obtain formal acceptance of the objectives of financial reports. Objectives are to be stipulated in the conceptual framework project of the FASB. However, these objectives will not represent a panacea for, unlike the natural sciences, accounting objectives change over time, even in a single country. Different objectives usually dictate different supporting frameworks.

Induction. The process of induction reasons from the particular to the general and is the method commonly used by the social sciences. Observations or measurements are made of particular actions or events upon which conclusions are made regarding the population concerned. The conclusions or generalizations are at once subject to refute by subsequent tests using the deductive process. In effect, it could be said that inductive processes often supply the premises to which deductive reasoning is applied.

Induction is valued for its ability to generate ideas without the shackles of undue constraints. Beyond that, most ideas in the social sciences remain theories—neither proven nor disproven—since few research efforts are replicable or can be applied to an entire population.

Pragmatism. The pragmatic approach simply looks to the real world for practices that are in general use and constructs concepts around those practices that have proved to be useful.

On the surface, this approach appears to be direct, productive, and logical. Yet, it could be, or become, a static approach. Given a list of generally accepted, useful practices today, how and where would new ideas be tested in order to have the opportunity to gain general acceptance? The problem of objectives is encountered also since the term "useful" must be described—to whom and for what purposes?

Ethics. The ethical approach to accounting theory rests firmly upon the concept of fairness, but fairness has yet to be resolved. Over the years, fair has been equated with equitable, truthful, accurate, unbiased, impartial, and factual, among others. Each of the alternate word-pictures is as subjective as fairness itself. Consequently, the ethical approach to accountancy is generally considered to be much too nebulous.

Nonetheless, fairness, however it may be construed, permeates the whole of the profession of accounting in the United States. In 1960, Arthur Andersen & Company suggested that fairness was "the one basic accounting postulate."[9]

Given the nature of the accounting profession in the United States today, the concept of fairness can be ignored only at great risk. Although often overshadowed, the basis and primary responsibility of the profession relate to third parties, or the investing public. Certified public accountants attest to the fairness of financial statements and their preparation in accordance with generally accepted accounting principles. Such attestations explicitly affirm: (1) pre-eminence of the concept of fairness; (2) existence of criteria for determining a fair presentation; and (3) the co-existence of accounting practices that are generally accepted because they result in fair representations to third parties. Like it or not, if the profession continues to testify that these concepts and practices exist, someone had better write them down. The someone currently charged with the task is the FASB.

Views of the Firm

The structure of accounting ideas and practices paralleled the evolution of the firm. As the notion of the firm increased in complexity, so did the nature, and the problems, of accounting.

Personification of Accounts. Until the twentieth century, persons or clerks were related with accounts in order to explain the workings of bookkeeping. Emphasis was placed upon *how* transactions should be recorded. The objectives of the recordings were limited to: (1) maintenance of a homogeneity of data in the accounts and; (2) the honesty of the accounts, portrayed as individuals responsible to the owner, yet separate and apart from him. Contemporary estate and trust accounting retain the essence of personified accounts.

Proprietary Theory. By 1909 the objective or the *why* of accounting had become focused upon the proprietor.[10] Records were maintained to reflect the capital of owner-managers and the changes in that capital over time. Since one or few proprietors were involved in business operations of those times, sophisticated classifications of revenues, expenses, and income distributions were unnecessary. Fairness of reports was of little concern other than in loan transactions with outsiders. Proprietor-managers were insiders; access to information needed was assumed.

By the time the proprietor was accepted as the objective of accounts and reports, the advent of the corporation rendered proprietary theory obsolete.

Entity Theory. As a legal entity, the corporation was given an existence separate and apart from its managers and owners. Significant changes occurred in the ways of thinking about business relationships.

Proprietors having a direct interest and association with business operations were transformed into stockholders with a residual interest and only limited liability and involvement. The ability of stockholders to market their shares transformed the concept of proprietorship into a constantly changing group of faceless persons.

Creditors could no longer look to individual stockholders for settlement of debts of the firm. In supplication, the law accorded creditors the status of equity-holders with a preference in liquidation.

Professional managers evolved as a class. They served as surrogates of the equity holders, accountable to owners and creditors alike for the costs and stewardship of the assets entrusted to their care.

The corporation focused the objective of accounting upon the entity. The firm became the center of interest since it existed, and therefore could function, separate from the equity holders. The function of external reporting centered upon accounting for the costs of assets owned by the entity (the left side of the balance sheet) to the equity holders (the right side of the balance sheet). Profit was considered as the excess of revenues (compensations for goods and services provided to others) over expenses (the costs of providing the goods and services). Profits accrued to the entity rather than to the equity holders directly. Accountings for the costs of assets and the distributions of profits by managements became founded in the concept of fairness to all equity holders, present and potential. Management information was of little concern since, as insiders, direct knowledge of operations and access to information by management was presumed.

William A. Paton introduced entity theory to accounting thought (in 1922) and, together with A. C. Littleton, firmly established it by 1940.[11]

The advent of the corporation and the professional manager presented accountants with mixed blessings. Accountancy was accorded the status of a profession serving the interests of the investing public and other equity holders. However, an intermediary was placed squarely between professional accountants and their publics. Over time, management acquired a natural interest in its self-perpetuation which was not necessarily congruent with the best interests of investors and creditors. Also over time, the image of the profession of accountancy was diminished by the virtual absence of any direct association between accountants and investors. Although unintentional (and unadmitted), investors became third parties; managements became clients. The role of accountancy became obscured. Public accountants assumed multiple functions: attestors to third parties; advisers to managements; advocates of business interests in tax and regulatory proceedings; and, occasionally, adversaries of management.

Fund Theory. In 1947, William Vatter argued that both the entity and proprietary theories were too personalistic (the former merely substituted an artificial, legal person for the real person). Accounting and reporting practices too often were determined by and reflected personal or vested interests. Depersonalization would enable accounting considerations to focus upon the nature of the problems instead of human nature.[12]

Vatter suggested that the firm should be viewed as a fund—an entity composed of groups of assets, with their related restrictions and purposes. Accounting and reporting could focus upon the multitude of purposes of complex corporations only by segmenting or layering the whole into its controllable, and therefore manageable, parts. Multiple purposes would require various concepts of value, accomplishment, and reporting.

In a sense, Vatter implied that large corporations were social organisms much too complex to account for logically in any macro context. Emphasis would best be directed to the control and accomplishment of the divisible parts. Compliance with budgets and similar restrictions constituted the objective of fund theory and, consequently, was more readily adaptable to the accounting for governmental units for which compliance reporting was of greater concern than efforts to measure accomplishment or profit. However, Vatter's emphasis upon the divisible parts of an enterprise is compatible with current efforts toward segmented reportings.

Enterprise Theory. Similar to the entity concept, yet broader in scope, is enterprise theory. Basically, the corporate enterprise is viewed as a social organism having a broad basis of interest and responsibility. Howard Perlmutter has collectively termed these interest groups "stakeholders," representing not only creditors, investors, and managers, but employees, trade unions, customers, governments, and the general public.[13]

The breadth of enterprise theory enables it to not only fit the multinational corporation as it exists today, but its probable successor, which Perlmutter termed "a transnational network, a TNN if you will, a global industrial system or constellation with linkages between companies."[14]

As a framework for accounting, enterprise theory provides a plethora of objectives. How can even multipurpose financial reports serve the needs of such a diverse group of users? Where various accounting or reporting practices exist, to which user group or groups should the basis of fairness be directed? For many stakeholders, views of asset valuation, accountability, income determination, income distribution, and necessary disclosure will differ widely —who should prevail?

In sum, enterprise theory dovetails rather neatly with the functions of even the largest enterprises as well as the interventions of governments as stakeholders of interest. The scope of the theory, however, is much too broad to serve as the basis of accounting objectives. Nonetheless, enterprise theory does serve to identify the many stakeholders having an interest in accounting information and the problems inherent in trying to satisfy most of the interests most of the time.

ACCOUNTING MODELS

Model building has become an honorific activity. The mystiques associated with mathematics, scientific methods, and electronic computers have done much to create this status. Basically, models represent simplified constructs of reality. The simplification process generally involves concentration upon the variables considered to be relevant. Models serve as frameworks for thinking—for analysis of problems and for decision making.

General Types of Models

Much like costs, models can be classified in many ways; such as according to structure, scope, time, certainty, and function.[15] Unfortunately, financial accounting, *as a practice,* doesn't fit neatly into any of these frameworks. Accounting is symbolic to the extent that arithmetic numerals are used to depict results of economic events. It is general in that it is widely applied across economies; it is also specific since it deals with micro units—firms as well as individual transactions.

With respect to time, financial accounting is essentially static insofar as the balance sheet is concerned. All illusion of dynamics is created by efforts of income, funds, and retained earnings statements to depict changes over time. However, the time referred to is past time rather than future time. In a sense, the best that financial reporting can achieve is to paint a still picture of a moving scene.

Although financial accounting is replete with estimates, it has been surrounded by an aura of certainty—or at least accuracy. This may be attributed in part to the exactness associated with numbers, together with some of the practices and language used by accountants.

Where function is concerned, financial accounting is essentially descriptive, although it attempts to depict the results of decisions that were made instead of how decisions are made.

The real problem in relating financial accounting to any type of decision model is the aspect of time. Financial accounting and reporting practices deal with past time. The model frameworks mentioned pertain to decision making, the province of the future.

The *setting of accounting standards,* however, is involved with selection from alternatives and, consequently, *is a process of decision making.* Some models have relevance here. As something of an applied art, accounting has focused attention upon standards as problems have arisen, usually over alternative practices either in use or proposed. Whether intentional or not, models or frameworks were constructed to examine the alternatives. Unfortunately, the potential benefits these frameworks could have provided have not been generally realized for reasons that can only be conjectured.

Normative (Simplex) Models

A normative approach to accounting standards is considered as simplex, in the author's opinion, since choices in action are determined by the constraints. Rules effectively supplant reason.

Normative approaches are founded upon several assumptions. Systems are closed, or virtually so, and free from external influences. Elements considered are alike (or reasonably similar) and can be well defined or programmed. Constraints, or decision criteria, are constructed to keep the choices within reasonable bounds as well as assist in their selection. Where tradeoffs are encountered, they are ranked in importance and cranked into the model.

The goal of the normative approach is identification of the best choice in action as indicated by the constraints imposed. Problem definition and structure of the constraints are all-important. Decision making is simplified since, by assumption, the best decision is identified by the workings of the model.

The more important constraints that have been employed in standard setting are usefulness, fairness, objectivity, and feasibility.

Situational (Complex) Models

Selection of accounting standards within a situational framework is complex in more than one respect.

At the outset, an open system is assumed. That is, not all internal factors relating to the problem at hand are known. Furthermore, the external influences of other environments, domestic and foreign, are recognized yet often prove to be intractable.

Of utmost importance is the recognition that all elements are not alike, although similarities exist. A single decision (or conceptual framework) is either logically impossible or must be generalized to such an extent that it represents an ineffective guideline.

Rather than identify decisions, the constraints actually function to separate the elements into like groups for which available alternatives would logically apply. In effect, the decision process would encompass the matching of elements (or situations) and available alternatives. Put another way, the situational approach would recognize the decision process as complex and attempt to break it down into several, similar parts to which normative measures could be applied logically.

The constraints used would not necessarily differ from those mentioned in the normative approach. They would only be employed in a different way—as sorting, rather than decision-making devices.

Another similarity of the normative and situational approaches should be recognized. For each, a change in basic objectives or constraints would require going back to the drawing board.

Managerial (Internal) Models

Any review of financial accounting frameworks would be incomplete without reference to managerial or internal accounting mechanisms.

Managerial accounting frameworks have few real constraints other than cost and ingenuity. A good system generally is considered one that provides the right information, to the right people, at the right time. On the other hand, managerial accounting is inherently more complex. While it deals in past time, considerably more involvement exists in present time (control of day-to-day operations) and future time (budgeting and planning) considerations. Internal reportings must not only be situational but must address themselves to many layers of authority having diverse objectives and information needs. The intricacies of complex organizations have required internal information to focus upon segments of a firm, rather than the whole, and to include nonmonetary data as well.

Although considered to be in its infancy, managerial accounting has flourished because of its flexibility in addressing the relevant needs of users. Some allege that managerial accounting was invented out of necessity, is a separate dialect of the language of business, and has little, if any, common ground with external reporting. Others argue that "all accounting is management accounting"; that there is a common ground upon which the needs of the users of financial statements converge.[16] (The author, for one, is becoming convinced that, not only is this latter observation sound, but that it actually is coming about. The move away from single-purpose consolidated statements, having limited value, to segmented reporting is one example. *Explanation* of the effects of changing price levels may well be another.)

THE PRESENT IN PERSPECTIVE

As the environmental frameworks of business grew in complexity over time, so did business and its attendant language.

Accounting thought paralleled the evolution of the firm. Theory was assembled in an eclectic fashion—much like a patchwork quilt—drawing upon deductive, inductive, pragmatic, and ethical approaches as necessary. Successive views of the firm—proprietary, entity, and enterprise theories—served as frameworks for accounting in order to portray what is now called "economic reality."

The most important constraints imposed upon the accounting models developed were:

- Methods should be applied uniformly.
- Procedures should be objective and verifiable.
- Presentations should be fair and not misleading.
- Reports should reflect economic sense.
- Reports should be useful and worth their costs.

Some argue that the current dilemma facing accountancy is the result of an obsession with uniformity. This does not appear to be valid, except for the recent past under the Financial Accounting Standards Board.

Prior to the FASB, it seems that uniformity was considered as desirable to the extent possible. Objectivity was sacrificed in some instances in order to increase the utility of information. Disclosures were increasingly recognized (and required) as: (1) the best means of preventing normative methods from producing misleading information, and (2) a reasonable approach to serve the needs of a variety of users. If anything, accounting was criticized for offering too many reporting options. Fault that could be related to the Accounting Principles Board would concern the absence of definitive guides for application of the alternatives permitted. The differing situations had to have been known and recognized in the consideration of the alternative methods. The situations and the preferred methods should have been stipulated, and appropriate mention by way of disclosure should have been required as well.

In the author's opinion, the greatest prostitution of financial reports, prior to the FASB, resulted from the surrender of accounting bodies (and accountants) to pressures from business and the Congress for tax relief. Accelerated methods of depreciation, investment tax credits, LIFO inventories, and the deferred income tax myths that resulted, effectively divorced accounting reports from the realm of economic sense.

Accountancy became a political arena; a much easier mark for achieving tax relief than the Congress. Political influence, tax bargaining, and vested interest supplanted the normal constraints upon the accounting process. As fictions replaced much of the common sense in accounting reports, the accounting profession emerged as the sole loser. User needs were protected reasonably well by the additional disclosure requirements levied by the SEC over time. (The additional costs connected with the disclosure process served to offset some of the gains realized by the tax hagglings of business. However, based upon the magnitudes of deferred income taxes appearing on the financial reports of most large firms, business has been a net winner despite its outcries over disclosure costs.) In the public eye, accountancy became associated with the vested interests of its big business clients rather than the public interest, whether real or imagined. The long-legged accountant's stool became rickety.

It has been said that "the FASB was created out of the ashes of predecessors burned up in the fires of the resulting political process."[17] Those ashes are still warm. They have also been stirred by the illegal payoff fiascos of the recent past and the cries of "where were the auditors?" Finally, inflation has fanned the coals

by challenging the validity of one of the basic tenets of accounting—
the stability of the U.S. dollar as the unit of measure.

A CONCEPTUAL FRAMEWORK

The FASB has chosen to return to its workbench and examine the
conceptual framework of accounting—and seek means of mending
the accountant's stool before it collapses. Undeniably, the FASB
has been (and is) in a difficult position. It attempted to perform
temporary repairs, by replacing the glue in some of the joints of the
stool, in order to acquire the time needed to reexamine the structure
itself. The FASB has not won many friends by either effort.

In its attempt at temporary repairs, the FASB selected a glue
composed of restrictive definitions and normative (or simplex)
approaches to apply to complex situations. The results flew in the
face of economic sense. Inflation accounting, the topic of interest
here, is an excellent example, as will be examined later at length.
The translation of foreign currencies, the treatment of research and
development expenditures, and accounting for the oil and gas industries are further examples of pronouncements criticized for their
irrational approaches and the uneconomic actions they motivated.

Although published materials imply that the conceptual framework project is in its early stages, it appears that the FASB is in
search of a holy grail in the form of immutable truths to serve as a
framework for accounting. It is believed that these truths would
point out solutions to problems as they arose. Furthermore, since
they were immutable, the truths would also serve to defend the
FASB from the political challenges of those with vested interests.

Based upon the results of similar searches over the past half-
century, there are no such immutable truths to be found. The quest
is an impossible dream. The many environments that affect business, the multiple needs of diverse stakeholders, and the dynamic
nature of the firm itself preclude a monolithic structure for accounting, in while rules can replace judgment, and in which a single,
normative treatment can be applied in all instances.

Yet, there is also a consensus that some standards must exist—
enterprises and their independent auditors can't have total freedom
of choice in reporting economic events.[18] Most interested parties
also agree that the standards should be set by the private sector

rather than the Securities and Exchange Commission. Thus, the FASB has the task of assembling the standards or conventions to guide financial accounting and reporting with not much more than judgment or common sense to serve as a foundation. Yet this foundation will determine whether or not the FASB will survive.

The considerations of the FASB can only be expected to achieve a more reasonable degree of uniformity in practice. In most cases, normative methods will be found wanting since they must treat unlike situations in a rigid manner with irrational results. Yet, like things should be treated alike. The FASB will be forced to spell out those circumstances in which the various alternatives are warranted. In other words, like things must first be determined—then treated alike.

Objectivity and verifiability will likely prohibit the adoption of many changes in *accounting practices*. This would not, however, preclude supplemental *disclosures* of various types of information. This observation is particularly relevant since the FASB has already determined that financial *reporting,* to be useful, should have *predictive* value—to assist users of reports in "assessing the amounts, timing, and uncertainty of prospective cash receipts."[19] The items italicized above cannot be overemphasized. As developed earlier, the accounting model is couched in terms of past time; it is not a predictive device. Therefore, it would be unwise to restructure basic financial accounting in attempts to predict future events. Information that is future oriented should be (and is) generated by the *managerial* accounting process and should be reported in supplementary disclosures. Well-managed companies generate future-oriented data routinely. Reasonable, selected disclosures are all that appear to be necessary.

Unless the waves of criticism encountered in the recent past have served to alter the FASB's approach to standard setting, the continued disregard of the criterion of economic (or common) sense will anchor the FASB in rough waters. Economic (or common) sense is not to be equated with so-called "economic reality"—the latter term is nebulous and in constant flux. Nor should it be confused with "economic consequences"—a word-picture applied to the concept that standard setters should (assuming they could) consider the future "ripple effects" of accounting rules before issuance. Economic (or common) sense simply means that accounting rules should produce accounting reports that appear to be reasonable and sound to the average user.

SUMMARY

The FASB has the task of setting accounting standards for the private sector in the United States. Its search for a conceptual framework or other model founded upon immutable truths—therefore shielded from political pressures or challenges—is not likely to be successful. Whatever rules are issued will have to be based upon—and subsequently defended by—nothing more profound than the collective judgment and common sense of the Board itself.

Challenges and political confrontations can neither be avoided nor overcome by the structuring of a framework. Accounting information must eventually stand or fall based upon the reasonableness or the soundness of the information as perceived by users. However, the characteristics of the information outputs and the acceptance they receive will be affected by the accounting model employed by the FASB.

Normative methods, while simpler to use, will tend to produce information that conflicts with economic sense. Defenses of challenges will not be likely to receive the support of the rank and file practitioner, user, or politician.

Situtational approaches to issues will require much more consideration, judgment, and time, although the resultant information should appear to be more reasonable and sound. Challenges by dissidents and vested interests will still occur since not all managements and users will be satisfied. However, it is much more likely that the majority of the rank and file could, and would, support practices that furnish reasonable and sound basic information—supplemented by disclosures and soft data geared to the needs of users and the times.

CHAPTER 2. NOTES

1. *FASB Discussion Memorandum: Conceptual Framework for Financial Accounting and Reporting* (Stamford, Conn.: Financial Accounting Standards Board, December 2, 1976).

2. In October 1978, the U.S. Treasury Department released the third annual prototype report, "Consolidated Financial Statements of the United States

Government, Fiscal Year 1977." Like its predecessors, this report was considered to be preliminary in that many problems of data conversion remained to be overcome. Nevertheless, a heretofore unavailable perspective of government operation was provided.

3. For example, see Marshall S. Armstrong, "The Politics of Establishing Accounting Standards," *Journal of Accountancy,* February 1977, pp. 76–79; and David Solomons, "The Politicization of Accounting," *Journal of Accountancy,* November 1978, pp. 65–72.

4. Comment by FASB member David Mosso, in an address to the Texas Society of CPAs and the South Texas Chapter of the Financial Executives Institute, in FASB *Viewpoints,* January 26, 1978, p. 1.

5. See Charles T. Horngren, "The Marketing of Accounting Standards," *Journal of Accountancy,* October 1973, pp. 61–66; and Leonard M. Savoie, "Price-Level Accounting, Practical Politics, and Tax Relief," *Management Accounting,* January 1977, pp. 15–18.

6. Gerhard G. Mueller, *International Accounting* (New York: The Macmillan Company, 1967), Chapters 1–4.

7. Results of the study were published in Robert H. Roy and James H. MacNeill, *Horizons for a Profession: The Common Body of Knowledge for Certified Public Accountants* (New York: American Institute of Certified Public Accountants, 1967). The experiment upon which the study was based was well designed and extensive. Unfortunately, when the results obtained did not correspond to their prejudgments, by their own admission, the authors substituted their personal opinions instead.

The body of knowledge recommended in the study, in this author's opinion, represented an excellent approach for a mathematician, engineer, or operations researcher simultaneously aspiring to become an accountant, but an inappropriate common body of knowledge for a CPA.

8. C. West Churchman, *The Systems Approach* (New York: Dell Publishing Co., 1968), p. 102.

9. *The Postulate of Accounting—What It Is, How It Is Determined, How It Should Be Used* (Chicago: Arthur Andersen & Co., 1960), p. 31.

10. Henry Rand Hatfield, *Modern Accounting* (New York: D. Appleton and Co., 1909).

11. William A. Paton, *Accounting Theory* (New York: Ronald Press, 1922); W. A. Paton and A. C. Littleton, *An Introduction to Corporate Accounting Standards,* Monograph No. 3 (New York: American Accounting Association, 1940).

12. William J. Vatter, *The Fund Theory of Accounting and its Implications for Financial Reports* (Chicago: University of Chicago Press, 1947), pp. 7–9.

13. Howard V. Perlmutter, "Alternative Futures for the Multinational," in *Proceedings, Second Annual International Business Conference,* Saint Louis University, December 16, 1976, pp. 17–25.

14. Ibid., p. 23.

15. Robert G. Murdick and Joel E. Ross, *Information Systems for Modern Management,* 2d ed., (Englewood Cliffs, N.J.: Prentice-Hall, 1975), pp. 502–504.

16. I. Wayne Keller, "All Accounting is Management Accounting," *Management Accounting,* November 1976, pp. 13–15.

17. David Mosso, op. cit.

18. There are supporters of free choice, however. See "Issue and Debate: Should Many Flowers Grow?", for the opinions of Abraham Briloff and Robert N. Anthony, *Journal of Accountancy,* October 1978, pp. 104–106; and Alan P. Mayer-Sommer and Stephen J. Laycock, "Financial Reporting: Let's Replace Compliance with Competition," *Management Accounting,* December 1978, pp. 14–19, 36.

19. *Statement of Financial Accounting Concepts No. 1,* "Objectives of Financial Reporting by Business Enterprises." (Stamford, Conn.: Financial Accounting Standards Board, November 1978), p. viii.

3
The U.S. Perspective

The magnitude and tenacity of inflation are new to most Americans. Until a cure is found, or the disease runs its course, most accountants have expressed concern over the impacts of inflation upon financial reports. These concerns will be examined since some have substance. A chronology of solutions considered in the United States will be developed, along with some conjectures to account for the lack of real progress.

ACCOUNTING CONCERNS

Inflation challenges some of the basic foundations upon which accountancy has been constructed in the United States. The decisions made by users of financial reports may also be affected adversely as a result.

Challenged Assumptions

Money performs two functions. It serves as a common denominator without which business would be reduced to barter and accounting would be impracticable. Money also represents a store of value, or a medium of future exchange. In the latter case, money could be considered an intermediate commodity, not desired for its intrinsic value, but rather for its expected command over future goods and services. The two functions are related inseparably. As the commodity value (or purchasing power) of money changes, it becomes a temporal common denominator at best. Dollars, for example, become nominal dollars requiring a reference in time—such as 1967 dollars—for complete meaning.

In the United States, as well as most other countries, accounting has been constructed upon the assumption of a reasonably stable monetary unit of measure. This stability supports:

- The use of historical cost as the basis upon which to measure assets and their consumption;
- The definition of profit as the amount that may be distributed while maintaining the *monetary* amount of shareholders' interest at the beginning of the year; and
- The expectation of reasonable comparability of financial statements at a given time and over time.

Most of the accounting frameworks mentioned in Chapter 2 rely upon historical cost as the most practicable means of accounting for the stewardship and operation of complex, capital-intensive organizations. Items having intrinsic value to the business (assets) are recorded, and subsequently accounted for, at their costs of acquisition. As the assets are consumed or expire, their representative costs (expenses) are related with the revenues generated (increases in equity) during the accounting period, with the difference represented as achievement (income or loss) and reflected as a number of dollars. Stripped to its bare essentials (and subject to compliance with the accepted definitions of accounts and their contents), historical cost accounting simply records and reports changes measured in numbers of dollars.

If the value of the dollar changes between the time assets are acquired and the time they are sold or expire, the reported income or loss represents a number of different dollars—a rather curious mixture of money and values.

Evaluation of achievement for the period becomes difficult, both in amount and nature. Similarly, evaluation of achievement over time (comparability) also becomes suspect—whether for the same firm, or for a given firm with others.

As a result, significant inflation has challenged the basic tenets of accountancy in the United States. Charges have been made that traditional financial reports are misleading, that operating decisions have been impaired, and that decisions made by third parties have been warped.

Misleading Reports

Allegations that financial statements make little economic sense today because of inflation are part fiction and part fact.

A classic example is the premise that conventional statements are "largely irrelevant because historical costs no longer reflect accurate and realistic values."[1] Historical costs have never purported to represent values. Cost and value are synonymous only at the time a transaction occurs. Thereafter, equality would be happenstance.

A related complaint is that assets are undervalued in financial statements. There is little question that, in times of rising prices, the net historical costs of most useful assets will be less than their values, however defined. Yet, those same complainants often conveniently ignore the prostitutions of inventories by LIFO costing, and long-lived assets by accelerated methods of depreciation. Also, value, like beauty, has several meanings dependent upon point of view. Value also has several determinants, of which inflation is but one. Value is an entirely different and severable problem.

Inflation is charged with producing "illusory profits" within the framework of historical cost. There is nothing imaginary about the differences between outputs and inputs measured in nominal dollars —they are quite real. Firms invest dollars in order to earn a larger number of dollars. In the long run success will be measured by that yardstick. During interim periods, however, problems arise in interpreting the results of operations, not because the dollars reported are fictitious, but rather because dollars representing different purchasing powers have been commingled. Interpretive problems can be lessened, if not resolved, by means much easier than changing the familiar frameworks of accounting.

The comparability of statements is impaired by inflation. However, the *real* impairment does not result from inflation, per se, but from the fact that inflation affects different firms in different ways— some derive net benefits, while others lose. Comparability is reduced by other factors as well. For a given firm over time, changes occur in sales mixes, geographical markets, and in the compositions of the conglomerate firms themselves. Among firms at a given point in time and over time, the multiplicity of generally accepted accounting conventions employed produces various results, not to mention the fact that few modern-day conglomerates are comparable at all. Consolidated statements have become very blunt, single-purpose measuring tools that conceal much more than they reveal. As a consequence, there is a long-overdue trend away from normative toward situational approaches to financial reporting. Other disclosures, such as segmented reportings, are examples of techniques used to increase the usefulness of financial reports. There is no overriding reason why the effects of price-level changes could not be *explained* in a similar fashion.

Management's concern that inflation produces defective financial reports is a myth. A moment's reflection would support the understandable, vested interest management has in reportings of high profits and returns on equities.

Impaired Internal Decisions

Charges that the absence of comprehensive methods of price-level accounting impairs management decision making are fictions.

No responsible manager uses (nor should consider using) financial accounting reports, prepared for external users, as the primary basis for making internal decisions. As mentioned earlier, financial accounting reports are necessarily couched in historical terms, and subjected to various precepts designed to protect third parties who ordinarily do not have access to information in any other reliable form. Managements, as insiders, are contrained only by ingenuity and cost in the design of internal information systems.

There is no doubt that changing price-levels complicate internal decisions. Access to larger supplies of cash and other quick assets often becomes necessary to finance the higher costs of inventories and day-to-day operations. Cash management has returned to the fore as a "new art."[2]

The costs of most factors of production have increased for most managements, just as living expenses have risen for most households. However, except for a relatively few technologically depressed industries, management has been able to factor inflation into standard costs, increase output prices regularly, and pass inflation along—

increased somewhat by means of markup policy. Many such firms benefit from higher margins at the net cost of the time required to revise and maintain up-to-date budgeting and standard cost systems.

Cost of capital has increased. This should not be surprising since capital is a commodity and, like most others, the price of money (interest) inflates in times of rising prices. Debt forms of capital often tend to have higher cash-flow costs than equity. Yet, for a plethora of reasons, many of which are difficult to comprehend, managements shy away from seeking out new equity capital. One reason often cited is that the market is depressed—whatever that means. If the market depression has occurred because investors perceive greater, regular returns in other forms of investments, then perhaps issuing firms have acted to depress the markets themselves; that is, by the willingness to pay a higher rate to debt rather than equity holders. If the depression results from the inability of short-run gamblers to foresee profits from trading shares rather than investing, well, that's a separate, unrelated abyss.

Increasing costs of replacing plant and equipment are often mentioned, usually with alarm. Generalizations are difficult, if at all possible, in this area of concern. Variables are many and interrelated. Examples include the type of industry (growing or mature); the condition of existing facilities; the effects of technology, present and projected; the timing of future replacements; the perception of future inflations, costs, and market levels; where new plants will be erected, in the United States or in other countries; the firm's replacement policy; and what the products of the future might be. These matters will be examined in detail later when the concepts of replacement value accounting are considered. However, two points are worthy of mention here:

- Firms in mature industries that find themselves with plants that are technologically outdated today are paying the penalty for the complacency of management yesterday. Most of the U.S. steel industry is an excellent example. Managements decided not to invest in new facilities in order to keep pace with the new, more efficient plants furnished the Japanese and Germans following World War II. The U.S. steel oligopoly had no fear of foreign competition—at that time.
- Most other firms were, admittedly, politicking for corporate

tax relief. On the one hand, it was argued that capital was being "immolated" or sacrificed.[3] On the other hand, using a simple, uncluttered example, Anthony illustrated that a "steady-state" company could be maintained in times of rising prices by basing selling prices on historical costs.[4]

Decisions regarding capital investments in new ventures were made more difficult by inflation. However, whether the problems were the result of existing inflation, or the uncertainty of future conditions, is not all that clearly defined. Most likely both factors were involved. Hurdle rates would have been increased because of higher present money prices and for the greater risk associated with future uncertainty as well. The point is that capital investment decisions were complicated, and surely some otherwise desirable long-term projects were spurned, and capital investment sagged, particularly in 1975.[5] The culprit, however, was inflation, not the absence of price-level accounting, nor the amount or quality of information available to management.

Performance evaluations of existing operations and their managers also became more complex. Studies indicated, however, that the methods of evaluation used by even the large, sophisticated multinationals had become suspect long before, if not invalidated, by:

- The creation of pseudo profits by ill-advised applications of transfer prices,[6] and
- The insistent use of profit-based measures, such as return-on-investment (ROI), to evaluate activities producing solely for internal distribution.[7]

Inflation merely represented the addition of a complicating variable to a series of fictions. The effects of inflation were tractable to isolation by also focusing upon quantities of goods and services produced, rather than only upon the quantities of money equivalents they represented.

Distorted External Decisions

The decisions made by external users of financial statements were obviously impaired by changing price levels. Some third parties, such as analysts and the banking community, were in position to request additional information. Most other users were restricted to the data included in financial reports, and vulnerable to the misleading effects mentioned earlier.

Government decisions concerning areas such as taxation are said to be biased by the higher levels of reported earnings during inflation. Government tax coffers were reportedly swelled by some $25 billions in 1973 due to the "inflation tax."[8] Since revenues are enhanced, government clearly benefits from inflation. Moreover, the additional revenues are skimmed without the trouble associated with raising statutory tax rates. However, that is not the same as stating that the government benefits unwittingly. On the contrary, governments know full well of the cause and effect, but simply choose not to index taxes for reasons which, in the main, are rhetorical rather than illogical.

Union demands for a larger share of the pie during periods of inflation are not necessarily distorted. Costs of living increase as well as do the costs of doing business. Higher reported profits do generate requests from labor for what unions consider their fair share. Such results are reasonable, not illogical. Management cannot expect to argue that reported profits are not real because their true costs are understated without anticipating labor's argument that wages are not real either. Distortions are interjected because the results of negotiations are, at least in the United States, more often determined by bargaining (or strike) power, rather than by economic factors, such as productivity. Such "squeaky wheel" techniques are not the product of faulty financial information but faulty social institutions.

Inadequate capital formation was mentioned earlier from the internal viewpoint. Externally, the effects attributed to distortions produced by historical cost statements during inflationary times are moot, at best. To the extent that one accepts the premise of the so-called "efficient market hypothesis," distortions cannot result in uneconomic decisions by those in the marketplace. Therefore, those who shun or desert the traditional equity markets do so for real, rather than imaginary, reasons beyond the *traditional* purview of accounting.

The word "traditional" has been stressed above, since it appears that the FASB now believes that the role of accounting should encompass more than reporting upon past performance. The new objectives connote a predictive function as well, in that

. . . financial reporting should provide information to help investors, creditors, and others assess the amounts, timing, and uncertainty of prospective net cash inflows to the related enterprise.[9]

The new objectives are laudable, but unattainable so long as financial reports remain couched in historical terms. Statements will only furnish information describing past performance, and then only in macro terms insofar as complex enterprises are concerned. Assessment of the future implies that:

- Users would adjust the aggregate historical data by their perceptions of the future in macro terms—a very blunt tool, at best—or,
- Users would be furnished with historical statements for each legal entity comprising the consolidated economic entity, in order to evaluate the performance, liquidity, and solvency— in past and prospective terms—of the legal segments of the economic whole, or
- Management would provide new "soft" data concerning the future prospects of the enterprise as a whole, as well as its segments; the future capital needs and sources, including the retention of earnings; and when, where, and to what extent physical assets are earmarked for addition or replacement.

The recent implementation of segmented reporting[10] is an initial step toward the lifting of the consolidated veil. Much remains to be done although, in the author's opinion, the area of soft data holds the greatest promise.

The argument that capital formation has been impeded by the inadequacy of capital consumption allowances to replace existing facilities has been refuted by Michael Schiff.[11] His findings have been reproduced and updated in Table 3-1.

Schiff's analysis was based upon data from the Bureau of Economic Analysis (BEA). Historical cost, perpetual inventories of total assets in the private sector, divided into 20 categories, are maintained by the BEA. At year end, the specific price index applicable to each

Table 3-1. Capital Consumption Allowances and Depreciation on Current Costs, 1960-1977 (billions of dollars).

YEAR	(1) TAX DEPRECIATION[a]	(2) DEPRECIATION ON CURRENT COST	(3) (1) - (2) DIFFERENCE	(4) INVESTMENT TAX CREDIT (ADJUSTED)[b]	(5) (3) + (4) ADJUSTED DIFFERENCE
1960	$24.0	$26.0	$-2.0	–	$-2.0
1961	25.1	26.9	-1.8	–	-1.8
1962	29.1	28.1	1.0	$1.5	2.5
1963	31.2	29.4	1.8	2.0	3.8
1964	33.4	32.2	1.2	2.4	3.6
1965	36.2	33.0	3.2	3.1	6.3
1966	39.6	36.2	3.4	3.6	7.0
1967	43.4	40.1	3.3	3.8	7.1
1968	47.6	44.2	3.4	4.3	7.7
1969	52.6	49.4	3.2	3.5	6.7
1970	56.3	55.2	1.1	1.6	2.7
1971	61.3	60.9	0.4	3.0	3.4
1972	68.0	65.9	2.1	5.4	7.5
1973	73.5	72.0	1.5	6.7	8.2
1974	79.7	81.7	-2.0	7.7	5.7
1975	84.9	96.8	-11.9	11.7	-0.2
1976	92.4	106.7	-14.3	16.5	2.2
1977	100.8	115.6	-14.8	N/A	

Notes: [a]A. H. Young, "New Estimates of Capital Consumption Allowances—Revision of GNP in the Benchmark," *Survey of Current Business*, October 1955, p. 14; amounts for 1975-77 from "Alternative Estimates of Capital Consumption and Profits of Nonfinancial Corporations, 1975-77," *Survey of Current Business*, September 1978, p. 47.

[b]The reported investment tax credit was adjusted for a 45% tax rate to equate the credit with the deduction for depreciation. Data for 1974-75 from *Survey of Current Business*, July 1978, p. 69; amount for 1976 from the U.S. Treasury, Office of Tax Analysis.

Source: Michael Schiff, "Depreciation Short-Fall—Fact or Fiction?", *Journal of Accountancy*, March 1977, Table 1, p. 41. Reproduced and updated (italicized data) by permission. Copyright ©1977 by the American Institute of Certified Public Accountants, Inc.

type is applied to restate the assets in current costs. Current cost depreciation is then computed by using 85% of the service lives stipulated in Bulletin F (of the Internal Revenue Service) and the *straight line method*. The straight-line, current-cost depreciation was compared with the total of: (1) tax depreciation, per the IRS, and (2) the depreciation equivalent of the investment tax credit, since the tax credit is a capital consumption allowance. The BEA data and the refinement added by Schiff attempt to relate tax and economic depreciation. The data in Table 3-1 indicate that tax depreciation alone has exceeded straight-line, current-cost depreciation by $25.6 billion during the 12-year period, 1962–1973, inclusive. When the depreciation-equivalents of the investment tax credits are added, the excess tax allowance for capital consumption is increased to $66.5 billion for the period.

During 1974 through 1977, a shortfall in tax depreciation, considered alone, did result—totaling $43 billion for the 4 years. However, the shortfall was more than offset by the depreciation-equivalent of the investment tax credit.

The Machinery and Allied Products Institute (MAPI) has perennially challenged the adequacy of capital consumption allowances. The methodology used was similar to the first three columns shown in Table 3–1; that is, tax depreciation was related to current-cost depreciation. Raw data were obtained from the same sources used by Schiff and 85% of Bulletin F lives were selected. However, the MAPI studies: (1) ignored the depreciation-equivalents of investment tax credits, and (2) calculated current-cost depreciation by the *double-declining-balance method* (at twice the straight-line rate). Naturally, quite a different picture was presented. Since April 1979, the MAPI has reverted to the straight-line basis stating that ". . . the difference no longer justifies departure. . . ."[12] The MAPI has not as yet reflected the investment tax credit as a capital consumption allowance.

The real challenge, therefore, is one of viewpoint. Professor Schiff attempted to relate capital consumption allowances on tax returns with their rational economic equivalents. The MAPI, on the other hand, depicted a depreciation shortfall by not considering the equivalent of the investment tax credit and, until 1979, using the most accelerated of depreciation methods.

Few would disagree that an increasing level of capital investment is essential to improve employment and productivity, as well as to remain competitive in international trade. However, rather than attempting to use inadequate depreciation as a crutch, a straightforward argument for lower corporate tax rates should be addressed. Accountancy call ill-afford any additional tax gimmicks such as the accelerated depreciation methods of the recent past.

The foregoing topics were examined in order to place the effects of changing price levels upon financial statements into context, not to brush them aside.

CHRONOLOGY OF U.S. CONSIDERATIONS

Lukewarm debate over how accountants should recognize the effects of inflation has occurred intermittently in the United States for over 60 years. Interest has risen and ebbed with the magnitude of inflation—and the probability of tax concessions as perceived by the business community. Accounting treatments suggested in the past will be reviewed since many have been resurrected, most with little revision.

Until the recent past, serious concern over the stability of the dollar coincided with the periods of chronic inflation during wars and their aftermaths.

For instance, in 1918, Livingston Middleditch, Jr., was concerned that the wholesale price index in the United States had nearly doubled during the 1914–1917 period. Accounting reports based upon historical costs combined dollars of changing value "without distinction." In his view, this was analogous to "mixing inches with centimeters or measuring a field with a rubber tape-line."[13] Middleditch suggested that the wholesale price index be applied to financial statements in order to express them in terms of dollars of current value. In this manner, neither the accounts nor the accounting process would need to be changed. The usefulness of the information contained in the historical accounts would be unimpaired and costs would be minimized. Only certain historical amounts reported in the financial statements would require restatement. Middleditch became the first published advocate of what is now known as reporting in units of general purchasing power.

A year later, in 1919, John Bauer suggested use of the second method widely discussed today—replacement value accounting. In brief, Bauer considered rising costs as potential threats to the ability of a firm to replace its long-lived assets and thereby "renew" itself. He recommended that depreciation be computed upon replacement rather than historical costs.[14]

Prices peaked in 1920 in the United States, declined until 1922, then remained rather stable until a further decline, precipitated in 1930, led to a trough established in 1933. The massive writeups of fixed assets that occurred in the 1920s were written down during the early 1930s. Interest in price-level accounting waned.

In 1936, Henry W. Sweeney regenerated some interest in the

topic through publication of his doctoral thesis, and he is often considered as the father of price-level accounting in the United States. Sweeney's work reflected the imprints of his earlier studies of accounting reports in Germany during the volatile 1920s. His thinking was also influenced by the works of the German professors Schmalenbach (who favored general purchasing power) and Schmidt (who advocated use of current costs). Sweeney argued that changing price levels caused dollars to become "rubber units of measurement."[15] His proposal, *stabilized accounting,* represented a hybrid form of price-level accounting and combined the teachings of Schmalenbach and Schmidt. In summary form, Sweeney's proposal required three steps:

- Restate opening and closing balance sheets into homogeneous units of purchasing power by applying the year-end cost-of-living index. Use surplus (retained earnings) as the balancing item.
- Segregate the gains and losses for the current year, obtained above, into those realized (by actual cash receipts or disbursements) and unrealized (all others). Include realized items in net income for the period. Report unrealized items after net income as a separate section of the income statement.
- Acquire replacement costs (by appraisals or other accepted means) for "real-value" assets (property, plant, equipment, inventories). Superimpose the replacement costs upon the indexed costs of these assets in the balance sheet, reflecting all differences in the unrealized segment of the income statement.

Sweeney attempted to report the effects of changes in general and specific prices, while retaining desirable accounting conventions, and increasing the usefulness of financial statements. He protected the concept of realization of net income. He used the unrealized segment of net income as a connecting link that retained the articulation between the balance sheet and income statement. The use of replacement costs for real assets on the balance sheet furnished, in Sweeney's opinion, values that many users had, rightly or wrongly, begun to expect from financial statements.

Professor Sweeney's ideas were the victims of time and circumstance. In 1936, inflation was not a real concern. Also, accountants well remembered the abuses of appraisals used during the 1920s. Finally, the computational procedures were complicated and time-consuming. Sweeney's ideas were never adopted.

The economic pressures following World War II rekindled inflation as well as interest in coping with higher costs.

In 1947, the American Institute of Accountants (predecessor of the American Institute of CPAs) and the Rockefeller Foundation formed the Study Group on Business Income. In that same year, the Institute's Committee on Accounting Procedure (forerunner of the Accounting Principles Board) considered the suggestion that depreciation be based upon current values in order to cope with rising costs. The suggestion was disapproved as impracticable and undesirable in *Accounting Research Bulletin No. 33*. Pressures from industry urged reconsideration, possibly more in an attempt to support efforts to reduce the corporate tax bite than over concern for better reporting.

In October 1948, the Committee on Accounting Procedure confirmed the position it had taken in *ARB No. 33* in a letter sent to members of the American Institute. In its letter, the Committee stated that no changes in depreciation methods would be considered pending receipt of the report of the Study Group. During the interim, the Committee charged management with the responsibility for coping with increased costs, as well as reporting to shareholders the perceived effects, and the actions taken.[16]

George O. May, a member of the Study Group, prepared a separate monograph, published in 1949, containing his suggestions for offsetting the *approximate* effects of inflation in financial reports.[17] May's recommendations stressed objectivity and ease of application. He suggested the use of LIFO to recognize the higher costs of replacing inventories, together with a depreciation charge in two parts:

- The customary amount based upon historical costs and credited to the regular accumulation accounts, plus
- An additional increment based upon the difference between the historical cost of an asset and that cost adjusted by the consumer price index at year end. This increment would be credited to a replacement reserve in the equity section.

In November 1949, the U.S. Treasury Department "reluctantly

approved" the use of dollar-value LIFO costing by all taxpayers (it was previously limited to retailers). The dollar-value method made LIFO costing practicable by treating inventory groups as pools, to which appropriate price indexes could be applied in order to cost inventory increments. This approval enabled industries to adopt LIFO costing and eliminate taxation of inventory profits, so long as LIFO was also used to determine income in financial reports.[18]

In 1951, the Committee on Concepts and Standards of the American Accounting Association supported continued use of historical costs in primary financial statements. The Committee suggested that supplementary statements be used to report the effects of inflation upon a given firm. Further study was recommended and, in this regard, the Committee expressed its favor for consistent application of a generally accepted price index to all financial statements.[19]

Price controls were imposed in 1951, and the Korean War being in progress, attention was diverted until 1952, when the final report of the Study Group on Business Income was issued. The report had a dampening effect since the Study Group agreed that inflation was impairing the usefulness of financial statements, but furnished no consensus on corrective measures to be taken.[20]

In 1953, *ARB No. 33* (and the letter of affirmation mentioned earlier) was restated as part of *Accounting Research Bulletin No. 43.* Dissenting opinions were also appended to the restatement and, in the main, reflected agreement with the recommendations of George May, cited above.[21]

The 1954 Internal Revenue Code permitted the use of accelerated methods of depreciation for tax purposes. This tax benefit effectively eliminated pressures from the bulk of the business community for price-level accounting. Prices remained relatively stable until the advent of stagflation (1956–1958).

During the ensuing 10 years, there were no official pronouncements on price-level accounting. The IRS abandoned Bulletin F in 1962 and relaxed constraints on the useful lives of depreciable assets. In October 1963, the AICPA issued *Accounting Research Study No. 6: Reporting the Financial Effects of Price-Level Changes. ARS No. 6* was the product of nearly 2 years' work by the staff of the Accounting Research Division of the AICPA. The study contained an excellent appendix covering index numbers (by Cecilia Tierney); a second appendix depicting the complete, step-by-step process of adjustment recommended; plus other appendices explaining the effects of holding money during inflation, price-level reporting examples from other countries, and results of experiments conducted by several U.S. firms. Unfortunately, *ARS No. 6* did not analyze the desirability of the several possible methods to reflect changing price levels. Instead, the study constructed and delineated a unified method of adjusting historical cost statements by the use of a general price index. In sum, *ARS No. 6* suggested that:

- Historical cost should be retained as the basis for preparation of the primary financial statements.
- Supplementary statements should be used to report the effects of price-level changes. The statements should be restated in units of purchasing power of common—*not constant*—dollars as of the date of the latest balance sheet.
- Restatement would be accomplished by application of a multiplier based upon the Gross National Product Implicit Price Deflator index:

$$\frac{\text{Numerator}}{\text{Denominator}} = \frac{\text{Index at latest balance sheet date}}{\text{Index at date of transaction, but}}$$
$$\text{not earlier than 1945.*}$$

(*The study group contended that the market baskets of goods and services supporting GNP indexes prior to 1945 were not comparable to those in 1963.)

- Gains and losses in purchasing power resulting from changes in holdings of net monetary assets (those fixed in money terms by law or contract) should be reflected in net income for the period. Changes in nonmonetary items (all others) should be reflected in net income as the items are used or expire.
- Income statements could be translated using the average index for the year (if operations were uniform) or quarterly indexes (if operations were cyclical). The exception, of course, concerned depreciation which would be based upon the restated costs of assets at their acquisition dates.
- In comparative presentations, statements of prior periods were to be rolled forward (restated) in units of purchasing power at the current year-end. (Thus, statements were to be expressed

in *common,* not constant, dollars. Data for prior periods would
be updated each year they were presented.)

The recommendations in *ARS No. 6* bore no weight of authority
since research studies are meant to encourage discussion. Use of the
supplementary statements would have been voluntary. Few firms
wished to be the minority of pioneers reporting lower (or higher)
earnings than others in their industries. Few firms adopted the
suggestions in *ARS No. 6.*

In 1969, the Accounting Principles Board issued its rather innocuous *Statement No. 3.*[22] As an official pronouncement, the *Statement* could have required the use of the methods in *ARS No. 6.*
Instead, *APBS No. 3* expressed only mild interest in reporting the
effects of price-level changes. Supplemental statements could be
used but were not required. The *Statement* was ignored by most of
the business community.

During 1973, the inexorable movement toward double-digit inflation became a reality in the United States. The Financial Accounting Standards Board had succeeded the APB as standard-setter
for the accounting profession. Motivated by the severity of inflation,
and the actions taken or underway by the professions and/or governments in other countries, the FASB issued a discussion memorandum
in February 1974. Following open hearings and the receipt of nearly
150 written comments, the FASB released its exposure draft, *Financial Reporting in Units of General Purchasing Power,* on December
31, 1974. Supplementary statements expressed in common dollars
were to be required for fiscal periods beginning January 1, 1976 and
thereafter. In effect, the FASB merely dusted off *ARS No. 6,* condensed it, changed the title, and published it in the form of an
exposure draft. No changes in thinking were introduced since 1963.
For a multitude of reasons, the exposure draft was not supported
by a majority in either the business or the professional community.
In fact, only 2 of the 600 firms represented in the AICPA's 1977
report, *Accounting Trends and Techniques,* issued supplementary
statements based upon general purchasing power units.[23]

Irked by the lack of any progress by the profession, the Securities
and Exchange Commission issued its *Accounting Series Release No.
190* on March 23, 1976.[24] The particulars of *ASR-190* will be
examined in a subsequent chapter concerning hybrid proposals.

However, suffice it to say here that *ASR-190* required the larger public enterprises to provide supplemental disclosures of selected information regarding replacement costs. The SEC termed *ASR-190* an "experiment" tentatively slated to be conducted over a three-year period.

In June 1976, the FASB tabled further action on its exposure draft pending developments in the project underway regarding the conceptual framework of accounting. During the 1976 Christmas holidays, required reading for most accountants and many business-men came in the form of a three-part, 462-page, "conceptual frame-work package" published by the FASB:

- *Scope and Implications of the Conceptual Framework Project* (24 pages)—A booklet serving as an introduction to the project.
- *Tentative Conclusions on Objectives of Financial Statements of Business Enterprises* (78 pages)—An exposure draft, of sorts, presenting the FASB's current opinions of the purposes of financial reporting.
- *Elements of Financial Statements and Their Measurement* (360 pages)—A three-part tome (discussion memorandum) encompassing the elements of financial statements, the characteristics of accounting information, and various bases for the measurement of the elements.

The "package" demanded considerable resolve of the reader. Many of the larger accounting firms prepared summary analyses for interested parties. One such firm, Ernst & Ernst, expressed its concern that the tenor and content of the package indicated a predisposition of the FASB to shift from reliance upon historical cost to some form of current value accounting.[25] Ernst & Ernst performed two significant services for accountancy in the United States, in the opinion of this author. They prepared and published the understandable analysis mentioned, together with their con-sidered opinions. In addition, they prepared and held numerous seminars throughout the country, "FASB Conceptual Framework: Issues and Implications."[26] The seminars emphasized the Ernst & Ernst concern that, *because of the narrowness of definition,* the path of the conceptual framework project could lead only to the adoption of current-value accounting. To what extent the FASB has deemed it advisable to reconsider its path remains to be seen.

On December 28, 1978, the FASB issued an exposure draft of a proposed statement *Financial Reporting and Changing Prices.* The draft called for various supplemental data based upon *either* general-purchasing-power or current-cost accounting. Since the draft actually represents a *hybrid* proposal, it will be examined in Chapter 7. For FASB *Statement No. 33,* see Appendix 9A.

The foregoing chronology illustrates that professional interest in reporting the effects of inflation varied directly with the degree of inflation. The interest of the business community typically varied with the probability and/or receipt of tax relief. A recent study indicates that little change has occurred in the financial and business community. Inflation accounting or reporting was found to be a "nonissue." Most business respondents expressed concern over their ability to "control" inflation, not how to measure and account for its effects. Moreover, management indicated a willingness to "live with" certain distortions in financial statements in exchange for the possibility of "tax relief to allow for capital formation."[27]

SUMMARY

The U.S. dollar is no longer a reasonably stable measuring stick. Consequently, the data in traditional financial reports based upon historical costs commingle changes in costs and values. The information is, at best, less useful and could be misleading unless the effects of inflation are also disclosed in some manner. The distortions in financial statements are viewed from different perspectives by the business and accounting communities. The different concerns and objectives are understandable; however, they should be remembered when proposals for corrective measures are considered.

The business community is concerned with coping with inflation on a day-to-day basis. However, interest in accounting or reporting for inflation primarily represents pressure for corporate tax relief. Tax relief for business is as sorely needed as it is for individuals. The question relates to means, not ends. As Schiff has illustrated, business cannot support requests for increased depreciation allowances to counteract inflation. Business pressures for lower tax rates or, preferably, for indexation could be supported without further prostitution of accounting. If business tax relief were to be granted tomorrow, inflation would not be cured or reduced—only the tax pains felt by the business sector would be lessened—and the accounting and reporting problems would remain unresolved.

The accounting community, in the main, is concerned over the effects of inflation upon financial reports and the distortions produced. Some sectors are concerned as much (or more) over the remedies proposed as the distortions themselves. Questions posed remain unanswered. Should the historical cost framework be discarded? If so, what should replace it? If not, how should the effects of inflation be disclosed in financial reports? Should the basic reports be restructured, or should new supplemental schedules be added? Should normative approaches be employed, or are economic entities affected in different ways and degrees? Should disclosures encompass the effects of both general and specific price-level changes? Do the solutions proposed reflect economic sense; are they worth their probable costs?

The accounting dilemmas are real and can be said to evidence less of a narrow-gauge, vested interest than the concerns expressed by business. Yet, if these dilemmas were also satisfactorily resolved, the disease would still remain.

Most likely no human being could lift, much less assimilate, all the literature produced on price-level accounting during the last decade in the United States alone. It is unfortunate, as well as surprising, that the accounting profession has not seen fit to devote as much effort toward affecting a cure for the disease as they have on methods of charting its effects. Perhaps the language of business has not yet achieved the degree of independence from business that the profession alleges. Accountancy is old enough, but maybe not mature enough.

CHAPTER 3. NOTES

1. Adolph J. H. Enthoven, "Replacement-Value Accounting: Wave of the Future?", *Harvard Business Review,* January–February 1976, p. 6.

2. "Cash Management: The New Art of Wringing More Profit from Corporate Funds," *Business Week,* March 13, 1978, pp. 62–66, 68.

3. Alfred C. Neal, "The Immolation of Business Capital," *Harvard Business Review,* March–April 1978, pp. 75–82.

4. Robert N. Anthony, "A Case for Historical Costs," *Harvard Business Review,* November–December 1976, pp. 69–79.

5. See, "Where Is The Capital Spending Boom?", *Business Week,* September 13, 1976, p. 64.

6. Itzhak Sharav, "Transfer Pricing–Diversity of Goals and Practices," *Journal of Accountancy,* April 1974, pp. 56–62.

7. Sidney M. Robbins and Robert B. Stobaugh, "The Bent Measuring Stick for Foreign Subsidiaries," *Harvard Business Review,* September–October 1973, pp. 80–88.

8. Milton Friedman, "Monetary Correction," in Herbert Giersch, et al. *Essays on Inflation and Indexation* (Washington, D.C.: American Enterprise Institute for Public Policy Research, 1974), p. 30.

9. Financial Accounting Standards Board, *Statement of Financial Accounting Concepts No. 1,* "Objectives of Financial Reporting by Business Enterprises" (Stamford, Conn.: FASB, November 1978), p. viii.

10. Financial Accounting Standards Board, *Statement of Financial Accounting Standards No. 14,* "Financial Reporting for Segments of a Business Enterprise" (Stamford, Conn.: FASB, December 1976).

11. Michael Schiff, "Depreciation Short Fall: Fact or Fiction?" *Journal of Accountancy,* March 1977, pp. 40–42.

12. George Terborgh, "Inflation and Profits," Machinery and Allied Products Institute Memorandum, January 1974. Revised and republished seven times; latest revision dated April 1979, p. 2.

13. Livingston Middleditch, Jr., "Should Accounts Reflect the Changing Value of the Dollar?", *Journal of Accountancy,* February 1918, p. 115.

14. John Bauer, "Renewal Costs and Business Profits in Relation to Rising Costs," *Journal of Accountancy,* December 1919, pp. 413–419.

15. Henry W. Sweeney, *Stabilized Accounting* (New York: Harper & Brothers, 1936), preface.

16. "Depreciation and High Costs," *Accounting Research Bulletin No. 33* (New York: American Institute of Accountants, 1947).

17. George O. May, *Business Income and Price Levels* (New York: American Institute of Accountants, 1949).

18. Herbert T. McAnly, "How LIFO Began," *Management Accounting,* May 1975, pp. 24–26.

19. American Accounting Association, Committee on Concepts and Standards, "Price Level Changes and Financial Statements," *The Accounting Review,* October 1951, pp. 468–474; also reprinted in *Journal of Accountancy,* October 1951, pp. 461–465.

20. Study Group on Business Income, *Changing Concepts of Business Income* (New York: The Macmillan Company, 1952).

21. *Accounting Research and Terminology Bulletins: Final Edition* (New York: AICPA, 1961), pp. 70–71.

22. Accounting Principles Board, *Statement No. 3: Financial Statements Restated for General Price-Level Changes* (New York: AICPA, June 1969).

23. American Institute of Certified Public Accountants, *Accounting Trends and Techniques,* 31st ed., (New York: AICPA, 1977), p. 72.

24. Securities and Exchange Commission, "Notice of Adoption of Amendments to Regulation S-X Requiring Disclosure of Certain Replacement Cost Data," *Accounting Series Release No. 190,* March 23, 1976.

25. Ernst & Ernst, "Conceptual Framework—Our Analysis and Response," June 1977. Retrieval No. 38608.

26. A 59-page booklet bearing the same title was furnished attendees of the seminars.

27. Allen H. Seed III, *Inflation: Its Impact on Financial Reporting and Decision Making* (New York: Financial Executives Research Foundation, 1978), p. xiv.

4

International Considerations

As inflation spilled over national boundaries, most countries wrestled with controlling as well as reporting the effects of inflation. This attenuated tour of selected countries is made in order to examine the remedies considered and adopted, as well as the conditions affecting the considerations.

THE INTERNATIONAL PERSPECTIVE

All industrial countries have been afflicted by inflation during the last decade. As the data in Table 4-1 indicate, the 1973 OPEC price orgy did not create inflation—consumer prices rose every year since 1968 in the countries listed.

Since 1974, the rate of increase in consumer prices has declined in all countries except Brazil. However, the post-1974 declines were to higher plateaus than those existing in 1968—Japan, the Netherlands, and West Germany are the only exceptions. This fact is also reflected in Table 4-2. Average increases in consumer prices for the past 3 years continue to exceed the average for the entire 1968–1978 period in all but Japan, the Netherlands, and West Germany. While OPEC's economic warfare did not create inflation, it redefined the levels of inflation in most countries.

The rate of inflation represented a signifcant element among those considered by countries in selecting options for combating and reporting the effects of rising prices. Other determinants were found

Table 4-1. Percentage Increases in Consumer Price Indexes, Selected Industrial Countries, 1968-1978.

YEAR	UNITED STATES	AUSTRALIA	BRAZIL	CANADA	FRANCE	JAPAN	NETHER-LANDS	WEST GERMANY	UNITED KINGDOM
1968	4.2	2.7	22.0	4.1	4.5	5.3	3.7	2.6	4.7
1969	5.4	2.9	22.6	4.5	6.4	5.2	7.5	1.9	5.4
1970	5.9	3.9	22.5	3.3	5.2	7.7	3.6	3.4	6.4
1971	4.3	6.1	20.2	2.9	5.3	6.1	7.5	5.3	9.4
1972	3.3	5.8	16.7	4.8	6.1	4.5	7.8	5.5	7.1
1973	6.2	9.5	12.6	7.6	7.3	11.7	8.0	6.9	9.2
1974	11.0	15.1	24.5	10.8	13.7	24.5	9.6	7.0	16.0
1975	9.1	15.1	29.0	10.8	11.7	11.8	10.2	6.0	24.2
1976	5.8	13.5	41.7	7.5	9.6	9.3	8.8	4.5	16.5
1977	6.5	12.3	44.0	8.0	9.8	8.1	6.4	3.9	15.9
1978[a]	8.9	7.9	38.9	8.7	9.3	3.3	4.2	2.1	7.8

[a]For 12-month period ended October 1978.

Sources of data: OECD *Economic Outlook*, No. 24, December 1978 (OECD members); IMF *International Financial Statistics*, March 1979 (Brazil).

Table 4–2. Consumer Prices, Average Changes, 1968–1978.

COUNTRY	AVERAGE CHANGE FOR PERIOD			
	1968–72	1973–75	1976–78	1968–78
United States	4.6	8.8	7.1	6.4
Australia	4.3	13.2	11.2	8.6
Brazil	20.8	22.0	41.5	26.8
Canada	3.9	9.7	8.1	6.6
France	5.5	10.9	9.6	8.1
Japan	5.8	16.0	6.9	8.9
Netherlands	6.0	9.3	6.5	7.0
West Germany	3.7	6.6	3.5	4.4
United Kingdom	6.6	16.5	13.4	11.1

Source: Averages of data in Table 4–1.

in the economic, political, legal, and tax structures, augmented by history and tradition.

Various measures were selected to combat inflation. For a variety of reasons, some countries were more successful than others. A few were helped by chance.

In most instances, interest in price-level accounting was affected by the success, or lack of success, in reducing the rate of inflation. Moreover, the approaches to price-level accounting were affected by all the environmental factors mentioned previously.

One caution is in order. Remedies proven successful in one environment are not necessarily transplantable in others. Economies, much like people, have different natures—in constitution, vigor, resistance to disease, tolerance of medication, and determination to help heal themselves.

LATIN AMERICA

Rampant inflation virtually wrecked the developing economies of most Latin American countries. Consequently, efforts were directed primarily toward arresting and curing the disease rather than charting its effects. Two examples—one at each end of the spectrum of success—are worthy of mention.

Argentina

As the eighth largest nation in the world, Argentina is endowed with many blessings: racial homogeneity, an educated populace, a large middle class, and a wealth of natural resources. Yet, it has been plagued by instability, endless strikes, and economic myopia. For some 30 years (1946–1976), the Peronistas concentrated upon giving to the people (labor), assuming a totally elastic wherewithal was available. The country has nearly been bankrupted.

Among Latin American countries, Argentina is second in size only to Brazil. Where inflation is concerned, Argentina is probably second to none, with increases in consumer prices of 182% in 1975, 443% in 1976, 176% in 1977, and 166% through October 1978.[1] A better context may be provided by U.S. Department of Labor statistics that report the cost of living in Buenos Aires zoomed from a base of 100 in 1970 to 13,274 by March 1977.

The gamut of control measures has been employed since 1970. The monetary unit (peso) was redefined several times, yet it is considered worthless by the populace and spent as soon as received. Price, wage, foreign investment, repatriation, and exchange controls have been applied. Since the peso became useless as a measuring unit, the government constructed general price indexes as the basis for the revaluation of transactions, assets, and taxes.

The major accounting institutes have required that price-level-adjusted information supplement the primary financial statements since 1972. The supplemental data were to be restated using the official government indexes and could be presented by means of complementary statements, use of a dual-column format, or by footnotes. Since the reporting requirement was not reflected in the law, compliance has not been widespread.

Brazil

Like most Latin American countries, Brazil has been faced with the twin problems of growing pains and persistent inflation for nearly 30 years.

Growth in aggregate terms has been remarkable. Gross national product has increased at an average rate of 10% per year since 1968 and reached $192 billion in 1978—eighth largest among Western nations. However, rapid growth came at a price. Whether the price is considered to be high or reasonable depends upon one's point of view.

Since Brazil depends upon imported capital and technology, inflation has ranged between 40-45% since 1976—roughly five times that of all industrial nations. On the other hand, when rates over 100% in the early 1960s are considered, as well as the decreasing trend to the low of 12.6% in 1973, Brazil's accomplishment is rather extraordinary. The reasons are worthy of mention.[2]

There is a consensus that Brazil's economy would have collapsed were it not for the adoption of indexation, or "monetary correction," and the innovative controls exercised by strong central governments.

Prior to 1964, the government experimented with the indexation of selected items—minimum wages, government salaries, rents, and personal income taxes—based upon movements of consumer prices. Fixed assets were revalued twice during the 1950s, but the revaluations were mostly cosmetic since they were either taxed, or the higher depreciation amounts were not deductible for tax purposes until after 1958. Exchange rates were centrally administered and reflected the typical infrequent but significant fluctuations. Speculation thrived while investment suffered. Financing was not to be found with usury laws at 12% and inflation nearly 10 times that amount.

Following the revolution in 1964, the government assumed the role of biggest consumer and investor while encouraging the supervised growth of free enterprise, both foreign and domestic.

Monetary correction was implemented in stages over the entire economy. Wages and pensions were indexed to the cost of living. Guidelines were provided regularly by the government based upon the present real wage, anticipated inflation, and productivity changes. In 1968, a refinement was added that corrected any differences, ex post, between anticipated and actual inflation. Government borrowings were indexed (both principal and interest) as well as all private financial contracts, including rents, life insurance, and savings deposits. Indexation improved the fiscal and monetary management of the government itself and enabled it to curb speculation. Price controls were used where necessary to control oligopolistic sectors.

Capital sources, internal and external, were enhanced by the indexation of fixed assets and working capital in 1964, and further refined in the 1976 company laws. In brief, two monetary corrections were required *for reporting and tax purposes*. All permanent assets (excluding inventories) were revalued monthly based upon special government indexes. Working capital (including inventories on the FIFO basis) was also revalued using general price-indexes constructed by the government. Offsetting credits were made to capital maintenance accounts in the equity section. Reported and taxable incomes were reduced by charges to "monetary correction" expense accounts for the increased depreciation and capital maintenance amounts. In effect, the government strove to attract and maintain capital investment by minimizing the confiscatory effects of taxation during periods of rampant inflation.

Several crucial factors should be recognized in the Brazilian experience:

- Indexation was a means, not an end in itself. It removed, or ameliorated, most of the so-called "textbook effects" of inflation.[3]
- Monetary correction was *nondiscriminatory*. It applied to individuals, foreign and domestic companies, as well as the government itself.
- Strong, yet positive, government directions were used to minimize, as well as manage, bottlenecks and oligopolistic influences. The government assumed the role of partner with free enterprise.
- The accounting model retained money as the unit of measure. Assets were measured at replacement costs based upon official indexes. Capital maintenance was achieved by protecting the purchasing power of the assets of the business.

Some consider the Brazilian experience miraculous in light of the circumstances. Growth was achieved while inflation was reduced and controlled. The sound judgment of the government must be given most of the credit. Free enterprise was encouraged yet inputs and outputs were guided to achieve goal congruence. Imports and exports were controlled in the interests of the total economy; businesses that cooperated were welcomed and encouraged. While American firms usually abhor any form of government restraint, most U.S. firms operating in Brazil will agree that the Brazilian government made the right decisions most of the time; solicited, rather than demanded, cooperation; and served as an understanding partner.

The real test may lie ahead. During the 1974–1978 period, governmental restraints and controls were relaxed or eliminated. Concurrently, the government became overly ambitious in spending for industrial development; government debt was increased, and so was inflation. A new military president assumed the reins of government in March 1979, along with its present and future challenges.

CONTINENTAL EUROPE

The price-level accounting practices of selected European countries will be reviewed since some are unique. All will prevail until superseded by directives of the European Economic Community. For convenience only, the United Kingdom will be considered separately in the section that follows, along with selected members of the British Commonwealth.

The European Economic Community

Since companies in member states compete for the same resources and markets, one goal of the European Economic Community (EEC) is to subject all companies to the same legal, tax, accounting, and disclosure requirements.

The process of harmonization is accomplished primarily by means of EEC directives and regulations. Following approval of a directive by the EEC Council of Ministers, member states normally have 2 years in which to conform their laws to the directive. EEC regulations are effective upon approval; no national legislation is necessary. The current status of relevant EEC directives and regulations is furnished in Figure 4–1. Two directives on company law (the Fourth and Seventh) will be reviewed, as well as the directive on corporate taxation.

The Fourth Directive. Following 7 year's debate and three revisions, the Fourth Directive on Company Law was approved in July 1978 by the EEC Council.

The first draft of the Fourth Directive was issued in 1971, prior to the entry of the U.K., Ireland, and Denmark into the EEC. As a

FIGURE 4-1. EEC DIRECTIVES AND REGULATIONS CONCERNING CORPORATE LAW, ACCOUNTING, AND TAXATION.

	DRAFT DATES	DATE APPROVED	TOPIC
I. *Directives, Company Law:*			
First, No. 68/151		3/68	Publication of balance sheet, profit and loss account. *Ultra vires* rules.
Second, No. 77/91		12/76	Public companies: capital formation and maintenance.
Third, No. 78/855		10/78	Intrastate mergers.
Fourth, No. 78/660		7/78	All limited liability companies (except banks/insurance companies): formats of statements; rules of accounts (except consolidations).
Fifth	1972		Structure, administration, and audit of public companies.
Sixth	1972,1975		Prospectuses: content and publication.
Seventh	1976		Consolidated accounts.
Eighth	1978		Statutory auditors: qualifications, independence, reciprocity.
II. *Regulations:*			
European Company— Societas Europa (SE)	1970,1975		Proposal for a European Company, subject to EEC (rather than member) laws. Similar to Federal Chartering in the U.S.
European Cooperative	1973		Joint ventures by companies in different member states.
III. *Directives, Taxation:*			
Corporate and Withholding Taxes	1975		Harmonization of rates; tax credit imputation system.
Parent/subsidiary Taxes	1969		Common system of taxing source/dividend incomes interstate.
Mutual Assistance		12/77	Tax information exchange among member states.

Source: Compiled by the author from announcements appearing in various issues, *EEC Bulletin,* Price Waterhouse & Co.

result, the original draft reflected German and French attitudes toward uniformity, conservatism, legalism, and tax-orientation. Since 1971, the "true and fair view" espoused by the U.K. and the Netherlands was gradually accepted and is the basis for accounting in the approved directive. Reporting guidelines call for disclosures of: tax-based items, such as additional depreciation; all reserves (often called "secret") through the income statement; assets and liabilities by category; and the cost of goods sold. The latter item will affect U.K. reportings primarily.

Uniformity is still reflected by the statement formats permitted— one for the balance sheet, two for the income statement. The amount of footnote disclosure varies with the size of the firm; the larger the firm, the greater the disclosures.

Historical cost has been retained as the basis of valuation. In fact, the German government was so adamantly opposed to the adoption of inflation accounting (for Germany or any other member) that the inclusion of any such Community-wide *requirement* would have jeopardized approval of the Fourth Directive. Member states are permitted to authorize departure from historical cost in certain conditions and for certain items (Articles 30 and 31). However, no method or system is suggested.

The Seventh Directive. Now in draft form, approval of the Seventh Directive on consolidated accounts will have been assisted by passage of the Fourth Directive. Basically, parent and subsidiaries (domestic and foreign) are to be consolidated using the equity method. Control of subsidiaries is patterned after the German concept of "effective control" rather than only upon percentages of ownership. The most unusual (and troublesome) feature is the requirement for a "horizontal" consolidation of EEC companies which are independent of each other but are owned by the same parent firm located outside the EEC. Also, the draft permits members to call for partial consolidation of joint ventures.

Tax Harmonization. The 1975 directive represents the initial step toward harmonizing the *systems* of corporate taxation. A common imputation system (between 45 and 55%) is required with a tax credit of similar rate for shareholders. Imputation systems are now used by all EEC members, except Germany, Luxembourg, and the

Netherlands. The draft also sets the withholding tax rate on dividends at a uniform 25% to discourage tax evasion.

The major criticism of the tax directive concerns the focus upon tax systems and rates while ignoring the different methods of determining the taxable income base.

The directives mentioned, together with many other less important proposals under consideration, will provide a starting point, and an atmosphere, conducive to further harmonization of accounting among EEC members. Historical cost has been retained as the basis of measurement, leaving members the option to require supplementary price-level-accounting information in the form and content considered necessary based upon the particular environments and circumstances. Consequently, some revisions will come about in the price-level-accounting methods and/or proposals within the member states mentioned below.

France

Operating within a civil law framework, French accounting methods represent uniform systems prescribed by the government.

There are approximately 900 quoted companies (compared with 500 in Germany and 3400 in the UK) and, as in Germany, shareholdings are primarily in the hands of banks, families, and government agencies. Accounting serves the needs of the government for statistics, tax purposes, and economic planning. Consequently, audits are geared to conformity with the laws.

The French government has protected its tax base zealously. Consequently, inflation accounting proposals have fallen upon deaf ears. However, the government has not been averse to levying price controls and other antiinflationary measures upon industry since that sector is seen as the real culprit.

In early 1977, a committee appointed by the government recommended that supplementary information based upon general-purchasing-power concepts be furnished by quoted companies. The proposal was rejected by being ignored. Shortly thereafter, at the urgings of the French Stock Exchange, finance acts were passed that permitted one-time revaluations of fixed assets, yet did not allow these write-ups to affect taxable income. Revaluations were compulsory for quoted companies, optional for others. All fixed assets could be revalued by using current or replacement costs, as of December 31, 1976, subject to a limit obtained by the use of indexes issued by the government.

No taxes were imposed upon the write-ups of nondepreciable assets. The amounts were to be added to an equity reserve not available for dividends.

Write-ups of depreciable items were not taxed either, merely credited to a special reserve. Depreciation for tax purposes was to be calculated on the revalued amounts, offset by the addition of a similar increment to income and a reduction of the special reserve. In effect, the revaluations were essentially cosmetic.[4]

Germany

The philosophy of German industry and government is simple and direct—keep inflation within reasonable bounds and you won't have to worry about how to account for it.

The German discipline results from vivid memories of the hyper-inflationary periods following the world wars. Savings and capital were destroyed. Also, during the reconstruction after World War II, the Germans learned what could be accomplished when government, business, and labor pulled in the same harness.

Several factors have enabled Germany to apply the harsh actions necessary to arrest inflation. Following the OPEC increases in 1973, the government cooled the booming economy since unemployment was of little concern—transient workers were sent home. Modern plant and a disciplined work force helped Germany retain (if not increase) worker productivity, increase exports, and minimize labor strife. Revaluations of the mark reduced imported inflation and the effective costs of oil (since contracts were in dollars). Costs of imports were lowered and, since many imports were intermediate goods processed for export, foreign market shares were enhanced. A strong currency and payments surplus permitted Germany to furnish trade credits and expand foreign markets. Auto exports were reduced, yet the strong mark made the acquisition of on-site plants, such as in the United States, practicable and reasonable. In sum, Germany's tough anti-inflationary measures were successful largely because social unrest was minimal. Some relaxation will be required in the near future to offset growing unemployment.

German accounting has been disciplined by the prescriptions of tax, civil, and company laws. Income statements must conform with tax returns. Shareholdings in the 500 or so listed companies are controlled mainly by the large banks and prominent families. Consequently, financial reports tend to be ultra conservative. Tax laws produce conservative income figures. Company laws protect the substance of the firm. Germany has long been noted for the use of *stille reserven* (secret reserves) since all earnings for the year, not reserved for particular puposes, are available for dividends.

Inflation accounting has been debated in Germany longer than in any other country. The controversy dates back to the running debates in the early 1920s between Professors Eugen Schmalenbach and F. Schmidt.[5] Schmalenbach advocated what is now called "general-purchasing-power" reporting, or the adjustment of financial reports using general price indexes. Schmidt, on the other hand, argued the case of current cost accounting since the volatility of the Germany economy in that era endangered the very survival of the firm in the short run. Schmidt's argument was considered more relevant:

With a background of severe inflation, it is important to devise an accounting system to safeguard the continued existence of the *entity* and its ability to provide jobs rather than to give a hypothetical average *investor* a revised profit to reflect the general decline in the purchasing power of money.[6]

In the author's opinion, German considerations were favorably influenced by the dominance of tax laws in financial reporting. First, arguments for tax concessions were relegated to the political arena where they belonged. Second, accounting debates centered upon the accounting effects of inflation upon the *particular* firm. Third, and most important, solutions proposed were forced to be practical; that is, in supplementary form rather than disrupting established reports.

In August 1975, the major committee (HFA) of the German Institute (IdW) released its proposal, "Accounting for Capital Maintenance in the Measurement of Company Profits," known as HFA 2/1975.[7] The proposal adhered to the use of money as the unit of measure, and historical cost as the basis for asset measurements in the official statements. Since German law forbids revaluations to be reflected in balance sheets, the Institute's proposal called for voluntary disclosure (in a supplemental note or statement) of the estimated *net* amount of "inflationary profits" included in the net income reported in the income statement. The supplemental disclosure reflects the estimated amount of current earnings needed to be retained in order to maintain the physical capital of the entity that is financed by equity.

The supplementary disclosure (called a "capital maintenance statement") could appear in the director's report (for public companies) or as an adjunct to the required financial statements (of other companies). The format suggested contains only two items and a total:

- The difference between depreciation of fixed assets (financed by equity) based on historical and current replacement costs;
- The difference between cost of goods sold and inventories, (financed by equity) calculated on historical and current replacement costs; and
- The total of the two above amounts, called "inflationary profits."

Given the above total, adjustment of reported profits is simplified, both for management and users. The determination of what fixed assets and inventoriable goods were financed externally (by debt rather than equity) does not appear to be that simple. (This problem has been ameliorated by subsequent proposals by the U.K. that will be examined later.)

As equally important as the above (maybe more so) is the Institute's requirement that *management must stipulate those measures taken and/or planned in order to maintain the substance of the company's capital.*

As side notes, the supplementary data provided by public companies are required to be audited; the data are not accepted for tax purposes, at least to date.

The Netherlands

A relatively small country, the Netherlands has been a center of maritime commerce since the Age of Discovery. Heavily reliant on foreign trade (more than one-half its GNP), the Netherlands became adept rather early at coping with fluctuating prices, both internal and external.

The government historically has taken the stringent fiscal and monetary actions necessary to control inflation and the strength of the currency (guilder). Taxes are high, relative to other EEC countries, but so is government spending (between 15 and 20% of the GNP as a rule). Tough wage and price controls have been used where necessary. As with many EEC countries, unemployment is not usually of real concern since transient workers are first and most affected. The Netherlands has also been a net exporter of oil; this factor has helped to reduce imported inflation significantly and to strengthen the guilder in currency markets.

Accounting in the Netherlands is constructed upon the micro-economic framework mentioned earlier. Tax and financial accounting are independent systems serving different purposes. Until 1972, the Company Law governing accounts consisted of only some 10 lines of the Commerical Code.[8] Present law provides only the broadest of guidelines. Accounting practices should follow sound business practices. Reports are to reflect a true and honest representation of the economic results and affairs of the enterprise. Dutch public accountants, therefore, must make their judgments without the assistance (or stricture?) of the myriad standards, rules, interpretations, and opinions confronting U.S. accountants. Yet, the Netherlands profession is noted for its auditing standards, rated among the most stringent anywhere. Dutch accountants do not purport to be tax experts, however. Firms submit relatively straightforward tax returns prescribed by tax laws. The tax authority subsequently calculates and bills the company for the amount due, less the advance payments made by the firm during the tax year (usually 80% of the prior year's tax).

To many, the Netherlands has become synonymous with current-replacement-value accounting (CRVA) over the last 50 years. Two reasons can be cited.

Professor Theodore Limperg, Jr., of the University of Amsterdam, developed and advocated CRVA in the 1920s. In brief, Limperg argued that the economic substance of the firm could be maintained only if the cost to replace the asset sold or consumed was recouped at the time of the transaction. The remainder, less any ancillary expenses, could be considered profit. Professor Limperg's ideas have not been widely adopted, even though CRVA is permitted in the Netherlands. Various studies indicate that, of the listed companies, about one-third apply some adaptation of CRVA in the income statement, but less than one-fifth reflect assets at current replacement values or report CRVA information at all.[9] Moreover, those companies using CRVA reportedly employ many adaptations and techniques.[10] The apparent lack of application of CRVA in the Netherlands may have several root causes: CRVA is sound in theory but difficult to apply; it is not acceptable for tax purposes; in times of rising prices, financial results appear to be excessively conservative; and smaller firms do not have the expertise or means to apply replacement value accounting.

One giant Dutch holding company, Philips N.V., has been the undisputed champion of replacement-value theory throughout the free world. Organized in 1920, Philips N.V. holds more than 95% of the oustanding shares of a network of Philips Industries operating in all parts of the globe. Over the years, Philips executives have readily admitted that the modified version of CRVA employed represents a highly sophisticated *managerial* accounting system, augmented by a unique responsibility accounting approach, and supported by elaborate standard cost methods based upon internally calculated indexes.[11]

Philips modifies replacement-value theory to suit the needs of management for decision making and evaluation. For example, backlog depreciation (under depreciation of prior years) is ignored. Replacement costs of buildings and equipment are provided by the Engineering Departments since the firm is continually constructing and replacing standardized facilities worldwide. General price indexes, adjusted for local conditions, are also used where they appear reasonable. Standards for product costing are projected to the following June 30th. Changes in the purchasing power of monetary items are not ignored; they are simply not recorded due to the financial structure and policy of the company. Debt financing reflects a normal yet monetary liability position which, in times of rising prices, produces net monetary gains. However, since the company recognizes such gains only to the extent of losses sustained, net monetary gains are never recorded.

In January 1976, the Netherlands Institute (NIVRA), which

recommends rather than requires accounting practices, published its opinions of the various methods of price-level accounting in an addendum furnished its membership along with *Exposure Draft No. 6* of the International Accounting Standards Committee, "Accounting for Changing Prices." The addendum has reproduced with permission in Appendix 4A. Paragraph III of the NIVRA addendum presents a supplementary schedule to reconcile current value and historical cost income, disclose separately realized and unrealized holding gains, and indicate the amount needed to maintain the purchasing power of equity. However, since "gearing" (financial leverage) is not included, the capital structure of the firm is not reflected.

Netherlands accountants take particular pride in their leadership in replacement value accounting. The conservatism reflected in financial reports is well received by the investment community due to the traditionally high debt-to-equity ratios common to Dutch firms. On the other hand, the profession must be somewhat concerned that, while it has been permitted for decades, replacement value theory has only been employed primarily by the larger firms.

THE BRITISH COMMONWEALTH

The United Kingdom has influenced and enhanced accounting thought since it imported Dutch practices in the days of Simon Stevin, refined them, and transplanted the practices in the American Colonies and the countries of the British Empire.

The United Kingdom introduced the third major concept of accounting for changing prices—current-cost accounting. These events will be reviewed, as well as the considerations in Australia and Canada.

United Kingdom

Since 1971 inflation in the United Kingdom has been roughly twice the level of that in the United States. (See Table 4–1.) Relatively old physical plant and equipment reduced productivity and slowed economic growth prior to the oil debacle. Unemployment was feared more than inflation; consequently, antiquated unions were able to press for and receive unwarranted wage gains. Relatively high public expenditures were directed toward welfare rather than reconstruction programs. Externally, the U.K. has traditionally been highly dependent upon imports, and therefore susceptible to imported inflation. Devaluation of the pound, credit restrictions, and price and wage controls enacted in 1973 were examples of too little, too late.

Discovery and production of North Sea oil rescued the British economy and the pound. Also, the effect of imports was ameliorated, the rate of inflation subsided, and the British government was given a breathing spell. The internal cankers, however, still remain virtually untreated.

Within a common law framework, the accountancy bodies in the U.K. have earned international respect for constructing the profession upon the concept of a "true and fair view." The presence of some 3400 listed companies, privately held, has influenced accounting practices to focus upon the investor. As one might expect, the process of establishing accounting standards in the United Kingdom is quite democratic. Consequently, change is deliberate and well considered.

Accounting standards in the U.K. are set by the Accounting Standards Committee (ASC), composed of representatives from the six major professional bodies in the U.K. and Ireland.[12] The ASC is a working committee authorized to prepare and issue exposure drafts of proposed standards for consideration. After revision as necessary, final drafts of the proposed standards are submitted to the council of each of the six professional bodies. Upon approval by the six councils, the approved draft becomes a Statement of Standard Accounting Practice (SSAP).

In January 1973, the Accounting Standards Steering Committee (predecessor of the ASC), issued *Exposure Draft No. 8: Accounting for Changes in the Purchasing Power of Money (ED-8)*. *ED-8* was similar to *APBS No. 3* (AICPA) and the FASB exposure draft that succeeded it in the United States. General-purchasing-power reporting was to be required of listed companies; however, the Consumer Price Index was to be used instead of the GNP deflator selected by the United States. Professional opinions were mixed. Considerable resistance was encountered in the business community. As a result, the government created a special Inflation Accounting Committee (later known as the Sandilands Committee) to consier the matter in January 1974—reportedly, a "common delaying tactic."[13]

In May 1974, the ASSC issued its *Provisional Statement of Standard Accounting Practice No. 7 (PSSAP-7)* titled and patterned after *ED-8*. Since *PSSAP-7* was provisional (adoption was voluntary), very few firms were interested. (A handful of the larger British firms, including Unilever and British-American Tobacco Company, had begun to establish reserves to cover higher replacement costs of plant during the 1950s and 1960s, but such simple measures to restrict dividend availability were a far cry from price-level accounting. Naturally, such measures can be practiced by directors without any recordings at all.)

The Sandilands Report. Unlike most government committees in the U.K. and the U.S., the Sandilands group took its charge seriously and issued a prodigious report in September 1975.[14] As is typical of charges given to such committees, those given the Sandilands group ran the gamut: to study the effects of inflation upon investment, management decisions, capital and resource markets, statement users, taxation, firms of all sizes, and the practices in other countries—particularly the EEC members.[15]

To the surprise of most, the Sandilands Committee performed a comprehensive, logical, well-structured study in a very short time (18 months) and recommended that:

- Primary financial statements—effective December 23, 1978— be based upon current-cost accounting (using various valuation bases to maintain the current value of assets employed by companies);
- General purchasing-power approaches be rejected as inappropriate; and
- The ASSC be charged with preparing the necessary SSAP to implement the findings.

The Sandilands Report was not only an excellent work, but it was unique in several other respects. The study was completed in a short time by a group having a minority of accountant members (Sandilands was an insurance executive). The venture represented the first government intervention into accounting standards in modern times. The report was issued during a time of indecision in the United States and overshadowed the efforts of the FASB. (It may also be reasonable to conjecture that the scope of the report, together with the lull in U.S. progress, led the Securities and Exchange Commission to issue its *Accounting Series Release No. 190*—which will be reviewed in the chapter covering hybrid proposals.

The Morpeth Committee. The ASSC organized the Inflation Accounting Steering Group, headed by Douglas Morpeth, vice chairman of the ASSC, to implement the Sandilands recommendations. Following eight revisions to satisfy a variety of different interests, the ASSC published *ED-18—Current Cost Accounting*—in November 1976. Actually, *ED-18* represented a combination of current-cost and general-price-level methods, the latter making use of a reserve to handle gains and losses on monetary items. In its democratic fashion, the membership of the English institute (the predominating member of the ASSC) decided to have none of it.

The Hyde Proposals. Following the rejection of *ED-18,* the ASSC was renamed ASC, and a working group, chaired by William Hyde, was created to prepare simplified guidelines that could be implemented quickly in order to report the impact of inflation upon accounting reports. In November 1977, the Hyde proposals were released by the ASC[16] and have been reproduced as Appendix 4B.

The proposals did not call for changes in accounting methods but, instead, that reported incomes be "adjusted" by three items: an increment to reflect depreciation based on "current costs," a cost of sales adjustment, and a "gearing adjustment." The adjustments were to be voluntary, applicable to fiscal years beginning after December 1977, and directed primarily at quoted companies.

The Hyde proposals were criticized for many short-comings. Adjustments were to be made only on the income statement. No changes were to appear on balance sheets. Consequently, financial statements would no longer articulate (no appropriation reserves were to be created). Assets could be revalued based upon "appropriate indexes" rather than deprival value (value to the business—upon which *ED-18* and Sandilands were founded).

The "gearing" or financial-leverage adjustment became the most controversial. In times of rising prices, companies whose monetary liabilities (both short- and long-term) exceeded monetary assets were said to be "geared"—a position common to most European companies. Since such firms benefited in times of inflation, the benefit should be added to operating income—to partially offset the deductions for additional depreciation and current cost of sales. A typical gearing adjustment is furnished in Appendix 4B, Annex 1B. Disclosure within the income statement is shown in Appendix 4B, Annex 1C.

By definition, the minority of firms reflecting net monetary assets were not geared; therefore, no gearing adjustment was to be made. Instead, such firms were encouraged to report the loss in purchasing power on the income statement as an "adjustment for net monetary assets"; see note to Appendix 4B, Annex 1C.

The Hyde proposals implemented by the ASC have also been challenged on theoretical grounds.[17] This is unfortunate since the Hyde Committee was charged with devising practicable, stop-gap disclosures that could be implemented quickly, not with the construction of a new system of inflation accounting such as attempted by Sandilands. The options afforded managements to use general or specific indexes to establish current costs of assets were also criticized for permitting variations. However, since inflation affects different firms and products in different ways, and since the adjustments must be audited, it would appear that firms could select those representations that most clearly reflect a "true and fair view" to which auditors could attest.

The Hyde proposals will conform with the EEC Fourth Directive with only one minor change: the three adjustments can be reflected in a footnote, (as suggested in the German HFA proposal), or, the current-cost income statement (Appendix 4B) can be provided as a supplementary statement.

The Hyde proposals also seem to be a good deal more practicable than the German HFA disclosures. While the same net effects are represented by the inflation adjustments, the German proposal requires that the gearing adjustment be apportioned between fixed assets and stocks in trade (which seems rather arbitrary), whereas the Hyde proposal merely calls for the disclosure of the effect of gearing on the company as a whole. Last, but not least, it seems that the simplified disclosures suggested by the German HFA or the Hyde proposals, attested for fairness by auditors, and augmented by management explanations, will be as far as European mandates on inflation reporting will go. *It may also well be as far as the United States need and should venture.*

In typical British fashion, however, the ASC is undaunted and plans to press forward. An Inflation Accounting Steering Group has been appointed and charged with the development of an exposure draft during 1979. Reportedly, the draft will require supplementary current-cost statements by all listed and the larger private companies. Simpler guidelines are expected for voluntary use by the smaller, private companies.

Australia

As a relatively young industrial country, Australia is still experiencing growing pains. Development of its natural resources required the importation of capital and people; both were welcomed, until 1973, and inflation was rather low considering the expansionary economy.

Since 1973, growth has been restrained to combat inflation. The subsequent era of stagflation led to various protectionist measures to favor domestic industry and reduce unemployment. Wage controls were applied extensively, personal income taxes were indexed, yet double-digit inflation has prevailed to date.

Australian accounting practices were conceived in the U.K. and the umbilical cord remains intact. Inflation accounting considerations paralleled those in the United Kingdom.

In December 1974, the Australian Accounting Standards Committee (AASC) issued its Preliminary Exposure Draft that reluctantly suggested general-purchasing-power reporting in supplementary statements (patterned after *SSAP-7* of the U.K.).[18]

Also in December 1974, the government appointed an inquiry group (the Matthews Committee) to study the effects of inflation, but upon taxation primarily. As a result of the Matthews Report, submitted in May 1975; personal income taxes were indexed; one-half the "inflationary profits" included in inventories was excluded from company taxation; and the use of some modified form of current-value income was recommended to be examined for implementation.[19]

In June 1975, the AASC published its second Preliminary Exposure Draft recommending that assets only be revalued, using current value methods, in order to protect the "operating capability" of the enterprise.[20]

Impressed by the Sandilands recommendations in the U.K., the

AASC issued a Provisional Standard on current cost-accounting in October 1976.[21] Although voluntary, the provisions called for current-cost accounting methods to be applied to the primary financial statements for periods beginning after July 1, 1977. Problems of implementation, together with bitter resistance from the major Australian accounting firms, led to an extension of the effective date to July 1, 1979, but, for all practical purposes, the measure was considered dead.

To mend the fences, a Current Cost Accounting Steering Group was formed with representation from both major bodies—the Australian Society of Accountants and the Institute of Chartered Accountants in Australia. The Steering Group prepared a revised recommendation (effective July 1, 1978) that, in supplementary notes, the current costs of fixed assets, depreciation, inventories, and cost of sales be disclosed. Concurrently, the Steering Group issued an exposure draft soliciting comments on how to treat monetary items (gearing) under current cost accounting.[22]

Progress beyond supplementary footnote disclosures is doubtful since the major accounting bodies remain firmly opposed to current-cost accounting in any form.

Canada

Until 1972, inflation in Canada was slightly less than that in the United States. Thereafter, consumer price increases in Canada have been somewhat greater.

In 1973, an Anti-Inflationary Board was established, personal income taxes were indexed, and controls on prices and incomes were imposed. In 1977, the government began to phase-out the price and incomes controls. The Anti-Inflationary Board was disbanded and replaced by a Centre for the Study of Inflation and Productivity—described as an "early warning system."

The Canadian economy and accounting profession are heavily influenced by close ties with the United Kingdom and with the United States. Economic benefits accrue to Canada as a result of both associations. Similarly, the Canadian accounting profession benefits from direct access to studies and pronouncements in both countries.

Uncommon care must be exercised by the Canadian Institute of

Chartered Accountants (CICA) since the decisions of its Accounting Research Committee, when published in the CICA *Handbook,* have the authority of law.[23] Consequently, the CICA is prone to digest the British and American accounting proposals prior to embarking on its own. The ability of the CICA to benefit from the mistakes of others while proceeding with its own endeavors can be construed as lagging behind, but such is not the case.

A discussion paper published by the CICA in 1971 supported retention of historical costs in published accounts, attached little value to general-price-level adjusted information, and stated that, if price-level changes were to be reflected in financial reports, specific price changes would be preferable.

Influenced by the earlier efforts of the FASB in the United States, the CICA encouraged the voluntary reporting of supplemental general-price-level data in a November 1974 guideline. (Guidelines do not bear the authority of *Handbook* decisions.) Subsequent issuing of the guidelines as an exposure draft in July 1975 met with nearly total rejection by the business community.

The Accounting Research Committee of the CICA published a discussion paper[24] in August 1976 that basically reviewed the various approaches to current value accounting. Comments were requested by June 30, 1977.

During June 1977, a committee appointed by the Province of Ontario issued its own suggestions calling for the interim use of a special, supplementary schedule, "Funds Available for Distribution or Expansion." The information would be optional and should include inventory profits; depreciation based upon replacement cost; availability of funds (internal and external) to finance the increased costs; and similar inflationary effects.[25]

As an aside, tax relief in Canada is generous insofar as depreciation allowances are concerned. However, inventory profits are taxed since LIFO costing is not permitted. Consequently, the Canadian business community is as eager as that in the United States to espouse a practicable reporting framework that will enhance the probability of tax relief.

Experimentation with various approaches to current-value accounting has been as widespread in Canada as anywhere outside the Netherlands. Touche Ross & Company has worked with industries and companies in Canada (known as the Current Value

Group) to encourage experimentation with various methods of implementation.[26]

Other than expressed preferences for supplemental disclosure, and maintenance of the general purchasing power of capital, the outcome of CICA considerations remains conjecture.

AN INTERNATIONAL OVERVIEW

The U.S. perspective on price-level accounting, together with the brief examinations of considerations in other selected countries, furnishes the information necessary to construct an overview.

Standard-setting bodies are faced with very few real choices in deciding how to revise the accounting model to reflect changing price-levels. The constraints, however, are many and very real. The available choices and the existing constraints are depicted in Figure 4-2. The choices available are shown in columnar form, not unlike a menu in a Chinese restaurant—selection from Column A restricts the possible choices from columns B and C, if a logical framework is to be constructed.

In fact, accountants must decide whether to continue to use money as the unit of measure (and change the basis of measurement), or, to change the unit of measure (and retain the existing basis of measurement).

If money is retained as the measuring unit, then assets could be measured based upon their current replacement costs, net realizable values, economic values, or some combination thereof, depending upon the nature of the assets and practical considerations. Profit, in turn, could be redefined as those earnings in excess of amounts required to maintain the financial capital (the purchasing power of either equity or assets) or the physical capital (productive capacity or the value-in-use of assets) of the entity. These methods and their variations will be collectively termed "replacement-value accounting" and examined in Chapter 6.

If the instability of the dollar as a unit of measure is corrected by placing the focus upon its purchasing power, then further choice is minimized. Accounts could retain their historical-cost basis, and profit would represent the amount available after the purchasing power of equity at the beginning of the year is maintained. In short, the accounting process would not require alteration; only the unit

FIGURE 4-2. PRICE-LEVEL ACCOUNTING CHOICES AND CONSTRAINTS.

Choices

A. Unit of measure	B. Basis for measuring assets	C. Definition of profit
1. Money	1. Historical cost	1. Amount that may be distributed while maintaining:
2. General purchasing power of money	2. Replacement cost at current purchasing prices	(a) Monetary amount of shareholders' interest at beginning of year
	3. Net realizable value	(b) Purchasing power of shareholders' interest at the beginning of year
	4. Economic value (the discounted present value of future cash flows)	(c) Productive capacity of assets (d) Purchasing power of assets at beginning of year (e) Value of assets less value of assets consumed

Constraints

- Methods should be applied uniformly.
- Procedures should be objective and verifiable.
- Presentations should be fair and not misleading.
- Reports should make economic sense.
- Reports should be useful and worth their costs.

Source: Adapted by permission of the *Harvard Business Review*. From "What's Wrong with Price-Level Accounting" by Elwood L. Miller. (November–December 1978, p. 117.) Copyright ©1978 by the President and Fellows of Harvard College.

of measurement reflected in financial reports would change. These methods will hereinafter be called "general-purchasing-power reporting" and will be addressed in Chapter 5 that follows.

The alternatives proposed and/or adopted in the countries reviewed thus far have been summarized in Figure 4–3 as a convenient form of overview.

As an aside, the FASB does not appear to have learned much from the efforts of the professions in other countries. According to the FASB, other countries ". . . have developed new types of financial reports which may be regarded as partial solutions. . . . none has yet produced a comprehensive solution that has been generally satisfactory."[27] That should not be considered unusual at all. There is no such solution.

FIGURE 4–3. PRICE-LEVEL ACCOUNTING AND REPORTING METHODS IN SELECTED COUNTRIES

COUNTRY	PRONOUNCEMENT/ METHOD	UNIT OF MEASURE	ASSET BASIS	CONCEPT OF CAPITAL MAINTENANCE	SALIENT FEATURES
Various	Historical cost (GAAP)	Money	HC	Monetary amount of equity	Compatible with tax/legal requirements.
United States*	FASB Exposure Draft, 12/74, General Purchasing Power	GPP of Money (GNP deflator)	HC	Purchasing power of equity	Supplementary statements in "common" dollars.
	SEC-ASR No. 190, 3/76	Money	RC	Productive capacity[1]	Supplementary disclosures of replacement costs of inventories, cost of goods sold, productive capacity, and current-cost depreciation.
	FASB Exposure Draft, 12/78 Current Cost Accounting[2]	Money	CC	Value of assets	Supplementary disclosures of: current replacement costs of "assets actually owned"; current costs of inventories, depreciation, and cost of goods sold; net holding gains/losses; net foreign exchange gains/losses.
	FASB Exposure Draft, 3/79, Constant Dollar Reporting[2]	GPP of Money (Consumer Price Index)	HC	Purchasing power of equity	Supplementary disclosures of: "constant dollar" net income; holding gains/losses on monetary items, foreign currency translations.
Argentina	Price-level Adjusted Reports	GPP of Money (official indexes)	HC	Purchasing power of equity	Supplemental statements; not part of law.
Brazil	Company Laws, 1976 (monetary correction)	Money	CC	Purchasing power of assets	Primary statements; all periods beginning Jan. 1, 1978.

*See Appendix 9A for FASB *Statement No. 33.*

FIGURE 4-3 (cont'd.)

COUNTRY	PRONOUNCEMENT/ METHOD	UNIT OF MEASURE	ASSET BASIS	CONCEPT OF CAPITAL MAINTENANCE	SALIENT FEATURES
European Economic Community	Fourth Directive on Company Law, 7/78	Money	HC	Monetary amount of equity	States are permitted to authorize departure from historical cost in supplemental statements or notes.
France	Finance Acts, 1977 and 1978	Money	HC—with one revaluation.	Purchasing power of assets	Cosmetic, one-time revaluation of fixed assets; no net effect on income.
Germany	*HFA 2/1975*	Money	HC	Value of assets financed by equity	Supplemental notes disclosing "inflationary profits" less gearing, plus *management explanations.*
Netherlands	Replacement Value (modified)	Money	RC/NRV/EV	Productive capacity of assets	Minority of firms have adopted.
	NIVRA note, appended to IASC's *ED 6.*	Money	RC/NRV/EV	Productive capacity of assets and purchasing power of equity.	Supplemental disclosure of realized and unrealized holding gains, plus GPP indexation of equity.
United Kindgom	*PSSAP-7,* 5/74, Current Purchasing Power	GPP of Money (Consumer Price Index)	HC	Purchasing power of equity	Voluntary, supplemental statements.
	Sandilands Report, 9/75, Current Cost Accounting	Money	RC/NRV/EV	Value of assets	Primary statements; ignored gains/losses on monetary items.
	ASSC-ED 18, 11/76, Current Cost Accounting (modified)	Money	RC/NRV/EV	Value of assets	Primary statements; monetary gains/losses reflected in reserves.

	ASC-Interim Recomm., 11/77, (Hyde Proposals)	Money	HC	Monetary amount of equity	Supplementary disclosure of: current costs of depreciation and cost of sales; plus gearing or loss on net monetary assets.
Australia	AASC Preliminary Exposure Draft, 12/74	GPP of Money (Consumer Price Index)	HC	Purchasing power of equity	Supplemental statements.
	AASC Preliminary Exposure Draft, 6/75	Money	RC/NRV/EV	Purchasing power of assets	Only assets to be revalued.
	AASC Provisional Std., 10/76	Money	RC/NRV/EV	Value of assets	Voluntary use; primary statements; effective 7/1/79.
	CCA Steering Group, 1977: Recommendation	Money	HC	Monetary amount of equity	Supplemental notes disclosing current costs of fixed assets, depreciation, inventories, cost of sales. Effective 7/1/78. Group solicited comments on treatment of monetary items.
Canada	CICA Exposure Draft, 7/75	Money	HC	Monetary amount of equity	Supplemental disclosures of general-price-level data.
	Ontario Committee Report, 6/77	Money	HC	Monetary amount of equity	Voluntary supplemental funds statement disclosing impacts of inflation pending development of current-value system.

Notes: (1) *ASR-190* disclosures were not designed for direct adjustment of reported incomes.
(2) Exposure drafts should be considered as a single effort encouraging experimentation. FASB *Statement No. 33* is examined in Appendix 9A.

CHAPTER 4. NOTES

1. IMF *International Financial Statistics,* March 1979, p. 35.

2. See also Alexandre Kafka, "Indexing for Inflation in Brazil," in Herbert Giersch, *et al. Essays on Inflation and Indexation* (Washington, D.C.: American Enterprise Institute for Public Policy Research, 1974), pp. 87–98.

3. Ibid., p. 95.

4. See Ernst & Ernst *International Series: France,* 1978. Retrieval No. 48382.

5. E. Schmalenbach, *Grundlagen dynamischer Bilanzlehere,* 3rd. ed. (Leipzig, 1925); and F. Schmidt, *Die organische Bilanz im Rahmen der Wirtschaft* (Leipzig, 1921); cited by Klaus R. Macharzina, "The Impact of Inflation on German Accounting: Theoretical Background and Professional Issues," in *The Impact of Inflation on Accounting: A Global View* (University of Illinois, Center for International Education and Research in Accounting, 1979).

6. Macharzina, op cit. p. 226

7. HFA, "Zur Berücksichtigung der Substanzerhaltung bei der Ermittlung des Jahresergebnisses." Stellungnahme 2/1975, *IdW Fachnachrichten,* No. 12, August 12, 1975; cited by Macharzina, *op cit.* p. 228.

8. Pieter C. Louwers, "The European Public Accountant: A Different View," *Management Accounting,* September 1975, p. 45.

9. See Macharzina, op cit. p. 230.

10. Jules W. Muis, "Current Value Accounting in the Netherlands: Fact or Fiction?", *The Accountant's Magazine,* LXXIX, No. 832, p. 379.

11. A. Goudeket, "How Inflation Is Being Recognized in Financial Statements in the Netherlands," *Journal of Accountancy,* October 1952, pp. 448–452; and "An Application of Replacement Value Theory," *Journal of Accountancy,* July 1960, pp. 37–47.

12. The ASC bodies are: the Institutes of Chartered Accountants in England and Wales, Scotland, and Ireland; the Association of Certified Accountants; the Institute of Cost and Management Accountants; and the Chartered Institute of Public Finance and Accountancy.

13. Brian D. Smith, "Sandilands Report," *The Arthur Andersen Chronicle,* April 1976, p. 26.

14. *Inflation Accounting: Report of the Inflation Accounting Committee,* F. E. P. Sandilands, chairman (London: Her Majesty's Stationery Office, September 1975), 364 pp.

15. Ibid, p. iv.

16. Accounting Standards Committee, *Inflation Accounting—An Interim Recommendation by the Accounting Standards Committee* (London: Institute of Chartered Accountants in England and Wales, 1977).

17. B. A. Rutherford and P. G. E. Boys, "The Hyde Proposals: A Critique," *The Certified Accountant* (London), August 1978, pp. 253–255, 257–259.

18. Australian Accounting Standards Committee, *Preliminary Exposure Draft:* "A Method of Accounting for Changes in the Purchasing Power of Money" (Melbourne: Institute of Chartered Accountants in Australia and Australian Society of Accountants, 1974).

19. W. J. Kenley, "Report on Inflation and Taxation," *Australian Accountant*, July 1975, pp. 338–340.

20. Australian Accounting Standards Committee, *Preliminary Exposure Draft:* "A Method of Current Value Accounting" (Melbourne: ICAA and ASA, 1975).

21. Institute of Chartered Accountants in Australia and Australian Society of Accountants, DPS 1-1, *Statement of Provisional Accounting Standards:* "Current Cost Accounting" (Melbourne: ICAA and ASA, 1976).

22. "Around the World: Australia," *Certified Accountant,* August 1978, p. 248.

23. Canada Business Corporation Act Regulations, Part V, Section 44.

24. Accounting Research Committee, Discussion Paper, "Current Value Accounting" (Toronto: CICA, 1976).

25. *Report of the Ontario Committee on Inflation Accounting*, M. O. Alexander, Chairman (Toronto: Ontario Government Bookstore, 1977), p. 24. Michael Alexander is now Director of Research with the FASB.

26. "Current Value Accounting: Economic Reality in Financial Reporting," Touche Ross & Co., New York, 1976, pp. 8–9.

27. Financial Accounting Standards Board, *Exposure Draft,* "Financial Reporting and Changing Prices" (Stamford, Conn.: FASB, December 28, 1978), p. i.

APPENDIX 4A.

NIVRA

Appendix to ED6: Accounting for changing prices

Accompanying note by the Council of the Nederlands Instituut van Registeraccountants

Accounting for changing prices is essential for giving a true and fair view of results and equity. The IASC draft, therefore, is concerned with an important subject. The draft derives significance not only from its rejection of information based on historical cost but also by stimulating an international discussion on alternative valuation principles.

In The Netherlands, business economics and accountancy as well as business practice have for a long time been engaged on the subject. The Council of NIVRA willingly accepts the invitation embodied in para. 14 of the IASC draft to express its opinion on the accounting methods for changing prices, that have been raised for discussion in a very general way in paras. 16, 17 and 18 of the draft.

The accompanying note has been prepared by the NIVRA Committee on Annual Accounts.

I. As far back as the Twenties a theory of business economics was developed in The Netherlands, with the aim of ensuring the continuity of the enterprise. The two principal conclusions were:

— that costs had to be calculated on the basis of the replacement value of the means of production used, and
— that profit had to be determined on current value basis.

In order to give a true and fair view of invested equity, it followed almost naturally, that balance sheet valuations also had to be on the same basis.

A number of Dutch enterprises adopted replacement value accounting in the course of time.

In an exposure draft issued by the Tripartite Discussion Group* ("Considerations on the Act on Annual Accounts," part 3, of 30th June, 1975) the opinion was expressed that determination of the amount of consumption of resources both on the basis of historical cost and on the basis of current value is acceptable, adding that in all cases where there is a significant difference between them, such difference shall be disclosed.

The NIVRA Council, therefore, expresses strong approval for para. 16 of the IASC draft, which specifies that information in the annual accounts may be based on current values.

II. In spite of strong pleas for the determination of equity and profit on the basis of current value, the theory has been applied in actual practice only sparingly in The Netherlands and not at all abroad.

Outside The Netherlands another path was followed when the high inflation of recent years demonstrated ever more clearly the inadequacy of accounting on the basis of historical cost: "general purchasing power accounting" (g.p.p.a.), being a conversion of historical cost accounts using a general purchasing power index.

Para. 17 of the IASC draft gives the option of providing information on a g.p.p.a. basis. Such a method has specifically been proposed by the Financial Accounting Standards Board in the USA and by the Accounting Standards Steering Committee in the UK.

NIVRA has serious objections to g.p.p.a., mainly because specific price changes relating to assets of individual enterprises, coincide only by chance with a general purchasing power index. G.p.p.a. information generally is of little value to users of annual accounts and is not relevant for the individual company.

It is worth noting that recent developments abroad suggest that this view is becoming more widely shared. After the accountancy bodies of Germany and Australia earlier in 1975 had published exposure drafts expressing a preference for current value methods, the Sandilands Committee in the UK and the SEC in the USA have recently declared a similar view.

III. The present inflation exposes the equity of enterprises to the risk of considerable erosion of purchasing power.

In 1974, when the British accountancy bodies were considering the introduction of g.p.p.a., NIVRA considered the possibility of combining elements of current value and g.p.p.a., as now stated in para. 18 of the IASC
draft.

In discussion with these bodies (see "de Accountant," June 1974) NIVRA
suggested, by way of example of such a combination, the following schedule
which might be presented as additional information with annual accounts
prepared on the basis of current value.

Net income on current value basis	a
Add: excess of replacement cost over historical cost of goods sold in the reporting period ("realized holding gains")	$\underline{b}$
Net income on historical cost basis	c
Add: "unrealized holding gains" of the reporting period	$\underline{d}$
Increase of equity as recorded	e
Equity in prior year's balance sheet f	
i.e. in current year's dollars (apply g.p.p. index) $\underline{g}$	
Increase needed to maintain equity in terms of g.p.p.	$\underline{h}$
Surplus/deficit	$\underline{i}$

The schedule indicates the extent to which general purchasing power of
equity is maintained in relation to the increase in value of the specific
assets.

Compared with g.p.p.a. this method is much less complicated because it is
the direct application of a general index to the equity.

The schedule also discloses (in item e) the total growth of equity: profit on
the basis of current value + realized holding gains + unrealized holding gains.

Separate issues are:

— whether it is desirable to disclose explicitly profit on the basis of historical cost (item c) as an intermediate step; this form has been chosen for
the schedule in connection with similar stipulations in a draft EEC
directive;
— whether it is necessary to disclose realized holding gains and unrealized
holding gains (items b and d) separately; in this connection it may be ob-
served that in the draft "considerations," part 3, the Tripartite Discussion
Group* has recommended to "disclose in the explanatory notes the extent to which the revaluation reserve has been realized."

The schedule is designed only to point to one method of combining a feature of
g.p.p.a. with the application of replacement value.

*The issue of the IASC draft "Accounting for changing prices" gives NIVRA the
opportunity of publicizing more widely the above schedule. This does not imply,
however, that NIVRA has already reached a final conclusion in respect of the
desirability of including the schedule in annual accounts.*

Interested parties are invited to comment on the significance of the information in the schedule as well as on the issues raised in connection with it.

Comments may be sent to
> Nederlands Instituut van Registeraccountants
> Mensinge 2, P.O. Box 7984
> Amsterdam — 1011

January 1976

* The Tripartite Discussion Group consists of representatives of
  - Confederation of Enterprises
  - Trade Unions
  - NIVRA.

It is a standing group, established at the request of the Minister of Justice,
1) to make an inventory of valuation bases used in business practice, and
2) to test these bases against what, in its opinion, may be deemed to be acceptable.

Source: Reprinted by permission of the Nederlands Instituut van Registeraccountants.

APPENDIX 4B

INFLATION ACCOUNTING—AN INTERIM RECOMMENDATION BY THE ACCOUNTING STANDARDS COMMITTEE

Introduction

1. In its statement of intent published on 27th July, 1977 the Accounting Standards Committee commented that it believed that:
   - (a) there is a wide recognition of the fact that the rapidly-changing price levels associated with inflation seriously distort results shown by accounts drawn up on the conventional historical cost basis, and
   - (b) there is a wide recognition of the urgent need to indicate the extent of this distortion.

2. The Accounting Standards Committee went on to say:
   - (i) that it had a continuing responsibility to propose to the Councils of the accountancy bodies, as soon as possible, an acceptable and workable system of price level accounting for promulgation as an accounting standard or standards, but
   - (ii) that recognition of the urgency of the need to show how accounts prepared on the historical cost basis are affected by inflation imposed a more immediate responsibility to give guidance, as an interim measure,

on how information as to these effects should be provided in the published accounts of, at least, all listed companies.

3. This recommendation, which deals only with the profit and loss account, is published in order to give that interim guidance.

4. The Accounting Standards Committee recommends that the published financial statements of companies listed on The Stock Exchange should include a prominent separate statement showing the financial results as amended by the adjustments described below. Wherever practicable, it is recommended that the statement should be prepared for accounting periods ending on or after 31st December, 1977. Whilst this recommendation is directed primarily to listed companies its wider adoption is urged in the interests of more informative reporting.

5. It is recommended that three adjustments should be made to the financial results as computed on the historical cost convention. Each adjustment should be shown separately.

Depreciation

An adjustment should be made for the difference between depreciation based upon the current cost of fixed assets and the depreciation charged in computing the historical cost result.

Cost of Sales

An adjustment should be made for the difference between the current cost of stock at the date of sale and the amount charged in computing the historical cost result.

'Gearing'

It is recognized that there are differing views on the question of how monetary items should be dealt with in inflation adjusted statements and that such differences are unlikely to be resolved quickly or without experiment. Nevertheless, it is considered that it would not be acceptable for the statement recommended to be limited to adjustments for depreciation and cost of sales. Such limitation would result in an incomplete and potentially misleading picture being given to shareholders and other users of accounts. Accordingly, the description of the gearing adjustment given below and the proposals which follow in paragraphs 16 to 20 are intended as an interim guide as to how this adjustment might be approached.

There are two different situations to be met, each of which calls for a different treatment:

(a) If the total liabilities of the business, including for this purpose preference share capital, exceed its total monetary assets, so that part of its operating capability is effectively financed by the net monetary liabilities, an adjustment should be made to reflect the extent to which the depreciation and cost of sales adjustments do not need to be provided in full from the current revenues of the business in showing the profit attributable to the shareholders.

(b) If the total monetary assets of the business exceed its total liabilities, an adjustment should be made to reflect the increase in the net monetary assets needed to maintain its scale of operation.

The form of each of these three adjustments is described below.

Depreciation

6. Where the business has already developed appropriate methods of computing current cost depreciation it is recommended that such methods should be used for the purpose of computing the adjustment.

7. Where other appropriate methods have not been developed, the charge for current cost depreciation may be computed by use of an appropriate index of price movements. For this purpose, the historical cost gross and net book values and current year depreciation charge should be analysed by reference to the year of purchase of each asset concerned. These amounts should be revised in accordance with the change in appropriate indices between the year of purchase and the current year. The depreciation adjustment is then the difference between the revised current year depreciation charge and the historical cost depreciation charge.

8. For assets in the United Kingdom the index, or indices, used may be selected from the industry specific or asset specific indices published in the Central Statistical Office booklet *Price index numbers for Current Cost Accounting*. For assets in the Republic of Ireland the index, or indices, used may be selected from those published by the Central Statistics Office of the Republic of Ireland. For buildings the index of the cost of new construction may be used.

9. For assets located in other countries, corresponding indices should be used where available. The Central Statistical Office booklet *Current Cost Accounting—Guide to price indices for Overseas Countries* may be helpful in indicating the indices available in certain overseas countries. If suitable specific indices for overseas assets cannot be obtained, a general price index for the country concerned may be used.

10. The method used to compute the depreciation adjustment, and the indices employed, should be disclosed in a brief note to the statement.

Cost of Sales

11. Where the business has already developed appropriate methods of computing the current cost of sales it is recommended that such methods should be used for the purpose of computing the adjustment. For example, where ac-

counting information is available from standard costing systems, or from base stock or last-in-first-out methods, it may be possible easily to compute the current cost of sales without resort to other methods. Where a more appropriate method cannot be devised and implemented in the time available it is recommended that, wherever possible, the cost of sales adjustment should be computed using the averaging method.

12. Using the averaging method, the current cost of sales may be computed by revising the historical cost of opening and closing stock to the average current cost for the year by use of an appropriate index. An example of the averaging method is given in Annex 1A. The index, or indices, used for this

Annex 1A. Example of the Use of the Averaging Method for Calculation of the Cost of Sales Adjustment

	£000
Historical cost data	
Opening stock	350
Add: Purchases	2,300
	2,650
Deduct: Closing stock	540
Cost of sales (historical cost basis)	2,110
Index Numbers for cost of stock	
Beginning of year	100
End of year	120
Average for year	110

	£000
(1) *Revise opening and closing stock to average current cost for the year £000*	
Opening stock: $350 \times \dfrac{110}{100} =$	385
Closing stock: $540 \times \dfrac{110}{120} =$	495

(2) *Compute current cost of sales using the revised amounts for opening and closing stock*

	£000
Opening stock	385
Add: Purchases	2,300
	2,685
Deduct: Closing stock	495
Cost of sales (current cost basis)	2,190

(3) *Calculate cost of sales adjustment*

	£000
Cost of sales (current cost basis)	2,190
Deduct: Cost of sales (historical cost basis)	2,110
Cost of sales adjustment	80

calculation may be selected from the same sources as indicated for depreciation in paragraphs 8 and 9.

13. Where progress payments are received from customers, the cost of sales adjustment should be computed on the amount of stock and work in progress after deduction of such payments. To avoid duplication, the progress payments deducted from stock and work in progress should be excluded from the calculation of the gearing adjustment.

14. The method used to compute the cost of sales adjustment, and the indices employed, should be disclosed in a brief note to the statement.

Gearing

15. It is acknowledged that some companies have already drawn up current cost statements including a gearing adjustment calculated by a method different from that described below, and that others may be planning to do so. Recognising that circumstances will differ, such companies are not discouraged from following their own methods providing these are disclosed in a note to the statement. The simple approach to the calculation of a gearing adjustment outlined below is recommended unless another method is preferred.

16. Where the total liabilities of the business, including preference share capital, exceed its total monetary assets, a calculation should be made of the proportion of:
    (a) the net balance of monetary liabilities, to
    (b) the net balance of monetary liabilities *plus* the equity share capital and reserves.

    In computing the amount of reserves to be used in this calculation, the difference between the current values and historical cost amounts for fixed assets and, if material, for stocks, should be added to the reserves shown by the historical cost accounts.

17. An amount equal to this proportion of the depreciation and cost of sales adjustments should be credited as a separate adjustment in the statement.

18. Where the total monetary assets of the business exceed its total liabilities, an adjustment should be calculated by applying to the net balance of monetary assets the percentage change in an appropriate index during the accounting year. This adjustment should be charged as a separate item in the statement.

19. In order to relate these adjustments as closely as possible to the current year's results, averages from the opening and closing balance sheets of the accounting year should be used, unless an alternative averaging method is considered necessary to give a fairer view. For the first year for which this calculation is made, it should be based upon the closing balance sheet if an appropriate average position cannot be obtained without an undue amount of work.

20. An example to illustrate this form of the calculation of the adjustment is given in Annex 1B.

Annex 1B. Illustration of the Gearing Adjustment

(1) *Total liabilities of the business exceed its total monetary assets*

Summarised balance sheet, after adjustment for the difference between the current values and historical cost amounts for fixed assets and, if material, for stocks:

	£000
Equity share capital and reserves	684
Long-term liabilities	350
Current liabilities	406
	1,440
Fixed assets	600
Stocks	540
Monetary assets	300
	1,440

(a) *Calculate net balance of monetary liabilities*

	£000
Long-term liabilities	350
Current liabilities	406
Total liabilities	756
Deduct: Monetary assets	300
Net balance of monetary liabilities	456

(b) *Calculate net balance of monetary liabilities plus the equity share capital and reserves*

	£000
Net balance of monetary liabilities	456
Add: Equity share capital and reserves	684
	1,140

(c) *Calculate gearing proportion*

	£000
Net balance of monetary liabilities	456 = 40%
divided by: Net balance of monetary liabilities plus equity share capital and reserves	1,140

(d) *Calculate gearing adjustment*

	£000
Depreciation adjustment	70
Cost of sales adjustment	80
	150
Multiply by gearing proportion	40%
Gearing adjustment	60

(2) *Total monetary assets of the business exceed its total liabilities*

In this case, the net balance of monetary assets should be calculated as shown in 1(a) above. The adjustment should be calculated by multiplying the net balance of monetary assets by the percentage change in an appropriate index during the accounting year.

21. The method used to compute the adjustment, and the index employed, should be disclosed in a brief note to the statement.

Presentation of the Statement

22. A suggested format for the presentation of the statement is given in Annex 1C. For the first year for which the statement is prepared, corresponding amounts for the preceding year should be omitted if they cannot be obtained without an undue amount of work. In the statements for subsequent years, corresponding amounts should be shown.

Annex 1C. Suggested Format for Presentation of the Statement

A Limited (a company with net monetary liabilities)
CURRENT COST STATEMENT
for the year ended 31st December 1977

	£000	£000
Turnover		2,940
Profit before taxation and interest as in historical cost accounts		395
Less: Adjustments		
Depreciation	70	
Cost of Sales	80	150
Operating profit		245
Interest payable less receivable		40
		205
Gearing adjustment		60
Adjusted profit before taxation and extraordinary items		265
*Taxation		90
		175
Minority interests		15
Adjusted profit before extraordinary items		160
Extraordinary items (net of taxation and minority interests)		20
Adjusted profit attributable to the shareholders		140
Dividends		110
Adjusted retained profit		30

*Companies may wish to take into account the proposals in Exposure Draft 19—Accounting for Deferred Taxation, in determining the taxation charge to be included in this statement.

Brief notes to this statement should disclose the method used to compute each adjustment and the indices employed.

For companies with net monetary assets, the gearing adjustment should be replaced by the adjustment for net monetary assets.

Note:
"A Limited" appearing in statement title is apparently the name of the fictitious company.

23. Brief notes to the statement should disclose the method used to compute each adjustment and the indices employed.

Comments on this Recommendation

24. The Accounting Standards Committee will be grateful to receive comments as soon as practicable, particularly from preparers and users of accounts in which the proposals contained in this interim recommendation are implemented, to assist them in considering how the evolution of inflation accounting should progress.

Source: Accounting Standards Committee, "Inflation Accounting: An Interim Recommendation." ICAEW, 1977. Reprinted by permission.

5
General-Purchasing-Power Reporting

As developed in the preceding chapters, general-purchasing-power methods represented the initial approaches considered by most industrial countries to recognize the impacts of inflation upon published accounts. In this chapter the rationale supporting general-purchasing-power methods will be assessed, along with the alleged benefits and disadvantages.

RATIONALE

The FASB, among others, adopted the dictionary definition of inflation as a persistent, upward trend in the level of *general* prices. Inflation accounting, then, should account for general price-level changes.

Inflation was perceived as a disease that manifested itself in the continuous decline in the *general*-purchasing-power (or stability) of money as a measuring unit. The logical alternative called for the use of units of general-purchasing-power (GPP) instead of units of money.

Two methods of application were possible but only one was considered practicable. Using an agreed-upon base period, account balances could be restated in units of purchasing power. Thereafter, all transactions would be recorded in those same units (general-purchasing-power accounting). For a variety of reasons, it was determined that the accounting process should not be revised; only the financial reports should be restated (general-purchasing-power reporting).

General-price-level financial statements could be accomplished in two ways, both of which yielded relatively similar results. In one, the purchasing power of current dollars (at latest balance sheet date) was to be used; in comparative presentations, statements of prior years would be "rolled forward" or inflated (common-dollar reporting). In the other, statements of the current and prior years would be "rolled backward" or deflated into the purchasing power units of a predetermined base period (constant-dollar reporting). In either case, the data would be presented in stable units of purchasing power as of a given point in time.

GPP reporting segregates accounts into two types: monetary and nonmonetary items. In inflationary periods, holders of net monetary assets suffer a loss in purchasing power. Conversely, net monetary debtors experience an increase or gain in purchasing power. These general-purchasing-power gains and losses should be recognized in income for the period. On the other hand, gains and losses on holding nonmonetary items occur for reasons other than inflation, consequently, recognition in income should be made only when the items are sold, used, or discharged.

In effect, GPP reporting serves to protect the purchasing power of the stockholders' equity at the beginning of the year. Income is defined as those resources that could be distributed as dividends without impairment of the purchasing power of equity.

ADVANTAGES OF GPP REPORTING

Advocates of GPP reporting argued that the process was reasonably objective and verifiable since it basically involved adjustments to existing historical cost accounts. Other benefits accrued as well (Figure 5-1) that made the process worthy of consideration.

A Stable Unit of Measure

The foremost benefit, of course, was recognition of the impact of inflation upon the purchasing power of money, a factor ignored by historical cost reporting.

GPP = CONSTANT DOLLAR

ADVANTAGES OF GENERAL PURCHASING POWER (GPP) STATEMENTS

1. GPP statements measure changes in general price levels now ignored by disclosing impact of inflation on the general purchasing power of the dollar.

2. Statements are reliable enough for reporting purposes since statements are primarily oriented toward third parties.

3. Statements are sufficiently objective and verifiable.

(a) All companies will use same index.
(b) Results are auditable.

4. GPP is relatively easy to apply.

(a) Accounting standards are not changed; only the unit of measure is.
(b) Restatement of prior years is simpler than with current replacement value accounting.
(c) Practices have been field-tested.

5. Statements facilitate comparability by using common unit of measure.

(a) Revenues and expenses are matched using common or constant dollars.
(b) Interperiod comparisons are more meaningful.

6. As a "dated dollar," the GPP unit replaces the "rubber" dollar. (The gross national product implicit price deflator is the best comprehensive index.)

7. Statements disclose effective or "real" tax rates and thereby enhance progress toward favorable changes in tax laws.

8. GPP represents a less drastic departure from historical cost.

(a) Historical costs must be retained in accounts for tax, legal, and other purposes.
(b) Few on-going changes in accounting are necessary; adjustments arise in preparation of reports, in the main.
(c) Reports are basically historical costs adjusted or restated in common (or constant) dollars.

9. Statements make more realistic income relationships possible.

(a) Statements relate dividends paid to real income.
(b) They help develop logical dividend policies.
(c) They help prevent accidental distribution of capital.

10. GPP aids management evaluation and use.

(a) GPP provides more realistic return-on-investment rates.
(b) GPP gains and losses reflect management's response to inflation.
(c) Statements give a better idea of purchasing power needed to replace assets consumed.
(d) They help internal management of cash.
(e) They aid in union negotiations by separating inflation and productivity gains.
(f) They can be used as public relations tools by certain industries.

Source: Adapted by permission of the *Harvard Business Review.* From "What's Wrong with Price-Level Accounting" by Elwood L. Miller. (November–December 1978, p. 113.) Copyright ©1978 by the President and Fellows of Harvard College.

FIGURE 5-1.

A cursory look at compound interest tables indicates that prices would effectively double (or purchasing power would be halved) in only 7 years at a 10% rate, 9 years at 8%, 11 years at 6%, and in 14 years at a modest rate of 5%. This compounding effect is the most insidious since it tends to be overlooked (as money earnings grow) until longer-lived assets need to be replaced or increased.

Adoption of either common dollars (as proposed in the 1974 FASB exposure draft) or constant dollars (in the March 1979 revision) would replace the "rubber" dollar now used. The gross national product implicit price deflator was favored initially as the broadest index available in the United States. Subsequently, use of the consumer price index was recommended in Britain and elsewhere, including the United States. In Britain, GPP reporting based upon the retail (consumer) price index was termed "current-purchasing-power reporting," but the difference was in name only. In the FASB's revised exposure draft of March 1979, the consumer price index was favored because it was considered more meaningful and familiar to users, as well as more readily available. Regardless of the index selected, the benefit achieved would be the use of a stable unit of measure that was additive.

Objectivity and Comparability

GPP statements were considered to be objective and verifiable. All firms would use the same indexes and the price-level-adjusted statements would lend themselves to audit as readily as have traditional reports.

Statements expressed in either common or constant dollars were reliable enough for external reporting. Not all assets would be replaced in kind and expressions in stable units of measure would reflect the general movements of prices. In that respect, users might be more comfortable with constant dollars since GNP data have been published in that context for years.

Comparability of operating data would be enhanced, both among firms at a given time and for the operations of a given firm over time. Revenues and expenses would be couched in common or constant dollars thereby separating real and inflationary results, and making interperiod comparisons more meaningful.

Ease of Application

Adjustments are relatively easy to make. Historical costs of transactions remain the "anchors" of accounts. Familiar accounting
conventions are retained; only the unit of measure in financial
reports is changed.

Presentations of data for prior years are simplified. Statements
expressed in constant dollars require no adjustments; those in common dollars are easier to roll forward than are reports based upon
value accounting. Restatements of existing nonmonetary items
would present problems whether common or constant dollars are
used, but only for the first year of implementation. GPP reporting
has been field-tested, particularly with a common-dollar base.

GPP reporting represents the least departure from historical cost.
Tax, legal, and other reporting requirements mandate that historical
cost accounts be retained for the foreseeable future. Very few
changes would be necessary in existing accounting systems since
GPP adjustments are made primarily in the process of statement
preparation. For this reason, GPP methods have also been called
general-price-level-adjusted historical-cost reporting.

Useful, Common-Sense Reports

More realistic income statements would be produced. With GPP
approaches applied to supplemental reports, comparison with net
incomes reflected in the primary historical cost statements would
disclose the effect of inflation upon the firm. Dividend distributions
could be related to "real income," logical dividend policies could be
devised, and accidental distributions of capital would be minimized.
Internally, management decisions and evaluations would be enhanced. The increased purchasing power required to finance inventories, receivables, and ongoing operations would emphasize the need
for improved cash management. Disclosures of inflationary profits
should prove helpful in management negotiations with unions, and
relations with the general and investing publics. Gains and losses
resulting from holding monetary items would reflect management's
response to inflation. The loss of purchasing power suffered by a
net monetary asset posture should be disclosed. Also, the debt ratios
or gearing positions of many firms are substantial enough that they

cannot continue to be ignored if statements are to be presented fairly. Finally, units of general purchasing-power would furnish management with more realistic bases for the evaluation of projects before and subsequent to their implementation.

Last, but not least, GPP statements would disclose the real or effective tax rates imposed upon companies. For the majority of nonleveraged firms, the real tax rates would provide ammunition for corporate tax relief.

DISADVANTAGES OF GPP REPORTING

Opponents of GPP reporting expressed their concerns that, among other problems, generalized attempts to isolate the effects of inflation upon companies might be as misleading, or more so than conventional historical cost presentations (see Figure 5–2).

DISADVANTAGES OF GPP STATEMENTS

---

1. **GPP does not account for changes in specific prices.**

(a) GPP should account for changes in both general and specific prices.
(b) GPP indexes applied to assets do not reflect the specific values of those assets.
(c) Gains and losses on nonmonetary assets are ignored.

---

2. **GPP is not logically consistent. While specific price changes are said to be ignored, price-level adjusted amounts reported for assets cannot be greater than their net realizable values.**

---

3. **General indexes are not always appropriate.**

(a) Not all goods and companies are affected in the same way.
(b) Specific indexes are more appropriate in some cases.
(c) "Relevance" of index depends on user. For management, wholesale or industrial indexes seem to be preferred; for stockholders, consumer price levels should be more meaningful.
(d) Indexes are not exacting measures.

---

4. **Results could be misleading.**

(a) While replacement costs of assets are not depicted, users will tend to make those assumptions.
(b) General price-level financial statements are not directly comparable with historical cost statements.
(c) Presented with multiple statements, users may wonder which set is real.
(d) Single net income figure includes "paper" gains and losses on monetary items as well as holding gains, which will be difficult for the layman to understand.

FIGURE 5-2.

5. Statements distort "normal" income.

(a) Highly leveraged, debt-laden companies will "look good."
(b) Paper gains on long-term debt are not necessarily equivalent to good management; funds are not provided for anything.
(c) Forecasting is hindered since focus is on past events.
(d) Gains and losses on monetary items should be separated into realized and unrealized segments, the latter deferred until they can be matched with expirations of costs of related assets.

6. Statements confuse profitability and liquidity.

(a) Companies willing or able to risk higher levels of borrowed working capital will be able to hedge.
(b) Companies with few nonmonetary assets are, by nature, automatically in a hedged position.
(c) Ability to hedge, either natural or created, will be combined with measurements of profitability.

7. Statements ignore other effects on prices, such as technology, competition, and economic environment of some companies.

8. Use of GPP of the dollar as the measuring unit mandates the use of unsound procedures for the translation of foreign operations.

(a) Use precludes "restate-translate-restate" procedures.
(b) It also assumes that all effects of inflation on foreign currencies are recognized by exchange rates.

9. The costs are not worth the alleged benefits.

(a) Companies may lose the ability to use LIFO for tax purposes.
(b) GPP may result in higher property tax assessments.
(c) Companies must roll forward (restate) prior years each time comparative statements are prepared if common dollars are used.
(d) Companies must also provide replacement cost information to the Securities and Exchange Commission (SEC).
(e) Investors may not attempt to understand the statements.
(f) There are better ways to disclose the effects of inflation on a specific company, its assets, its operations, and its future.

Source: Adapted by permission of the *Harvard Business Review*. From "What's Wrong with Price-Level Accounting" by Elwood L. Miller. (November–December 1978, p. 114.) Copyright © 1978 by the President and Fellows of Harvard College.

Unsound Theory

Changes in general price-levels are macrophenomena that can affect microunits (individual firms) in different ways. Accounting reports, on the other hand, are concerned with microunits. Consequently, attempts to report the effects of general price changes on individual companies using any *normative* method would make economic sense only by accident.

The problem associated with attempts to use macro measures, such as price indexes, for micro purposes has been described as

". . . analogous to tracing the movement of a swarm of bees. The relative movements of the individual bees in the swarm are very irregular; nevertheless the movement of the swarm as a whole is well defined."[1]

Consequently, indexes are logical measures to track movements of the "whole," such as a sector of, or an entire economy. Failure to recognize the changes in specific prices of key commodities (such as oil) renders GPP reporting an illogical method to be applied by *all* companies. Industrial price indexes would be appropriate if and only if applied to firms in a single industry or to industrial segments of conglomerates and/or multinationals. Consumer price indexes have relevance for the day-to-day activities of individuals, but must be considered suspect in relation to the operations of most businesses.

Theoretically, the validity of the assumption that any index produces a common or constant dollar unit of measure has been questioned. Since all indexes are constructed for a given bundle of goods or services, GPP reports are measured in common bundles of goods or services rather than dollars.

Application of general indexes to the historical costs of non-monetary items produces results that are neither costs nor values. The differences upon restatement are not disclosed but are lumped into equity and flow through income over time.

Logical consistency is flawed insofar as nonrecognition of specific prices are concerned. Although specific price changes are said to be irrelevant, price-level-adjusted amounts for assets cannot be greater than their net realizable values. GPP data admittedly ignore the effects on prices of oftentimes important variables such as technology, competition, and the economic environs of firms.

Finally, adoption of general purchasing power of the dollar would require the use of questionable procedures to translate foreign operations of multinational firms. The statements of foreign operations would necessarily have to be first translated into dollars, then restated into units of general purchasing power (the so-called "translate-restate" method). Prohibition of the restate-translate-restate approach would: (1) Ignore foreign inflation, or (2) assume that the relative inflation rates (U.S. and foreign) are recognized by the exchange rates applied in translation.

Misleading Results

General price-level statements are not directly comparable with those produced using historical costs. When presented with multiple statements, users may wonder which set is "real."

Although replacement costs or values of assets are not depicted, users may well tend to make those assumptions. Also, while the restated amounts of most nonmonetary assets will be higher than their historical costs, the real benefits of plant and equipment in place would be ignored. For example, inflation and related increased risks serve to discourage new intruders into market areas; this competitive edge is not recognized.

GPP income statements may prove to be difficult for the layman (and many accountants and analysts) to comprehend. A unit of purchasing power, or a dated dollar, may be sound in theory but neither the entity nor the statement user can do much with it. It may be more foreign to the understanding than a unit of foreign currency.

The relaxation of the original requirement (in the 1974 exposure draft) for comprehensive restatement can assist user understanding somewhat. Two options are made available for supplementary presentation of operating results: a condensed constant-dollar statement, or a reconciliation of the constant-dollar and traditional income statements. The condensed statement alternative (Figure 5-3) appears to present at least four problems:

- Unless the supplemental income statement appears beside the traditional one, users will have to flip pages back and forth to make comparisons. Even then, the causes of differences in items other than sales, cost of goods sold, and depreciation will be not be stated.
- Users may still be led to believe that the inflation gain or loss reflected on monetary items is the total impact of inflation upon the entity.

CONDENSED STATEMENT OF CONSTANT DOLLAR INCOME
FROM CONTINUING OPERATIONS IN DECEMBER 31, 1978
DOLLARS AND OTHER DATA PERTAINING TO
CHANGING PRICES.
(For the Year Ended December 31, 1978)

Net sales and other operating revenues	$*52,000
Cost of goods sold at restated historical cost	21,200
Depreciation and amortization expense at restated historical cost	11,800
Other operating expenses	9,360
Interest expense	1,040
Provision for income taxes	5,200
Constant dollar income from continuing operations	$* 3,400
Inflation gain on net monetary items	$* 600
Foreign exchange loss net of tax†	$* 500

$* December 31, 1978 Dollars.
†It is assumed that the foreign exchange loss is stated at the same amount as in the basic income statement.

Source: Exposure Draft, "Financial Reporting and Changing Prices," December 28, 1978, p. 23. Copyright © by Financial Accounting Standards Board, High Ridge Park, Stamford, Connecticut 06905, U.S.A. Reprinted with permission. Copies of the complete document are available from the FASB.

FIGURE 5-3.

• Separate disclosure of the difference produced by translation of foreign currencies is an improvement over previous requirements. Nonetheless, the translation difference is still termed an exchange "gain or loss" which commingles translation differences (unrealized paper gains and losses) with conversion differences (realized economic gains and losses).
• The two separate disclosures mentioned above may cause the users to question whether or not they are included in the constant dollar amount of income reported.

The reconciliation-format alternative (Figure 5-4) appears to be a better choice since it alleviates the need to flip pages in financial reports in order to make comparisons, and the format itself enhances the explanations of differences in incomes. Also, the separate disclosures on monetary items and foreign exchange differences are clearly identified as separate disclosures. The only source of possible

RECONCILIATION OF INCOME FROM CONTINUING
OPERATIONS AS REPORTED IN THE INCOME STATEMENT TO
CONSTANT DOLLAR INCOME FROM CONTINUING OPERATIONS
IN DECEMBER 31, 1978 DOLLARS
AND OTHER DATA PERTAINING TO CHANGING PRICES
(For the Year Ended December 31, 1978)

Income from continuing operations as reported in the income statement	$ 4,500
Differences caused by changes in the general purchasing power of the dollar from the dates of transactions to December 31, 1978	
Net sales and other operating revenues	2,000
Cost of goods sold	(1,200)
Depreciation and amortization expense	(1,800)
Other operating expenses and income taxes	(600)
Exclusion of foreign exchange loss net of tax	500
Constant dollar income from continuing operations	$* 3,400
Inflation gain on net monetary items	$* 600
Foreign exchange loss net of tax†	$* (500)

$* December 31, 1978 Dollars.
†It is assumed that the foreign exchange loss is stated at the same amount as in the basic financial statements.

Source: Exposure Draft, "Financial Reporting and Changing Prices," December 28, 1978, p. 24. Copyright © by Financial Accounting Standards Board, High Ridge Park, Stamford, Connecticut 06905, U.S.A. Reprinted with permission. Copies of the complete document are available from the FASB.

FIGURE 5-4.

confusion concerns the treatment of the so-called foreign exchange "gain or loss." In Figure 5–4, the foreign exchange "loss" is added back to the traditional income figure in order to arrive at the constant dollar income. Users might wonder, and rightly so, why that item is considered a "loss" in one context but not in another.

The 5-year comparison of selected operating and financial data (Figure 5–5) discloses trends in constant dollars. However, the restated cash dividends and market prices per share will undoubtedly have more relevance to management than to investors. The latter group is more concerned with the relationship between cash dividends received and share prices actually paid in dollars.

The most misleading aspect of GPP reporting arises from the confusion of profitability and liquidity. Firms suffering critical ailments (such as high leverage or cash and capital deficiencies)

**FIVE-YEAR COMPARISON OF SELECTED FINANCIAL DATA
IN DECEMBER 31, 1978 DOLLARS.**

	YEARS ENDED DECEMBER 31				
	1974	1975	1976	1977	1978
Net sales and other operating revenues	$*XX	$*XX	$*XX	$*XX	$*XX
Constant dollar income from continuing operations	XX	XX	XX	XX	XX
Inflation gain (loss) on net monetary items	XX	XX	XX	XX	XX
Foreign exchange gain (loss) net of tax	XX	XX	XX	XX	XX
Net assets at year-end	XX	XX	XX	XX	XX
Constant dollar income from continuing operations per common share	XX	XX	XX	XX	XX
Cash dividends declared per common share	XX	XX	XX	XX	XX
Market price per common share at year-end	XX	XX	XX	XX	XX

$*December 31, 1978 Dollars.

Source: Exposure Draft, "Financial Reporting and Changing Prices," December 28, 1978, p. 25. Copyright © by Financial Accounting Standards Board, High Ridge Park, Stamford, Connecticut 06905, U.S.A. Reprinted with permission. Copies of the complete document are available from the FASB.

FIGURE 5-5.

would be diagnosed not only as healthy but also as steadily improving since incomes would be inflated. The "gain" on long-term debt may or may not be indicative of sound management: funds are not provided for any purpose; and estimates of future cash flows are certainly not enhanced. At minimum, these so-called "gains" should be recognized only when realized. The ability to hedge—whether natural or created—will be combined with measurements of profitability, and commonsense reporting can only suffer.

Perhaps the loudest complaints from the business community concerned charges that the costs associated with GPP reporting were not worth the alleged benefits. Initially, firms complained about the high start-up costs associated with restatements of non-monetary items; particularly inventories, prepayments, plant and equipment, as well as the deferred income tax labyrinth. (The latter complaint was corrected by the reclassification of deferred income taxes as a monetary item in the March 1979 exposure draft.) A second out-of-pocket cost concerned the laborious roll-forward requirements of the initial common-dollar proposal—often referred to as "galloping numbers" that changed every year.[2] (This complaint also was ameliorated by the option to use a constant-dollar base—restatements of prior years would only be required when and if the base year of the consumer price index were revised.) Many companies objected to the additional costs of GPP reporting since they also were burdened with furnishing the SEC data regarding replacement costs.

Perhaps the most worrisome concerns pertained to the costs of possible repercussions. The benefits of LIFO costing for tax purposes could be lost should the Treasury Department decide to follow the letter of the law (since GPP-adjusted inventories are not necessarily the equivalent of LIFO costs for financial reporting). It should be noted that the IRS has proposed liberalization of the LIFO conformity rule, effective in September 1979. This would permit references in annual reports to inventories, cost of sales, and earnings based upon FIFO as well as LIFO costs. Moreover, property tax assessors might be prone to base assessments upon the higher restated amounts for assets in GPP reports.

The last complaint required the FASB several years to appreciate—if, in fact, they have. That is the fact that most investors would not make the effort needed to understand GPP reports, and there were better ways to disclose the effects of inflation on a specific company, its assets, its operations, and its future.

CRITIQUE

Many of the anticipated effects of general-purchasing-power reporting have been confirmed by field tests. Other possible effects remain conjectures since GPP reporting has not been applied on any sizeable scale over a period of time. The evidence, together with logic, furnish a reasonable basis for critique.

Industry Appraisals

Following the release of its 1974 exposure draft, the FASB field-tested the proposed common-dollar reporting methods with a representative group of companies in more than a dozen industries.[3]

Field Tests. As expected, capital-intensive firms reported lower "real" incomes and higher effective tax rates. Labor-intensive companies reported no real impact. Debt-intensive firms, such as utilities, reported significantly higher "real" incomes due to holding gains (for 11 firms in 1974: lowest, nearly 40%; median, 105%; highest, 311%).[4] Cash-intensive firms, such as financial institutions, reflected lower common-dollar incomes (10 institutions reported a median reduction of nearly 60% in 1974).[5]

Within capital-intensive industries, however, differences between nominal and common-dollar incomes varied over a significant range. These variations represented the effects of several differences in the financial and operating structures: ages of plant and equipment, as well as patterns of replacement and acquisition; different turnover rates of inventories and receivables; financial leverage or gearing; and similar factors. It was evident that inflation affected firms in different ways; what was not evident was whether or not GPP reports made economic sense. Since a sample size of 20 oil companies reported a median decline of nearly 10% in 1974 common-dollar income, the economic realism of GPP reporting suffered.[6]

Support and Opposition. Naturally, support for GPP reporting was generated by those managements which were inclined to espouse any practice that would lend support for reductions in corporate taxes and thereby assist capital formation. Beyond that facade little support was found.

Management objections ran the gamut of disadvantages mentioned previously: problems of implementation, user interpretation, and recognition of gains on long-term debt. Utilities and financial institutions were vehemently opposed to the virtual reversals in earnings patterns that would be reflected. Generally, other managements did not welcome the prospects of reporting lower incomes and rates of return. On the one hand, the more conservative reportings might represent only a temporary concern *if*: all firms reported similar downturns; investors understood the results and did not rush to change portfolios; and traditional financial structures and markets would not be disrupted. For most managements the uncertainties loomed rather large.

Considered Opinions

When compared with the constraints imposed upon the accounting model in Chapter 2:

- GPP reporting receives high marks for uniformity, objectivity, and verifiability.
- Low marks must be assessed insofar as the fairness, economic sense, usefulness, and cost of GPP are concerned.

General-purchasing-power approaches to reporting the effects of inflation attempt to do the impossible with bad theory ill applied.

To merely change the unit of measurement is to adopt a simplex approach to a complex problem. Dictionary definitions notwithstanding, inflation manifests itself in myriad forms other than an unstable monetary unit. Reporting the effects of inflation is not that easy a task. Different firms are affected in different ways. Any *normative* method that is attempted can only produce economic nonsense, since it must treat alike that which is not.

Burdensome, comprehensive restatements are unnecessary and often irrelevant, if not misleading. Supplementary disclosures of a *uniform* set of selected, restated items reduces costs of implememmentation but cannot increase relevance.

The necessary ingredients (often mentioned but never taken seriously in pronouncements) are the expertise and judgment of those in the only positions to assess and disclose the impacts of inflation on a specific entity—its management and independent auditors.

Management knows more about the enterprise and its affairs than investors, creditors, or other "outsiders" and accordingly can often increase the usefulness of financial information by identifying certain events and circumstances and explaining their financial effects on the enterprise.[7]

Management of an enterprise is periodically accountable to the owners not only for the custody and safekeeping of enterprise resources but also for their efficient and profitable use and for protecting them to the extent possible from unfavorable economic impacts of factors in the economy such as inflation or deflation and technological and social changes.[8]

The role of the independent auditor concerns attestation of the fairness of management's reports and representations. The nature and scope of the analytical review procedures required of independent auditors pertain to examinations "using dollars, physical quantities, ratios, or percentages" and "may be applied to overall financial information of the entity, to financial information of components such as subsidiaries or divisions, and to individual elements of financial information."[9]

The means exist to provide statement users with meaningful *inflation explanation.* The means should be used.

FASB Statement No. 33

Since the SEC warned the FASB that GPP data, standing alone would be unacceptable, the FASB elected to call for *both* GPP (constant dollar) and current cost disclosures. The details of FASB *Statement No. 33,* "Financial Reporting and Changing Prices," September 1979, are examined in Appendix 9A.

CHAPTER 5. NOTES

1. Irving Fisher, *The Purchasing Power of Money* (New York: Macmillan, 1911), p. 194; cited by Livingston Middleditch, Jr., "Should Accounts Reflect the Changing Value of the Dollar?", *Journal of Accountancy,* February 1918, p. 115.

2. John C. Biegler, "Common-Sense Accounting for Inflation," *Financial Executive,* December 1977, p. 37.

3. Statistical summary of results in six industry groups is provided in Financial Accounting Standards Board, *Exposure Draft,* "Financial Reporting and Changing Prices" (Stamford, Conn.: FASB, December 1978), p. 42.

4. Ibid.

5. Ibid.

6. Ibid.

7. Financial Accounting Standards Board, *Statement of Financial Accounting Concepts No. 1,* "Objectives of Financial Reporting by Business Enterprises" (Stamford, Conn: FASB, November 1978), p. x.

8. Ibid., p. 25.

9. Auditing Standards Executive Committee, *Statement on Auditing Standards No. 23,* "Analytical Review Procedures" (New York: AICPA, October 1978), p. 3.

6
Value Accounting

Many of those who became disenchanted with general-purchasing-power reporting joined the ranks of those who advocated value accounting. For this and a variety of other reasons, methods of value accounting gained increasing support in late 1975 in the United States and elsewhere. In this chapter, the reasonings, benefits, and shortcomings of value accounting proposals will be addressed.

RATIONALE

In the theory of business economics, income is defined as the earnings residual after capital has been recovered. Capital maintenance, therefore, becomes the overriding concept. At that point, unfortunately, agreement ends. Although there are several other minor differences in opinion among the various schools of thought, basic disagreements involve three issues: the concept of capital, the basis of value determination, and the recognition of holding gains.

Concepts of Capital

Two concepts of capital have been debated. One school of thought seeks to protect the *physical capital* or the *equivalent productive capacity* of the firm. Neither replacement of existing assets in kind nor their money values are involved. Instead, the effects of technological change upon the firm's products, as well as the nature and scope of the physical plant needed to maintain present levels of production are considered in determining replacement values. The other school of thought allegedly seeks to preserve the *financial capital* or the money value of the firm's *existing net assets.* (Both schools must express the values assigned to the firm's resources in money terms for reporting purposes. Consequently, the physical-financial dichotomy that has become popular may not be the most appropriate. One group recognizes the effects of technological change; the other holds technology constant.)

Determinants of Value

A second conceptual difference concerns the basis upon which values are determined. Two general approaches have been developed:

- *Entry* prices (input costs)—the current costs to repurchase or reproduce the asset or its productive capacity.
- *Exit* prices (output values), based upon either:
  —net realizable values, or
  —economic values (the present values of future cash flows).

In theory, there is a consensus that the discounted present value of future cash flows produces an accounting income closely resembling economic income. Consequently, economic value would be the most appropriate basis for measurement. Unfortunately, these same theorists agree that economic values are the least practicable for most applications. If future net income streams are to be determined by the expirations of the current values of assets, and if these current values are to be determined by discounting future net income streams, the model contains two unknowns and is insoluble.

Following extensive discussions in the literature, a consensus has emerged that favors the use of entry prices (current replacement costs) for most nonmonetary assets, such as fixed assets in use and goods purchased or produced for sale in the normal course of business. Economic (or present) value is considered appropriate for those monetary items for which an objective, external interest or discount rate is available. Net realizable value (or current disposal value less normal disposal costs) is seen as feasible for nonroutine (deprival) sales of assets not normally held for sale, and for those monetary items for which determinations of economic value would be impractical. Finally, in cases where all three values may be determinable, conservatism requires that current replacement cost should prevail except in those few circumstances in which it would be greater than both economic and net realizable values.[1]

Holding Gains

The third conceptual issue that has been debated concerns *holding gains*. In value accounting, a holding gain is defined as the difference between the historical acquisition cost of an item (net of depreciation where applicable) and its current cost or value at a specific time.

Disagreement surrounds whether or not holding gains should be included in the profit to be reported for the period. (All holding gains are involved, not simply whether they are realized, by sale or disposal of the items; or unrealized—the items are still on hand at the end of the accounting period.) Both sides agree that profit represents the amount that could be distributed without impairing the firm's capital. Consequently, the financial capital school would include holding gains in profit. The physical capital school would exclude all holding gains since, if the items are to be replaced in kind or equivalence, provision must be made for the increased replacement cost otherwise the physical capital would be diminished. Most advocates of value accounting agree, however, that holding gains (as well as extraordinary gains) should be disclosed in some fashion since the information is useful, but should not necessarily be considered as a part of distributable profit.

It should be noted that the foregoing comments on holding gains pertain only to nonmonetary items. Value theorists treat money as a unit of measure not as a commodity to be valued. Therefore, monetary items are not to be adjusted since they are stated in units considered to be constant in value.

Variant Forms

While many hybrid forms of value accounting exist, recognition of one of two dichotomies will apply in most cases:

1. Concept of capital:
   a. Financial capital
   b. Physical capital
2. Basis of values:
   a. Current cost—the amount required to replace an existing item in kind at current prices (technological change is ignored).
   b. Replacement cost—the amount required to replace the equivalent productive capacity considering technological change.

Regardless of the particular or variant form of value accounting under consideration, it may prove helpful to recognize the procedural differences between conventional and value accounting. Conventional accounting practices focus upon the matchings of revenues and expenses for presentation in the income statement; the balance sheet reflects the residuals or balances resulting from the matching process. Value accounting methods focus upon the values (however defined) of specific resources for balance sheet presentation; the income statement reflects the results of changes in those values during the period.

It should also be recognized that replacement-value methods would require changes in day-to-day accounting procedures. Unlike GPP *reporting* (in which historical cost accounting data are merely restated for reporting purposes), replacement-value methods represent an entirely different, comprehensive *accounting* system (historical cost data needed for tax and other purposes would require a supplementary set of records). Consequently, the current-cost *reporting* alternative proposed by the FASB in December 1978 will be examined in the chapter that follows dealing with hybrid proposals.

As a final note, the characteristics of current-cost and replacement-cost accounting proposals are similar enough to warrant collective evaluation as value accounting in the balance of this chapter.

ADVANTAGES OF VALUE ACCOUNTING

Advocates of value accounting were convinced that their methods were superior from both theoretical and practical standpoints. Theoretically, the recognition of specific price changes applied microconcepts to microunits and related concepts to entities. Practically, accounting for changes in the values (both specific and general) of the productive assets of a firm, and retaining the familiar monetary unit of measure, addressed the only real concerns of any consequence. Other benefits accrued as well (see Figure 6-1).

ADVANTAGES OF REPLACEMENT VALUE OR CURRENT COST ACCOUNTING

1. Statements are interpretable.

(a) Familiar monetary unit is retained as the unit of measurement.
(b) Assets will approximate the "values" often assumed by users of historical cost statements.

2. Current replacement value accounting (CRVA) provides closer approximation of real income.

(a) Revenues are related to costs in common dollars.
(b) Income is not contaminated by changes in price levels since these are excluded and set up in capital maintenance accounts.

3. The capital of the enterprise, however defined, is protected from involuntary diminution by management.

4. CRVA measures real effects of inflation.

(a) Balance sheet items reflected at current values take into account changes in both general and specific prices on these items; no additional price changes are relevant to the company.
(b) CRVA will correct prostitution of balance sheets by LIFO inventories while retaining current matching benefits on income statements as well as protecting continued use of LIFO for tax purposes.
(c) Current values can also recognize the effects of technology, competition, industry peculiarities, and so forth.

5. Effective or real tax rates are disclosed.

6. Value accounting is a better management tool. Concepts are future-oriented, which is the realm of managers, analysts, and other informed users of financial statements.

7. Value accounting is gaining support.

(a) The SEC requires certain replacement cost information now; it may require supplemental statements later.
(b) Professional groups in other countries and regions (such as the European Economic Community) are considering trial and/or adoption in various forms.

Source: Reprinted by permission of the *Harvard Business Review*. From "What's Wrong with Price-Level Accounting" by Elwood L. Miller. (November–December 1978, p. 115.) Copyright © 1978 by the President and Fellows of Harvard College.

FIGURE 6-1.

Interpretability

Retention of the familiar monetary unit of measure poses several benefits. The same money unit would continue to serve as the common denominator by all accounting entities, and the unit would not change from year to year. Moreover, a unit of money, such as the dollar, is real. Statement users can relate to a unit of money much more readily than to a unit of general purchasing-power or a dated dollar.

Perhaps interpretability (or user understanding) would benefit most from the fact that the amounts ascribed to assets would closely approximate the "values" now often assumed by statement users.

Realism

As mentioned earlier, economic reality is a nebulous concept that is colored by various interpretations and subject to constant change. Therefore, realism here refers to common sense reporting.

Assets would be reported at their "real values" to the firm, with or without recognition of the effects of changing technology (although the former would be more realistic). Operating income would not be contaminated by changes in price levels since the results of these changes would be set up in capital maintenance accounts.

Profitability would not be confused with liquidity. Since money is considered a unit of measure rather than a commodity with a changing value, gains on holding net monetary liabilities would not be computed and reflected in income. The current and potential effects of gearing or leverage are considered useful information that merits disclosure, but not within income statements.

Profits reported under value accounting would furnish a more realistic basis for decisions by all "stakeholders," not only investors. The separation of operating and holding gains would provide unions and employees with data that would enable them to separate their "fair share" of profits from those sums needed to maintain productive capacity and future employment. Creditors should find that the reported net values of assets furnish more meaningful relationships with risks assumed than either the residuals of historical costs or general-indexed amounts. Governments, as influential users of accounting information, would have *timely* data upon which to compute the effective rates of corporate taxation—data reported by the Bureau of Economic Analysis and the Treasury Department have a 2 to 3-year lag-time (see Table 3-1).

Last, but not least, the impacts of changes in general and specific price levels reflected in value accounting reports would support efforts for general indexation. Monetary correction will be needed to maintain the substance of economic life should the political sector prove incapable of reducing inflation to a tolerable level.

Comparability

Current values would take into account changes in both general and specific prices upon balance sheet items of all firms. No additional price changes are relevant in depicting the impacts of inflation upon the productive parts of entities.

Replacement cost, in particular, would recognize the effects of changes in technology and competition, as well as industry peculiarities ignored by other methods of accounting. Ownership of modern, technologically efficient plant and equipment of adequate scale represents an inflationary hedge and a competitive edge. A firm with up-todate facilities in desirable locations is not faced with impending modernizations or realignments at inflationary prices, nor the problems of obtaining debt or equity capital in unfavorable markets. Moreover, at least two competitive advantages accrue. Modern, efficient facilities in place represent a formidable barrier to potential new entrants into the market area, and a competitive "leg up" over existing competitors that have permitted themselves to become fossilized.

Replacement-value accounting would correct the prostitution of balance sheets by those firms using LIFO-cost inventories. Comparability would be improved while retaining the benefits of matching current costs and revenues on income statements. Approval of the Treasury Department or Congress (or both) would be necessary to replace LIFO with replacement cost for tax purposes. However, little opposition could be expected since, for the large majority of firms, effects on taxable incomes would be negligible; balance sheet amounts would return to the realm of economic sense. No longer would one read of a loan negotiated for $10 million secured by inventories reported at a LIFO cost of say $2 million—a form of off-balance-sheet financing.

The reportings of stewardship by all firms should be enhanced. Although not all gains would be included in operating profit, as such, the disclosure of total gains—properly earmarked as realized, unrealized, holding, extraordinary, and operating—would reflect the total results of activities during the period. In fact, many of the present dilemmas concerning what should or should not be reported as operating profit would disappear since all gains would be disclosed. For firms in certain sectors (such as the trading of commodities or real properties), holding gains may be as relevant, or more so, than current operating profits. In all cases, presentations of all gains and losses would enable users to assess the performance of a firm or a group of firms using the measures considered to be most appropriate given the circumstances.

Usefulness

Value accounting methods are considered to be much more useful tools for decision-making purposes, internally and externally.

Management is furnished routinely with data that serve to protect the capital of the firm from involuntary diminution. The development of fiscally sound dividend policies would not only be enhanced but should be better understood by third parties. Value accounting methods are future-oriented and provide a more realistic basis for the development of pricing policies and strategies.

External uses (as well as internal, ex-post project evaluations) would benefit significantly from the ability of value accounting to differentiate between the return *of* and the return *on* investment. A more rational basis for the making of economic evaluations of past performances would be furnished all stakeholders—investors, creditors, analysts, government agencies, and other concerned users of accounting reports.

Insofar as certain decisions pertaining to the future are concerned —such as the FASB's current interest in the prediction of future cash flows—the jury is still out. Proponents of value theory, and the tentative findings of some studies, indicate that much depends upon conditions and circumstances. However, there appears to be an emerging consensus that, in the majority of inflationary situations, current-value data represent a superior basis for the estimation of future cash flows.[2]

Time and circumstance have improved the cost-benefit ratio of value accounting. Many of the larger corporations have implemented systems for compiling the replacement-cost information required by the SEC's *ASR-190* experiment. Replacement cost methods (and to a lesser extent those of current cost accounting) conform closely with the SEC requirements. Should value accounting be adopted, a reduction in the redundancy (if not the total cost) of reporting should result. Downstream, the SEC might be inclined to discontinue or conform its experiment. For those firms that have not been subjected to compliance with *ASR-190,* consideration could be given to the use of the specific price indexes that the Bureau of Economic Analysis maintains and applies to 20 categories of plant assets (see Chapter 3).

DISADVANTAGES OF VALUE ACCOUNTING

Critics were quick to challenge the subjectivity necessarily related to assessments of condition (value or current cost) to be measured. Other challenges questioned the underlying logic of the proposals, problems of implementation, the alleged usefulness, and the adverse repercussions possible should value accounting continue its rise in popularity and become adopted (see Figure 6–2).

Subjectivity

There is little doubt that concerns over subjectivity represented the initial reverberations to value accounting proposals.

Value was an elusive concept to most individuals but particularly so to accountants. The worth of a thing was considered to be what it would bring, and that could only be determined in the marketplace (eventually) or by looking ahead (during the interim). Interim values required a point of reference: Value to the business, value in use, replacement value, deprival value, realizable value (from a regular or forced disposition), among others.

Many American accountants feared a return to the appraisal fiascos of the 1920s. This may, in part, account for the earlier consideration of current-cost accounting in Britain. The British business community was accustomed to using the services of professional appraisers for many years prior to the publication of the Sandilands Report in 1975.

DISADVANTAGES OF REPLACEMENT VALUE OR CURRENT COST ACCOUNTING

1. Income statements are defective.

(a) Changes in the purchasing power of money are not reflected in the period in which they occur.
(b) Comparability is impaired.

2. Balance sheets are defective.

(a) Subjective evaluations and asset appraisals may signal a return to the abuses of the 1920s.
(b) There is no uniformity; combinations of current cost and current value will be used.

3. There are problems and costs of implementation and administration.

(a) Necessary specific indexes are not generally available.
(b) CRVA represents a complete departure from historical costs; two sets of records will be required.
(c) Costs and problems of implementation will seriously affect small companies; there is no practicable way to implement CRVA in complex companies.
(d) Replacement values may result in increased property tax assessments.
(e) Audit costs will increase.

4. CRVA may initiate price increases to further aggravate inflationary conditions.

5. CRVA systems are not logically sound.

(a) In a competitive environment, company survival cannot be taken as a given.
(b) Maintenance of productive capacity is neither a necessary nor a sufficient condition for survival and growth of an enterprise.
(c) Increases in assets on balance sheets are not reflected in income statements.
(d) Recovery of historical costs plus costs of capital will produce a steady state company as long as selling prices are based on historical costs.

Source: Reprinted by permission of the *Harvard Business Review*. From "What's Wrong with Price-Level Accounting" by Elwood L. Miller. (November–December 1978, p. 115.) Copyright © 1978 by the President and Fellows of Harvard College.

FIGURE 6-2.

Quite likely, many American accountants were concerned that value accounting would attach precisions in measurement to the accounting process that were unwarranted since they did not exist. Public accounting practitioners expressed their reservations regarding attestations of value appraisals in which they had no reasonable expertise—particularly replacement values that required the recognition of technological change.

All in all, subjectivity generated a cloud enshrouding the whole of value accounting.

Faulty Logic

As with all models, the logic (or set of assumptions) supporting value accounting supplied ample grist for the mills of critics.

Value accounting methods did not measure or report the effects of inflation as normally defined. Inflation was not considered a disease but rather only a symptom of the many deficiencies attached to reliance upon the historical cost model. Value accounting, then, was not really a proposal to account for inflation, but rather a rejection of the historical-cost model regardless of the degree or absence of inflation.

In a competitive environment, company survival could not be taken as a given. The vigor and growth of business entities are functions of management and the marketplace. Accounting involves the measurement and reporting of economic results, both internally and externally, and should act as an evaluative and communicative device rather than as an active conservator of business.

The maintenance of productive capacity is neither a necessary nor sufficient condition for survival and growth of a firm. Those who would disagree rely upon the textbook assumptions of free, competitive markets in which prices are not manipulable by firms but are competitively determined. Few, if any, such markets exist today. Firms can decrease production and increase prices whereby they can realize stable or increased net incomes. Moreover, as mentioned earlier, Anthony has demonstrated that recovery of historical costs, plus costs of capital, will produce a steady-state company in times of inflation as long as selling prices are based upon historical costs.[3]

Value accounting methods "account" for quantities of goods and services, not for money. Proponents of value accounting have adopted, knowingly or otherwise, an incomplete business cycle of money-to-goods-to-money-to-goods that is appropriate for a barter economy. Goods in themselves cannot function as a common denominator in an accounting system.

The amounts reported for most nonmonetary assets in balance sheets are unsound, if not misleading. Several fallacies may be represented. Emphasis is placed upon *current* replacement values or costs. For items with rapid turnovers (such as inventories), that emphasis seems to be appropriate. For longer-lived items to be replaced in the distant future (such as plant assets), the approach does not seem logical. Modern businesses may well choose to relocate operations in a different economic environment (such as in a different country), and quite possibly in a different form (due to needs and technological advances). Also, many assets are not reproducible currently or at any future time. Managements are free to use the assets entrusted to their care much as they please, but the one thing they cannot do is acquire them again.

Current cost proposals have been criticized for ignoring technological change and flaunting reality. Replacement cost approaches attempt to rectify that shortcoming, however, to conjure and then quantify the present effects of future change requires a vivid imagination indeed.

Problems of Implementation

Theoretical problems aside, the practical difficulties of implementing value accounting created significant resistance within the business community.

Value accounting represented a complete departure from historical costs and, for the foreseeable future, two sets of records would be necessary in order to satisfy legal and tax requirements. Small firms would be faced with inordinate costs. Implementation would be impracticable for large, complex companies and multinationals.

Many companies did not have the internal expertise needed to generate replacement costs, however defined. The necessary specific indexes required as alternative measures might not exist or be generally available.

If operating capability is to be maintained, value accounting methods would have to cope with the knotty problems of "backlog" depreciation, unless the entities concerned were large enough to adopt and practice a policy of continuous, partial replacement of plant assets.

A particularly troublesome problem would arise in consideration of the income tax treatment to be applied to the differences between historical and current-replacement costs. If unrealized holding gains (not subject to tax concurrently) were not reflected net of tax, equity would be overstated. If the potential tax effects were to be recognized, estimated due dates for payment would be needed in order to reduce the deferred liabilities to their present values.

A final problem of implementation that is somewhat more conceptual than practical surrounds the recognition that the business of accounting cannot concern itself with *mythical* measurements of economic income or the value of a firm.

Comparability and Usefulness

A majority of advocates and critics alike tend to agree that the usefulness of value accounting reports would depend very much upon the peculiarities and circumstances of the particular firms.

All firms are not alike. All assets do not lend themselves logically or practically to measurement by normative means. Uniformity across and among firms would tend to suffer since various forms of current value and current cost would be used in combination. Reporting firms and users of reports would often be faced with tradeoffs between the nonsense products of normative means and the commonsense results produced by selected applications of various measures determined by judgment and circumstance.

Balance sheets may appear to be defective in that the values of assets reported do not, a priori, reflect or indicate the replacement policies of management. These important factors can only be *explained*.

Income statements may also be considered faulty. Increases in asset values on the balance sheet would not be reflected in income. Would users comprehend the holding gains reported? Conceptually, the reported impacts of price changes would be overstated as long as the beneficial effects of debt financing (gearing) were ignored.

Since value accounting methods are based upon tracking flows of goods, the resulting reports could assist in the prediction of future operating cash flows *if* the flows were assumed to be a function of changes in physical units only, not changes in selling prices. Theory aside, many individuals (including the author) are convinced that future cash flows cannot be predicted by external parties using data provided in any reports of past events. The future cash needs of a firm will be affected by many variables other than those gleaned from reports: technologies; price and demand elasticities; competitive positions; planned capital expenditures—discretionary, mandatory, expansionary, and otherwise; pursuits of new markets and ventures; acquisitions of new companies or dispositions of current units; and where management plans to acquire the capital needed to do all these things. These "soft data" are critical needs not to be found routinely in present or proposed reports.

Some allege that the natures of complex firms—both domestic conglomerates and multinational enterprises—are so diverse that consolidated reports have become single-purpose statements of limited value. Investors of the parent firm can obtain a macroconcept of the organization's absolute or relative size but very little else. Size and diversity are said to have rendered ratio analyses and funds statements of most firms meaningless. Segmented reporting methods, long overdue and still in embryonic form, represent a step in the direction needed to restore a semblance of usefulness in financial reports.

Uncertain Repercussions

Few things generate as much concern as uncertainty. Fears of imagined repercussions often bear more weight in considerations of change than do real and present problems.

Some fear that value accounting methods will institutionalize inflation. Price increases may be generated without due consideration given their ability to further aggravate inflationary conditions. To the extent that market structures have been rendered defective by oligopolistic collusion such results are possible. However, there is little reason to believe that selling prices are not currently being increased at will by those industries and sectors enjoying relatively inelastic demands for their outputs. The introduction of value accounting may have little net effect on price increases. As an aside, value accounting methods may well disclose the "price gougers," provided that reports are segmented in the necessary detail.

Management fears were usually fourfold. The potential adverse effects upon stock markets were foremost concerns. Efficient market ideas made good topics for conversation but few firms were anxious to put them to the test. A second concern involved the certainties of higher accounting and audit costs. Revisions would be necessary to internal information systems—already a sore spot for many companies insofar as cost-benefit relationships were concerned. Spiraling audit costs were certain to escalate even further, not to mention the additional management advisory services that would be required by many industries. A third irritant was the possibility that local assessors would use the higher reported asset values as an easy means to increase property tax revenues. The last and very real fear was the threat of reconsideration (and possible withdrawal) by the Treasury

Department of LIFO and accelerated methods of depreciation for tax purposes. As mentioned in the preceding chapter, the IRS proposal to liberalize its LIFO conformity rule should allay concerns over the possible loss of LIFO benefits. No similar assurances exist or can be foreseen regarding accelerated depreciation benefits.

Many accountants considered "value-itis" as a disease to be dreaded more than inflation itself. Memories of the valuation fiascos of the 1920s and early 1930s were rekindled. How much these fears really represented concerns over subjectivity and how much they merely reflected reluctance to depart from familiar ways of doing things can only be conjectured.

CRITIQUE

New ways of thinking are generally suspect. Value accounting proposals, even though they have been credited with gaining momentum, are relatively untried outside of a small group of select holding companies in the Netherlands. Also, as mentioned previously, the microeconomic environment of the Netherlands, together with the nature of the firms organized there—as well as the structure of stock ownership—lend themselves rather well to value accounting. How well such methods would transplant within different economic environments is not certain by any means.

While it is said that two wrongs cannot make a right, adoption of value accounting would eliminate some of the nonsense and much of the mechanical problems associated with the translation of foreign currencies under *FASB-8*.[4] According to the temporal method of translation prescribed by *FASB-8*, the use of current values would enable the use of current exchange rates in translations of financial statements. If nothing else, the "essence" of foreign financial statements of subsidiaries would be restored and retained. Beyond this benefit (which could be gained by much simpler means), value accounting poses more problems than solutions.

If accounting should report changes in both general and specific price levels, then the effects upon the values of all commodities should be addressed—including changes in the values of monies held (purchasing power) and the finances obtained externally (gearing). To do less would fall short of accounting for inflation.

Those who look to value accounting reports (or any reports based upon past events) as surrogate predictors of future events are treading on thin ice indeed. There simply is no way in which financial statements can tell stockholders what the future has in store in the way of dividends or market values of their shares.

Company survival, capital formation, and tax reform are important endeavors that must be addressed by managements within the parameters of the economic and political environments. However, they are not appropriate functions for accounting to address. Accounting is a language of business, not a mechanism to be used to accomplish economic or social reforms.

In mature economies, the magnitude and complexity of firms have dictated that objective and fair reportings of past economic events be structured around the historical cost model. Inflation has not presented any valid challenges to the objectivity of the historical cost model; it has questioned the validity of the unit of measurement employed in some, but not all, circumstances. Value accounting proposals do not attempt to correct the measuring stick but, instead, seek to change the nature of the property to be measured. Reports of accomplishments (profits) reflect the residuals of changes in estimated values at the ends of consecutive periods and have no stable reference point or benchmark. In a sense, then, an unstable unit of measure is replaced by an unstable or varying basis of measurement. In short, a nominal measure is applied to relative characteristics.

Although value accounting may be defended in the sense that it is theoretically more useful than other methods, it simply is not practicable.

CHAPTER 6. NOTES

1. For an excellent analysis of the hierarchy of value determinants, see *Inflation Accounting: Report of the Inflation Accounting Committee,* F.E.P. Sandilands, Chmn. (London: Her Majesty's Stationery Office, September 1975), pp. 58–61.

2. For example, see George M. Scott, *Research Study on Current-Value Accounting Measurements and Utility* (New York: Touche Ross Foundation, 1978).

3. Robert N. Anthony, "A Case for Historical Costs," *Harvard Business Review,* November-December 1976, pp. 69–79.

4. Financial Accounting Standards Board, *Statement of Financial Accounting Standards No. 8:* "Accounting for the Translation of Foreign Currency Transactions and Foreign Currency Financial Statements" (Stamford, Conn.: FASB, October 1975), para. 12b.

7
Hybrid Proposals

Considerations of general-purchasing-power reporting and value accounting, in their pure forms, were incapable of convincing a majority to favor either method, at least in the United States. That should not be surprising at all given the nature of the disease in question.

Inflation manifested itself in changes in both general and specific price levels. The total effects upon a given firm were, more often than not, found to be dependent upon the structure of the business (the nature and composition of assets and debt) and the sources of its earnings. Accounting or reporting methods proposed should disclose all the effects if they are to present the impacts of inflation. Each method was found wanting. Moreover, serious disadvantages were attributed to both approaches—theoretical and practical. Reason dictated that the search be continued for a better way.

PROFESSIONAL EXPERIMENTATION

To encourage further discussion and in the search for a better way, an experimental program was initiated in April 1977 by the AICPA. The program consisted of a field test of four accounting models constructed to depict the effects of changing prices. The tests were conducted by 23 major public companies that agreed to participate voluntarily as long as the test results would be confidential, at least for a period of time.[1] Evidently, the participating firms were unwilling to publicize concurrently operating results that departed from those portrayed in their official reports.

The four accounting models examined in the experiment were:

- *Model A*—A simplified version of general-price-level-adjusted historical-cost reporting as proposed by the FASB's 1974 exposure draft. Condensed, supplementary *schedules* were to be used (rather than complete supplementary statements), requiring only the restatement of selected items in constant (rather than common) dollars.
- *Model B*—A modification of historical cost reporting in which inventories were based upon LIFO cost, and depreciation was computed upon the acquisition costs of assets adjusted by specific indexes (not replacement costs).
- *Model C*—A hybrid form of replacement cost reporting making use of historical costs, current costs, and current values dependent upon the items involved. Operating income was to be distinguished from value changes, both realized and unrealized.
- *Model D*—A comprehensive, hybrid value-accounting model employing all the value approaches—replacement cost, net realizable value, and economic value—together with recognition of the effects of changes in general price-levels on shareholders' equity. The resulting financial statements would include a statement of changes disclosing net operating income, value changes (realized and unrealized), and the amount needed to maintain the general purchasing-power of equity.

The experiment did not provide the AICPA task force with a clear consensus. Like many such experiments, the answer to the question of which method best portrayed the effects of inflation upon a company was an unequivocal "it all depends." The AICPA and the FASB (with whom the results were shared) concluded that the number of firms that participated in the study was rather small, and that the experiment was worthy of continuation on a revised but much broader scale. Consequently, the FASB initiated its current program of *mandatory experimentation* by large, public companies (with more than $125 million of plant and inventory *or* $1 billion of total assets). The FASB's December 1978 *Exposure Draft*, "Financial Reporting and Changing Prices," will require an estimated 1000 companies[2] to disclose supplementary information for fiscal years ending on or after December 25, 1979 using either a simplified version of (1) the historical cost/constant dollar, or (2) the current cost method. (The former is a modification of the GPP reporting model proposed by the FASB in 1974 and was reviewed in Chapter 5. The current cost option is a hybrid form of reporting and will be examined later in this chapter.)

Two studies of the effects of general-price-level reporting upon several hundred North American companies were conducted for the Society of Management Accountants of Canada. They are worthy of mention here because of their findings and recommendations. General-price-level-adjusted historical-cost data were found to portray more realistic risk information for only three industry groups: "(1) textiles, paper, and printing; (2) steel and other metals; and (3) machinery and electricals."[3] For other classes of firms, the restated data did not convey any information not furnished in the traditional historical cost reports. Generally, other than a downward bias in the absolute data, the relationship between historical cost and GPP-adjusted data were essentially the same—and this could be expected. The study suggested that the relative benefits and costs of GPP reporting be reexamined prior to implementation.[4]

In an earlier study, GPP reporting was considered to be only marginally superior to historical cost and contained "timing errors." Consequently, the study suggested that consideration of "supplementary GPL restated current value data . . . is necessary if accountants are to properly inform financial statement users."[5]

More likely than not, the FASB experiment was motivated (and rather hastily) because of: (1) The SEC pressure that something be done, and (2) the division existing among many of the large CPA firms. At least two firms, Ernst & Ernst and Price Waterhouse, were adamantly opposed to the abandonment of historical cost. Two others, Arthur Andersen and Touche Ross, encouraged the adoption of variant forms of value accounting. A fifth firm, Coopers and Lybrand, as well as other major practitioners, professed a "sort of open-minded neutrality."[6] (Yet, two major partners of Coopers and Lybrand edited a book on value accounting for businessmen.)[7] The hybrid methods espoused by the SEC and the major firms will be addressed in the sections that follow.

ALTERNATIVES PROPOSED

The alternative approaches to accounting for or reporting the effects of changing price-levels are classified here as *hybrid* proposals since they deviate from the basic general price-level and value-accounting methods. Several proposals attempt to combine the desirable features of the two basic methods. Others are clearly maverick approaches. Still others differ only in shadings of opinions that make classification difficult and subjective. The author, therefore, is forced to invoke the privilege of literary license regarding classifications of the proposals that follow.

Replacement Cost Reporting

There are probably very few *advocates* of replacement cost reporting. However, there are those who *accept* replacement cost reporting as preferable to ignoring the effects of changing price-levels upon historical cost reports.

Replacement cost reporting is a hybrid form of value accounting in that the supporting accounting system based upon historical cost is not changed drastically or discarded. Only selected elements in traditional reports are to be disclosed as supplementary information, restated at replacement cost—the amount required to replace the equivalent productive capacity considering the effects of technological change.

Securities and Exchange Commission. Irked by the lack of any real progress by the FASB toward disclosing the effects of rising prices upon published accounts, the SEC issued its controversial *Accounting Series Release No. 190 (ASR-190)* on March 23, 1976.[8] (Psychologically, the issuance of the Sandilands Report in Britain during the lull in FASB activity must also have been a factor.) *ASR-190* represented a temporary, stop-gap experiment scheduled to last 3 years, or until the FASB could devise alternate means acceptable to the SEC.

According to the SEC, the function of financial accounting should not involve attempts to measure the value of a firm or economic income—the former was indeterminate, the latter was impracticable.

General-price-level reportings were considered to be relatively easy to apply but capable of misleading statement users—the costs were not worth the benefits. Replacement cost information was considered to be meaningful and desirable, yet fraught with many problems. Therefore, the SEC implemented *ASR-190* as the first step *toward* replacement cost reporting based upon input costs (as opposed to output values). At the outset, only selected information in supplementary form was required. Downstream, if the experiment proved to be practical and meaningful, the requirements could be expanded to encompass complete supplemental statements based upon replacement costs.

ASR-190 was applicable to large, industrial firms (financial institutions were excluded) whose inventories plus gross plant and equipment exceeded $100 million *and* represented more than 10% of total assets. The effective date pertained to financial statements for fiscal years ending on or after December 25, 1976. The data required to be disclosed were:

- Inventories—at current replacement cost. If net realizable value was lower, the fact and the difference were to be disclosed.
- Cost of Sales—at current replacement costs of goods and services at the dates of sale.
- Plant and Equipment—at the estimated current replacement cost of the remaining productive capacity. Assets obtained under financing leases were to be included. Land as well as assets not to be replaced were to be excluded.
- Depreciation—based upon current replacement costs, using regular service lives and salvage values, and calculated by the *straight-line* method. Depreciation equivalents of investment tax credits were not required to be reflected.
- Additional supplementary information was *encouraged* to be provided by management in order to prevent the above data from misleading users, and to help them understand the effects (good and bad) of changing price-levels upon the particular firm.

The above disclosures could be in the form of a footnote or a separate section of the financial statements. The information was to be labeled "unaudited," yet the independent accountants were considered to be "associated" with the information; that is, the auditors were expected to assure themselves that the data appeared to be prepared on a reasonable basis and presented in good faith. This last feature served as a foundation for a "safe harbor" rule issued by the SEC to protect firms and auditors from liability for fraudulent disclosures.

Costing techniques permitted were: Specific pricings, for individual assets in excess of $20,000; unit or standard costs, for inventories; specific indexes, where appropriate; and functional approaches, for process-costing firms and those engaged in sectors confronted with dynamic technologies. Actually, no reasonable basis of determining replacement cost was precluded so long as it was explained adequately.

The most unusual (and troublesome) requirement involved the replacement cost of productive capacity, not of the existing assets in kind. Also, the estimated efficiencies afforded by technological change were to be described and reflected. Managements were reluctant to speculate on the replacement costs of different assets to be acquired in the future.

The SEC did not require (but did permit) disclosure of the effects of inflation upon monetary items since they could be approximated by use of various indexes generally available to the statement user.

The SEC cautioned users against attempting to use the disclosures to reconstruct an adjusted net income figure since historical and projected data could not, in combination, depict true current income. Nonetheless, many undoubtedly tried. In fact, Davidson and Weil[9] suggested that multiple profit figures might be more informative than one. They favored replacement cost disclosures, similar to those of *ASR-190,* since such data were extremely difficult to "guesstimate" from traditional statements. By the integration of holding gains on debt (based upon changes in interest rates), and changes in general price levels, Davidson and Weil illustrated how three measures of income could be estimated based upon *ASR-190* disclosures: (1) Sustainable (distributable) income; (2) realized income (sustainable income plus realized holding gains); and (3) economic income (the foregoing plus the unrealized holding gains).

Perhaps the most relevant observation made by Davidson and Weil concerns hybrid forms of inflation accounting. Given a choice limited to one method, they preferred replacement cost. However, they stipulated that the "ideal" method combined both replacement-cost and general-price-level elements.[10]

Following implementation of *ASR-190*, studies of the 1000 companies subject to the disclosure rules indicated almost universal disapproval (99%), if not contempt, for the experiment. Oddly enough, management's initial concern, costs of implementation, did not prove to be formidable. Average costs of first-year implementation for capital intensive companies was reported at $64,000; primary fabricators and manufacturers incurred higher costs, averaging $100,000; lowest costs were reported by controlled companies, such as utilities and transportation ($13,000 on average), reflecting the benefits of records oriented toward asset costs, and the ready availability of replacement-cost data for the types of assets employed. For continued compliance, the mean estimate of cost was lowered to less than $38,000 per year.[11]

In addition to almost universal opposition to *ASR-190* by management, studies also indicated that the disclosures were not considered to be very useful by sophisticated investors and analysts.[12] Both managements and users surveyed considered disclosure of the impact of inflation upon a given company as a relevant and timely concern; yet, both respondents were uncertain how the impact could be best presented.[13] Almost one-half (45%) of the respondents expressed a preference for inflationary disclosures to be contained in commentaries by managements.[14]

Surveys conducted by the large CPA firms also yielded similar conclusions. Very few issuers and users approved of the *ASR-190* disclosures. Almost all cautioned that the information did not portray current value (76%), "true income" (80%), nor the intended replacement plans of management (92%). Moreover, 88% warned that the data were subjective and imprecise.[15] Results did indicate that, although only a slight (1%) average difference was reflected in replacement costs of sales, the gap in replacement cost depreciation was significant: an average of 1.68 times, and a median of 1.62 times greater than historical cost.[16] (It should be noted that the studies compared differences between depreciation expenses shown on financial reports, not tax returns. Also, no study considered the added benefits of the depreciation-equivalent of the investment tax credit.)

The most unusual, yet rarely mentioned, aspect of *ASR-190* (at least in the author's opinion) is the fact that, while management generally considered the required disclosures to be suspect, if not misleading, *few firms attempted to supply the additional information considered necessary to explain the real effects of inflation, as encouraged by ASR-190.* This neglect is particularly surprising in view of the findings of a major study that:

- Current management information systems are now well developed in all corporations affected by *ASR-190.* These systems typically portray the impact of inflation in great specificity— in some cases, down to the detail of an individual piece part.
- Top management reporting as well as profit and cash forecasting systems are also well developed in major corporations. The information generated through these systems assists management in dealing with the impact of inflation.[17]

It seems clear that meaningful information and the opportunity for disclosure existed. Yet, most managements became so immersed in and incensed over the specific, *normative* requirements of *ASR-190* that their opportunity to do what they all considered to be important—*explain* the effects of inflation upon their companies— was completely overshadowed.

Price-Level-Adjusted Current-Cost Reporting

One of the oldest (and newest) hybrid proposals for disclosing the effects of inflation can be termed price-level-adjusted current-cost reporting. Advocates argue that changes in both general and specific price levels must be reported. Inflation accounting is not recommended (since the underlying historical cost systems would be retained); instead, inflation reporting is suggested (only the financial reports would be restated, in whole or in part).

Basically this method (PLACC reporting) seeks to: (1) Maintain the general purchasing power of equity, or financial capital; (2) use a stabilized measuring unit; and (3) report the gains and losses, both realized and unrealized, caused by changes in the value of money.

The feature that distinguishes PLACC reporting from a similar hybrid proposal—price-level-adjusted replacement-cost reporting (PLARC)—is that PLACC relates to *existing* assets and technology. (PLARC will be examined in the section that follows.)

Henry W. Sweeney was the originator of PLACC reporting ideas in the United States. His suggestions for combining the use of general (consumer) price indexes to balance sheet data, and superimposing the specific prices of "real assets" (using appraisals or specific indexes) were reviewed earlier in Chapter 3. Sweeney called his approach "stabilized accounting," although adjustments were only to be made during the preparation of financial reports.

Financial Accounting Standards Board. As mentioned earlier, the FASB's December 1978 *Exposure Draft,* "Financial Reporting and Changing Prices," is a mandatory experiment. It was designed to produce broad-based inflation disclosures for fiscal years ending on or after December 25, 1979.

Current-cost experiment. The *Exposure Draft* is a hybrid proposal in several respects. Companies can disclose supplementary data on operations using: (1) Historical cost/constant dollar, or (2) "current cost" reporting methods, dependent upon the circumstances. The constant-dollar provisions were reviewed with other methods of GPP reporting in Chapter 5. In this section, the current-cost disclosures proposed will be examined since they constitute a hybrid proposal in themselves.

Both methods of supplementary disclosure proposed in the *Exposure Draft* retain the historical cost framework. Inflation-related information is to be reported or disclosed in ancillary schedules. Consequently, references to constant-dollar and current-cost *accounting* appearing in the *Draft* itself, and in the literature concerning it, should be more appropriately referred to as *reporting* mechanisms. Also, the two methods proposed are not free-choice alternatives. Constant-dollar reporting can be used *if*: (1) The amounts of cost of sales and depreciation are not material, *or* (2) the specific price changes for those items closely paralleled changes in the general (consumer) price index. Firms not permitted to adopt constant-dollar reporting must follow the current-cost measures specified.

The applicability provisions of the *Draft* are similar to yet broader than those of *ASR-190.* All large public companies meeting the quantitative criteria are involved, including financial institutions exempted by *ASR-190*. Criteria are gross inventories, plant, and equipment of $125 million or more (versus $100 million for *ASR-190*), *and* total assets of $1 billion or more as of the *beginning* of the fiscal year. As a result, most public companies subject to *ASR-190* will also be subject to the *Draft* disclosures; that is, about 1000 large firms.

The major difference between the current-cost provisions of the *Draft* and *ASR-190* is the concept that separates all current-cost from replacement-cost proposals: the former concerns estimates of current replacement costs of assets owned in kind, without consideration of technological changes. Also, the current-cost provisions of the *Draft* apply to all assets owned or leased, whereas *ASR-190* excluded land as well as those assets management did not intend to replace in the future. Finally, the *Draft* disclosures include some effects of changes in general price-levels: inflation gains and losses on holding monetary items, domestic and foreign. Other than the differences mentioned—which can be significant for some industries—the measures proposed in the *Draft* are similar:

- Inventories—at current input cost (or net realizable value or value in use, if lower).
- Cost of Sales—at current replacement costs at the dates of sale (noncyclical industries can assume an even distribution of sales over the year).
- Plant and Equipment (including land and capital leases)—at current costs of replacing the "remaining service potential" (the same technology, capacity, and operating efficiency) of the assets concerned.
- Depreciation—based upon average current costs for the year, using the same methods used for computing historical cost depreciation, *unless* the latter were "chosen partly to allow for expected price changes." This feature will resurrect the tenuous arguments supporting use of accelerated methods of depreciation.

Supplemental current-cost disclosures regarding operations can be presented (as with constant-dollar disclosures) by means of either the statement format (Figure 7–1) or the reconcilation format (Figure 7–2). In addition, current-cost disclosures must also include

CONDENSED STATEMENT OF CURRENT COST INCOME FROM CONTINUING OPERATIONS AND OTHER DATA PERTAINING TO CHANGING PRICES.
(For the Year Ended December 31, 1978)

Net sales and other operating revenues	$50,000
Cost of goods sold at current cost	21,900
Depreciation and amortization expense at current cost	12,100
Other operating expenses	9,000
Interest expense	1,000
Provision for income taxes	3,000
Current cost income from continuing operations	$ 3,000
Net holding loss on inventories and property, plant, and equipment resulting from a holding gain ($4,500) less inflation component ($4,000) and less income tax ($2,000) on amounts realized	$(1,500)
Inflation gain on net monetary items	$ 575
Foreign exchange loss net of tax	$ (500)

Source: *Exposure Draft,* "Financial Reporting and Changing Prices," December 28, 1978, p. 20. Copyright © by Financial Accounting Standards Board, High Ridge Park, Stamford, Connecticut 06905, U.S.A. Reprinted with permission. Copies of the complete document are available from the FASB.

FIGURE 7-1.

RECONCILIATION OF INCOME FROM CONTINUING OPERATIONS AS REPORTED IN THE INCOME STATEMENT TO CURRENT COST INCOME FROM CONTINUING OPERATIONS AND OTHER DATA PERTAINING TO CHANGING PRICES.
(For the Year Ended December 31, 1978)

Income from continuing operations as reported in the income statement	$ 4,500
Excess of current cost of goods sold over historical cost of goods sold	(1,900)
Excess of current cost depreciation over historical cost depreciation	(2,100)
Exclusion of income tax on realized holding gains	2,000
Exclusion of foreign exchange loss net of tax	500
Current cost income from continuing operations	$ 3,000
Net holding loss on inventories and property, plant, and equipment resulting from a holding gain ($4,500) less inflation component ($4,000) and less income tax ($2,000) on realized gains	$(1,500)
Inflation gain on net monetary items	$ 575
Foreign exchange loss net of tax	$ (500)

Source: *Exposure Draft,* "Financial Reporting and Changing Prices," December 28, 1978, p. 21. Copyright © by Financial Accounting Standards Board, High Ridge Park, Stamford, Connecticut 06905, U.S.A. Reprinted with permission. Copies of the complete document are available from the FASB.

FIGURE 7-2.

a schedule of total inventory and plant assets showing the net historical and net current costs upon which the financial statements and the disclosures were based (Figure 7–3).

A 5-year comparison of selected data is also required of those using the current-cost approach (Figure 7–4). There are two basic differences between this schedule and that required of constant-dollar reporters (see Figure 5–5):

STATEMENT OF ASSET VALUES AT DECEMBER 31, 1978.

	NET HISTORICAL COST PER BALANCE SHEET	NET CURRENT COST
Inventory	$ 5,435	$ 6,920
Property, plant, and equipment	40,000	50,000
	$45,435	$56,920

Source: *Exposure Draft*, "Financial Reporting and Changing Prices," December 28, 1978, p. 21. Copyright © by Financial Accounting Standards Board, High Ridge Park, Stamford, Connecticut 06905, U.S.A. Reprinted with permission. Copies of the complete document are available from the FASB.

FIGURE 7–3.

FIVE-YEAR COMPARISON OF SELECTED FINANCIAL DATA

	YEARS ENDED DECEMBER 31				
	1974	1975	1976	1977	1978
Consumer price index average for year	XX	XX	XX	XX	XX
Net sales and other operating revenues	$XX	$XX	$XX	$XX	$XX
Current cost income from continuing operations	XX	XX	XX	XX	XX
Holding gain (loss) on inventories and plant assets net of inflation and tax	XX	XX	XX	XX	XX
Inflation gain (loss) on net monetary items	XX	XX	XX	XX	XX
Foreign exchange gain (loss) net of tax	XX	XX	XX	XX	XX
Net assets at year-end	XX	XX	XX	XX	XX
Current cost income from continuing operations per common share	XX	XX	XX	XX	XX
Cash dividends declared per common share	XX	XX	XX	XX	XX
Market price per common share at year-end	XX	XX	XX	XX	XX

Source: *Exposure Draft*, "Financial Reporting and Changing Prices," December 28, 1978, p. 22. Copyright © by Financial Accounting Standards Board, High Ridge Park, Stamford, Connecticut 06905, U.S.A. Reprinted with permission. Copies of the complete document are available from the FASB.

FIGURE 7–4.

- The average consumer price indexes for the years reported are to be shown on the first line, leaving users to adjust the nominal-dollar data themselves, if they wish. (A preference has been expressed for a specific index "tuned to the product being sold" rather than the CPI.[18] This would be a desirable improvement for single-line companies, of course. It would also be useful if these disclosures were feasible for and made applicable to the segmented reportings of conglomerates, multinationals, and other multiproduct firms.)
- Holding gains and losses which, naturally, are not generated by constant-dollar methods (and which, if the truth were known, current-cost advocates wish they did not have to try to defend).

Overview of FASB's current-cost experiment. General acceptance of the FASB's experiment with current-cost disclosures will face many of the hurdles confronting all current-cost proposals (see Chapter 6), plus some unique to the *Exposure Draft* itself.

The FASB's experiment will benefit from the fact that virtually all companies subject to current-cost disclosures will have gained experience and a reasonably similar data base by complying with *ASR-190.* Also, as with *ASR-190,* there is no overt, immediate goal of chucking out the historical framework. Moreover, the proposed IRS liberalization of the LIFO conformity rule will preclude any threat to the loss of tax benefits by LIFO companies. Finally, if the SEC agrees to the acceptability of the FASB's current-cost disclosures, then *ASR-190* would presumably be discontinued. (Companies may be eager to free themselves of attempts to "guesstimate" the impacts of future technological changes now required by the SEC. Many firms may also believe that the FASB would be more receptive to requests for future changes than the SEC.)

Problems confronting acceptance are real and imagined. Requirements are complicated, even for professional accountants. Gaps and doubts exist regarding implementation; probably as much, or more, the result of haste in preparation as the intent to experiment. A very real problem concerns the disclosure of gain or loss on holding monetary items, or financial leverage. This same problem of "gearing" has reverberated through considerations in the EEC and among some of its members, as mentioned earlier. If a gain accrues, is the gain taxable, and if so, when? The FASB has hedged, thus far at least, by requiring the monetary gain to be reported in gross amount, leaving the user to construe any future tax effect as he chooses. (This should, but will not, convince standard-setters that toleration of deferred income tax myths can only lead to the procreation of additional myths.) It has been suggested that the nonrecognition of the tax effects on monetary gains is offset by the nonrecognition of backlog depreciation—a prime example of one oversight correcting another.

Many observers are concerned that the generality as well as the normative characteristics of the disclosures will create confusion among users, resulting in virtual disdain for the data. This point is moot and can only be addressed by trial and an open mind.

Conceptual problems are stickier. The stated goal of the current-cost disclosures in the *Exposure Draft* is maintenance of the purchasing power of investors. This further supports the FASB's change from use of the GNP deflator to the consumer price index. Yet, changes in the consumer price index may be irrelevant in predicting the future cash flows of a particular firm—another FASB avowed purpose.

Perhaps the most incompatible aspect of the current-cost portion of the *Draft* concerns end and means. In paragraphs 59 and 60 of the *Draft,* a good case is made for the preservation of financial rather than physical capital. Yet, all value accounting concepts, including current cost, are specifically designed to protect the physical capital of an enterprise. It appears that the FASB has used the idea of an experiment to permit it to stand on both sides of the fence.

Auditors are naturally concerned over their expected role. *ASR-190* was clear in its stipulation that auditors were considered to be "associated" with the required disclosures, wherever they might appear in the financial reports, or in the SEC's Form 10-K. The FASB has hedged, quite probably at the insistence of the AICPA. Paragraph 16 of the *Exposure Draft* stipulates that a company must provide the required disclosures (either constant-dollar or current cost, as applicable) "in the annual reports that contain its financial statements." In an "unofficial" article by the AICPA's vice-president-auditing, it was made clear that the disclosures "would not be part of audited financial statements," but little else was clarified.[19] The FASB has assumed, and properly so, its responsibility to establish standards for financial reporting, defined as the financial statements and all supplemental *required* information. The FASB has notified the AICPA that auditor involvement would be essential in order to attach the desired credibility to required supplementary disclosures.[20] The AICPA is understandably uneasy. It realizes that the tenor of emphasis of the FASB and the SEC has focused upon supplemental information, ranging from statistical and analytical to future-oriented, "soft data." Such disclosures are increasingly being considered necessary to accommodate the various needs of users of statements of complex companies. Smaller, less complicated firms may not be subjected to the same range of supplementary disclosures, and this is understandable. The real problem, however, will only be defined, not resolved, when some rule of thumb is agreed upon to determine what firms will or will not be required to furnish what disclosures. The question of auditor involvement in the required cases will remain. The tack adopted by the AICPA is clear: "Some supplemental information might be auditable, but that does not mean it should be audited."[21]

That innocuous statement contains enough weasel words to signify the AICPA's aim to remove auditor involvement from all parts of financial reports other than the statements and related footnotes. That is not only a sorry position for a profession to advocate, but it disavows the recommendations made by the Cohen Commission on Auditors' Responsibilities:

Reporting requirements should be made consistent by requiring the auditor to report on all unaudited financial information with which he is associated, including that appearing in a document containing audited financial statements.

If contact between the auditor and users is deemed valuable by the users, such added communications should be encouraged.[22]

Moreover, it seems that the profession would be well advised to consider carefully the full omen of the above reference to the *perceived value* of auditor-client contact. A profession should not imply one role yet perform another lesser service. If the FASB proves incapable of prodding the AICPA into accepting its perceived function, the SEC will probably be forced to "bell the cat" again.

The characteristic reluctance of public accounting firms to interpret financial information, and to accept involvement with disclosures other than the primary statements and notes, represent poor hallmarks for a supposed profession. The FASB and the SEC should make certain that users of financial reports receive what they have assumed (rightly or wrongly) for some time—assurance that auditors have examined the *reasonableness* of all required disclosures appearing in reports. Moreover, such assurance should be required to be expressly stated by the auditors in an introduction to the section containing the required, supplemental disclosures.

In summary, the FASB should be congratulated for recognizing, albeit belatedly, that inflation affects different firms in different ways. The *Exposure Draft* permits companies to select the type of price-level reporting that most closely resembles the movement of prices in their specific circumstances. Conglomerates and multi-nationals present problems that can only be resolved by adequately segmented disclosures; these will require time. Also, certain industries (banking, insurance, real estate, oil and gas, forestry, and mining) have argued that they have peculiar problems; these will be addressed separately by the FASB. (See Appendix 9A.)

Unfortunately, the FASB appears to be unyielding in its pursuit of the "elusive"—a normative set of raw data that can portray the effects of changing prices on diverse companies. Also, the AICPA can only be charged with low marks for its attempts to renege on its professional responsibility as perceived by the public whose interests it purports to serve. As some wise man once said some time ago, it's time to put the "public" back into the title of certified public accountant.

Price-Level-Adjusted Replacement-Cost Reporting

Proponents of price-level-adjusted replacement-cost reporting (PL-ARC) suggest a hybrid method quite similar to PLACC. The primary difference is that PLARC reporting considers the effects of technology upon the future replacement of existing productive capacity, and the economies (or diseconomies) that will affect the costs of product and service outputs.

Although the advocates of PLARC reporting are relatively few in number, their hybrid proposal appears to be the most logical of all. Attempts are made to reflect the impacts of specific price changes as well as technological changes upon nonmonetary assets. Both are considered to be necessary if real, as opposed to hypothetical,

replacement costs are to be reflected. The final step involves adjustments to report the changes in the general purchasing-power of
money.

The goals of PLARC reporting are to: (1) Maintain the physical
capital of the enterprise, defined as its productive capacity; and (2)
report the impact of general price changes by adopting the general
purchasing power of money as the unit of measure.

Evolution of the Ideas. Many of the current advocates of PLARC
reporting originally suggested that historical cost systems be supplanted by adoption of price-level-adjusted replacement-cost accounting.[23] As it became evident over time that the large majority,
in the United States and elsewhere, favored retention of historical
cost accounting, the emphasis was changed to call for PLARC
reports.

Revsine and Weygandt stipulated that specific indexes might be
appropriate for use by small, single-line firms to value assets so long
as the assumption of replacement with "essentially similar assets" is
recognized and valid. General indexes, such as the GNP deflator,
were considered appropriate for use by conglomerates and other
complex firms that are capable of reinvesting in assets of any type
that may be required in the future. Whether replacement costs were
estimated by indexes or other means, the reporting of specific prices
was preferred in order to maintain the physical operating capacity
of the firm. Consequently, recognition of backlog depreciation was
also recommended to assist predictions of expected cash flows. The
supplemental inclusion of general price indexes in financial reports
was considered a courtesy to investors useful primarily for restatement of dividends received.[24]

In a later article, Revsine and Thies demonstrated how the basic
replacement cost model (then popularized by *ASR-190* requirements)
could be converted into a PLARC reporting framework by means of
simplified, "wash entries." Essentially, the process was of four parts:

- Preparation of replacement cost information to determine
  holding gains (increase in equity).
- Rollforward of beginning equity (using end-of-year dollars)
  to isolate that part of the holding gain necessary to maintain
  the purchasing power of equity.

- Comparison of replacement costs and price-level-adjusted costs of assets to isolate the "real" components of "gains" to be reflected in income.
- Computation of the monetary gain or loss from holding cash equivalents—also to be reflected in PLARC income.

In effect, Revsine and Thies suggested a simplified method of converting replacement-cost statements into PLARC reports in order to report monetary gains or losses, and separate holding gains (on nonmonetary items) into two parts: the general-price-level effect and the "real gain."[25] However, the writers adhered to their preference for adoption of basic replacement cost systems; the above adjustments were suggested to satisfy the urgings of those who required that the effects of general price changes also be disclosed.

In 1975, Robert Sterling argued that financial reports should be *relevant* and *interpretable* insofar as the accounting model (not user needs) was concerned. Relevance meant that the attribute was appropriate for use in decisions. Interpretability implied that the information could be explained and understood outside of the modeling framework employed. In Sterling's opinion, command over goods (the commodity value of money) represented the attribute of accounting that was both relevant and interpretable. Using simplified cases, Sterling concluded that historical cost and price-level-adjusted historical cost reports were neither relevant nor interpretable; current value reports were interpretable but not relevant; only price-level-adjusted current-value reports satisfied both criteria.[26]

Richard Vancil suggested a similar hybrid form that he termed "specific and general price-level accounting (SPLA)."[27] To be more precise, Vancil stated that SPLA was "an extension" of current-replacement-value accounting. Reportings in constant dollars were superimposed to preserve the "real value" of equity. Vancil considered value accounting and GPP reporting to be "complimentary methods"; both were needed. Value accounting functioned to preserve the physical capital of an enterprise, defined as its productive capacity. The recognition of general price changes separated holding gains into their inflationary and economic components, while highlighting the effects of holding monetary items. Reportings in constant dollars would involve restating the results of prior years using general price indexes. The extra effort would enable managements to protect either the physical *or* the financial capital of their companies depending upon the particular circumstances:

- Firms committed to one or few lines of business would seek to preserve physical capital (productive capacity). Holding gains would not be considered part of distributable income.
- Conglomerates and holding companies might wish to maintain financial capital (purchasing power of assets). Consequently, holding gains could be included in operating income.

Vancil recognized two hurdles facing his proposal: (1) The recognition of gains on monetary items, and (2) the problem of implementation. He solved the first by recommending current recognition of gains. Resolution of the second problem called for experimentation. In sum, Vancil called for the incorporation of both specific and general price changes since the combination of the two produced information more useful then either method used alone. It should also be noted that Vancil defended the superiority of information produced by SPLA as measures of operating (internal) and investment (external) performance.

Evaluation of the Ideas. To the extent that it is desirable for accounting income to closely approximate economic income, PLARC reporting is theoretically sound. All important effects of changes in specific and general price levels are disclosed and classified in a manner that serves multiple needs, internal and external. The primary objection concerns problems of implementation, and adoption appears highly unlikely in the foreseeable future. A prolonged period of double-digit inflation in the United States, for instance, would more likely encourage some form of *monetary* correction, rather than correction by adoption of a new accounting or reporting system.

Continuously Contemporary Accounting

Professor Raymond Chambers (of the University of Sydney, Australia) invented another hybrid proposal—continuously contemporary accounting—and a new acronym, COCOA, in 1966.[28]

COCOA is a unique proposal combining concepts based upon the current sales values of most assets and general purchasing power. Chambers suggests that most assets be valued at their "current cash equivalents" (an exit-value form of replacement-value accounting). These values are similar to the more familiar net realizable values assuming an orderly, rather than forced, disposition. The asset excepted is inventory which is to be valued at current replacement cost (an entry price).

Assets are presumed to be resources waiting to be used to buy other goods and services; consequently, their market values are most relevant to users. This ability of a firm to adapt by changing its bank of assets as the economic climate changes is one of Chambers' key concepts.

The capital maintenance concept employed is preservation of the general purchasing-power of the stockholders' equity. However, money is retained as the unit of measure rather than the general purchasing-power unit.

Chambers considers net income to include the difference between increases in sales values and the GPP-indexed values of assets. This treatment presents some interesting issues. First, depreciation becomes relegated to the status of "just another kind of price variation"; that is, the difference between sales values at the beginning and end of each year. Second, all holding gains on assets (increases in sales values over GPP-adjusted amounts) are to be reflected in income for the year. As a result, significant amounts of unrealized gains (to be realized in subsequent periods) would be capitalized in the current period.

Evaluation of COCOA. This hybrid approach to accounting for inflation represents the most drastic departure from historical costs. The use of exit values (or current cash equivalents) would possibly report the collective value of the business to certain statement users, particularly creditors. However, exit values become opportunity costs which would be valid to apply only to those assets that the firm normally sells, rather than buys, in the marketplace. Even then, operating income would be anticipated prior to the sale of the items concerned.

Few, including Chambers himself, have approached the actual

problems of implementation and changeover from one accounting system to another. Nonetheless, the practical problems would appear to loom rather large.

Fair Value Accounting

Another alternative mentioned occasionally in the literature is fair value accounting.

The presentation of dual statements is recommended. One set would continue to be the traditional statements based upon generally accepted accounting principles and historical cost, bearing the expression of an opinion. The second set would be based upon "fair value" accounting and, preferably, would also contain the expression of an auditor's opinion. Proponents believe that historical cost statements should be furnished along with those based upon fair value in order to enable users to recognize the "economic differences" between fair values and historical costs.[29] This concurrent comparability would be desirable.

Fair values would primarily be based upon professional appraisals, similar to the means suggested in the Sandilands Report. Statements based upon fair values would depict the results of changes in general and specific price levels, singly or in combination, depending upon the natures of the assets concerned.

The proposals do not indicate the degree of change required in accounting systems. Since historical cost results would continue to be reported, it is assumed that the fair-value data would be processed in ancillary records. Consequently, this hybrid form would more closely resemble fair-value reporting.

The major objection raised concerns the use of appraisals, the fairness of which public accountants would have to attest in order to express an opinion. As cited earlier, this objection would be of much more concern in the United States than, say in the United Kingdom where professional appraisals have been used for some time.

Eclectic Proposals

Several hybrid methods selected and combined features considered appropriate from a variety of possible approaches.

Three models will be examined, representing the proposals made by Arthur Andersen & Company, Touche Ross & Company, and Morton Backer. Each proposal is a hybrid method that combines the use of general and specific price changes. Each is also eclectic in that a gamut of value bases is employed. All three proposals can be described as models since they represent comprehensive systems of accounting and reporting. The models are similar in that each would require a new system of accounting, yet each has peculiarities that differentiates it from the others. For the sake of brevity, the Arthur Andersen model will be examined in some detail, followed by a review of the differences attributed to each of the other models.

The Arthur Andersen Model. As one of the largest international accounting firms, Arthur Andersen & Company has taken an active interest in accounting standards, not only in the United States, but in most other countries as well. In 1974, the firm published the latest in a series of recommendations for international accounting standards.[30] Proposals for the treatments of changing prices and values are but a portion of the contents and are found throughout the 17 chapters of the booklet.

Workings of the model. The Andersen model purports to maintain financial capital by preserving the general purchasing-power of equity. This is accomplished by applying the change in the consumer price index to the weighted average balance of equity during the year. Yet, income is determined by changes in values (less the amount needed to maintain the GPP of equity) and, like all value accounting models, relates to physical capital. Actually, the maintenance of both concepts of capital are addressed and the perceived precedence of one form over the other would be irrelevant in normal operating periods. However, in abnormal times, the maintenance of equity would prevail. For example, if income (values of resources earned less values of resources used) was less than the amount needed to maintain the GPP of equity, a loss would be reported.

The primary thrust of the model is upon value accounting. The purpose of financial statements is stipulated to be the communication of information regarding the "nature and value of the economic resources of a business enterprise" and their changes over time.[31]

Accountings of legal, social, and similar responsibilities are to be made in separate reports.

Value is defined as the price an item "commands in exchange"—its fair market value. All other values are considered as alternative prices. These may be past prices (historical cost), present prices (reproduction cost, replacement value, net realizable value), or future prices (present values of future cash flows). The appropriate alternate prices to be used would depend upon the items and the circumstances.[32] Where several values are determinable for an item, fair market value should represent the "highest value realizable," although competitive market forces would normally interact to cause replacement cost to become the *ceiling* value on most depreciable assets.[33]

Depreciation would become a part of the valuation process rather than only a vehicle for cost allocation. Appraisals by members of the National Institute of Appraisers were the preferred methods of assessing values. (The use of specific price indexes was considered to be acceptable only if the item was to be replaced in kind.) Technological change was to be reckoned with in determining the net values of plant and equipment as well as the outputs produced. Available tax incentives would also be considered as reductions in the net replacement values of facilities. Depreciation was to be calculated by application of the *straight-line* method based upon the last appraisal values.[34]

Inventories were to be valued using the FIFO basis only, with historical costs applied to high turnover items, and replacement cost reflected for items with lower turnovers. (Evidently, LIFO was considered to be a tax gimmick, not a valid accounting process.)

Certain items (such as natural resources or assets leased out for their economic lives) should be assigned their economic values. Where market prices were not available, price-level-adjusted historical-cost was an acceptable alternative.

Unusual aspects. The Andersen model is unsual in at least two respects. Internally, the model contained some novel aspects in advance of their time. Moreover, the approach to accounting in general was uncommon.

The internal features considered to be somewhat unusual were:

- In common with basic value-accounting models, holding gains and losses on monetary items were not recognized. Yet, in several places in the booklet, Andersen stipulated that the recognition of "gains" arising from holding debt was under consideration and might be revised. ("Gains and losses" from the translations of foreign currencies were to be taken up in income since the process of consolidation automatically created imbalances that had to be recognized. See Figure 7–5.)

- Problems of goodwill and deferred income taxes were eliminated. Purchased goodwill was to be deducted from equity. Tax deferrals and other investment incentives were to be deducted from the values of assets acquired that led to their creation.
- The model permitted, but did not emphasize, reporting in common or constant dollars.

The attitudinal approaches to accounting and reporting were refreshing in many ways. Values were recognized to be "difficult areas of judgment," yet were considered necessary. Value was believed to be an "unbiased" concept if approached with the proper care and attested by auditors. Problems of attestation were not viewed as significant.

Consolidated reportings were considered to be necessary but not sufficient standing alone. Separate statements of parent companies were often deemed to be useful. For conglomerates and other diverse companies, segmented reportings by lines-of-business and geographic areas were considered absolutely necessary. In these segmentations, operating expenses were to be segregated into variable and fixed categories, and any assets and expenses that would require arbitrary allocation should be treated as common items. (See Figure 7–6.)

The accounting standards supporting the proposed model attempted to strike a reasonable balance between objectivity (verifiability) and subjectivity (relevance). In that respect, mere disclosures of raw data did not satisfy measurement responsibilities. Disclosures were to be used to *explain* matters that could not be measured fairly. Disclosures required, among others, were:

- Commitments of resources, projected capital requirements, and the sources of financing available.
- The methods of valuation employed.

XYZ INC.
CONSOLIDATED STATEMENT OF INCOME
FOR THE YEARS ENDED DECEMBER 31, 1974 AND 1973

	1974		1973	
	(000 omitted)			
Net revenue		$4,000		$3,800
Operating expenses—				
Fixed expenses	$1,230		$1,210	
Variable expenses	1,780	3,010	1,700	2,910
		$ 990		$ 890
Other operating items—				
Increase in replacement cost of inventory held during the year	$ 100		$ 90	
Equity in net income of affiliated companies	100	200	90	180
Operating income		$1,190		$1,070
Less—Expenditures for intangibles (Statement of Intangibles)		100		110
Operating income less expenditures for intangibles		$1,090		$ 960
Nonoperating items—				
Holding gains and losses—				
Increase in replacement cost of property, plant and equipment (Note 1)	$ 150		$ 100	
Gain on translation of accounts of foreign subsidiaries (Note 1)	—		20	
Loss on bonds payable in Swiss francs resulting from revaluation of the Swiss franc	—		(25)	
Total holding gains and losses	$ 150		$ 95	
Unusual item—excess of fire loss over amount recovered from insurance company	(30)		—	
Provision for maintenance of capital (Note 1)	(150)	(30)	(125)	(30)
		$1,060		$ 930
Provision for income taxes, attributable to—				
Operating income	$ 620		$ 555	
Expenditures for intangibles	(50)		(55)	
Translation gain	—		10	
Unusual item	(15)	555	—	510
Income before interest expense and minority interests		$ 505		$ 420
Interest expense, less related reduction in income taxes of $80,000 in 1974 and $90,000 in 1973	$ 80		$ 90	
Minority interests in income of subsidiaries	25	105	20	110
Net income		$ 400		$ 310

Source: Arthur Andersen & Co., *Accounting Standards for Business Enterprises Throughout the World,* 1974, p. 147. Reproduced with permission.

FIGURE 7-5

The company is engaged in two lines of business, the manufacture of bicycles and the manufacture of garden tools and equipment, primarily for homeowners. The following tabulations present (1) items of income and expense before interest expense and adjustments for minority interests and (2) assets that are directly assignable to each line of business and those that are common to both and cannot be assigned on a reasonable basis.

	1974			1973		
	Bicycles	**Garden**	**Common**	**Bicycles**	**Garden**	**Common**
			(000 omitted)			
Items of Income and Expense						
Net revenue	$2,000	$2,000	$ —	$1,500	$2,300	$ —
Operating expenses—						
Fixed	$ 375	$ 425	$ 430	$ 375	$ 400	$ 435
Variable	850	800	130	625	975	100
	$1,225	$1,225	$ 560	$1,000	$1,375	$ 535
	$ 775	$ 775	$ (560)	$ 500	$ 925	$ (535)
Increase in replacement cost of inventory	45	55	—	40	50	—
Equity in income of affiliates..	100	—	—	90	—	—
Operating income	$ 920	$ 830	$ (560)	$ 630	$ 975	$ (535)
Holding gains and losses	70	70	10	60	50	(15)
Expenditures for intangibles..	(70)	(30)	—	(60)	(50)	—
Unusual item	—	(30)	—	—	—	—
Maintenance of capital	—	—	(150)	—	—	(125)
Income taxes	—	—	(555)	—	—	(510)
Income before interest expense and minority interests	$ 920	$ 840	$(1,255)	$ 630	$ 975	$(1,185)
Assets						
Cash	$ —	$ —	$ 430	$ —	$ —	$ 300
Temporary investments	—	—	350	—	—	400
Accounts and notes receivable	700	500	—	525	575	—
Inventories	650	550	—	500	500	—
Prepaid interest and insurance	10	10	20	10	15	25
Investments in affiliated companies	650	—	—	600	—	—
Property, plant and equipment	1,750	1,450	250	1,400	1,400	200
Rights to use leased buildings.	—	700	—	—	800	—
Total assets	$3,760	$3,210	$1,050	$3,035	$3,290	$ 925

It is not practicable to allocate interest expense, and it is considered more meaningful, for comparative purposes, to present results prior to adjustment for minority interests.

Source: Arthur Andersen & Co., *Accounting Standards for Business Enterprises Throughout the World*, 1974, pp. 155-156. Reproduced with permission.

FIGURE 7-6. PROFIT CONTRIBUTIONS BY LINE OF BUSINESS

The Andersen philosophy was summed rather well by the following statement: "No system of accounting practices established in the past is wholly valid today, and no system established today is likely to be valid in even a few years' time."[35]

The Touche Ross Model. In 1975, Touche Ross & Company proposed that "economic reality" might be introduced into financial reports through experimentation with a hybrid form of current-value accounting.[36]

Similarities. The Touche Ross and Andersen models were similar in purpose: the maintenance of financial capital, or the general purchasing power of equity. Yet, the value concepts also concerned the maintenance of physical capital.

The value approaches were eclectic. Present values (the discounted value of future cash flows) were preferred, although practical problems would usually limit their application to monetary items. Current cost was considered to be an acceptable alternative for inventories and depreciable assets. Net realizable values were suggested for use with all other nonmonetary items.

The Touche Ross approach also called for: (1) Comprehensive revisions in ongoing accounting systems over time; (2) revision of the income statement to reflect value changes, realized and unrealized (Figure 7–7); and (3) the exclusion of intangibles from reports.

Differences. Unlike the Andersen model, the Touche Ross proposal:

- Placed less emphasis upon the need for supplemental reports. Comparative statements were specified, however, together with an *explanation* of "reasons for the changes."[37]
- Recognized gains and losses resulting from changes in the market values of liabilities subsequent to issuance, as interest rates changed. (Andersen was studying this aspect.)
- Segregated value changes into realized and unrealized categories. The former concerned past cash flows. Unrealized changes were related to potential future cash flows; most value-accounting proposals obscured these changes in reserves.
- Reported the impacts of changes in general price-levels upon the value of money. Use of the GNP deflator was suggested until a better index was developed. (This hybrid feature cor-

CURRENT-VALUE EXAMPLE COMPANY

STATEMENT OF NET RESULTS OF OPERATIONS
AND CHANGES IN VALUE

	Current-value basis December 31,		Conventional (historical cost) basis December 31,	
	19X1	19X2	19X1	19X2
Results of operations:				
Sales	$ 90	$ 90	$ 90	$ 90
Cost of sales	50	65	50	50
Current expenses	10	14	10	15
Depreciation.................................	15	20	10	10
	75	99	70	75
Net results of operations	15	(9)	20*	15*
Changes in value of non-monetary re-sources:				
Realized changes from inventory sold after increase in value.....................	—	5		
Unrealized changes:				
Inventory held at year-end	10	5		
Long-term investment	50	(10)		
Equipment	50	45		
	110	40		
Impact of decline in general pur-chasing power on value changes	(26)	(37)		
	84	8		
Changes in value of monetary re-sources and obligations:				
Unrealized changes in long-term debt due to change in interest rates	(10)	19		
Economic advantage from decline in general purchasing power on net monetary items held	6	9		
	(4)	28		
Total of net results of operations and changes in value for year	$ 95	$ 27	$ 20*	$ 15*

---

*In conventional financial reporting these amounts are designated as net income.

Source: Touche Ross & Co., *Economic Reality in Financial Reporting*, 1975, p. 24. Reproduced with permission.

FIGURE 7-7

IMPLEMENTING CURRENT-VALUE ACCOUNTING

PHASE I—to obtain overall information about alternative valuation methods and their usefulness for management decisions and financial reporting.
- Identify which needs to address and outline priorities for information:
  - performance measurement
  - cash forecasts
  - pricing
  - dividend distribution
  - capital budgeting
  - financial reporting
- Identify alternatives to produce needed information and analyze each valuation alternative:
  - replacement cost
  - present value
  - net realizable value
- Apply each valuation alternative in gross terms
- Evaluate usefulness of information produced by each alternative
  ◇ **Decision 1**—specify information to be collected and reported.

PHASE III—to develop additional detail for preparation of current-value reports and to prepare more detailed management reports.
- Determine organizational units to be included
- Determine the most relevant approach for various resources and obligations
- Identify elements that will be revalued
- Collect detailed data on items
- Prepare reports using data
- Present to management and get feedback
- Start education of outside users
- Publish data to users
- Solicit reaction of outside users and assess impact
  ◇ **Decision 3**—decide whether to continue to produce the reports, and in what form.

PHASE IV—to determine what system changes are necessary to generate current-values on an ongoing basis.
- Assess desirability of making systems changes
  ◇ **Decision 4**—decide what system changes need to be made.

PHASE II—to prepare examples of management reports and to determine the costs and benefits of obtaining additional details for these reports.

• Identify what data are needed, for example:

–*Land and buildings:* appraisals; recent purchases; existing leases and dates; capital expenditure plans; depreciation policies; inefficiencies in plant layout; economic use of land.

–*Machinery and equipment:* inventory of machinery and equipment; types of specialized machinery and equipment; suppliers; machine capacities in units of production; capital expenditure plans; depreciation policies.

–*Inventory and cost of sales:* percentages of labor and material components of finished products; other significant costs of production, such as fuel; price increases throughout the year; types of variances reported; details on cost of sales information; turnover statistics; valuation bases; stockpiling.

• Identify what data are now available
• Analyze costs of obtaining additional data
• Prepare mock up of management reports
• Review reports with users and assess benefits
• Assess costs relative to benefits of data
◊ **Decision 2**—decide what additional data to obtain for current-value reports.

Source: Touche Ross & Co., *Economic Reality in Financial Reporting,* 1975, p. 9. Reproduced with permission.

FIGURE 7-8

169

rected deficiencies attributed to most value-based models, such as the Andersen and Sandilands versions.)
- Called for a program of phased experimentation and assessment (Figure 7–8).

The Backer Model. Professor Morton Backer conducted a study of value accounting in 1973 that began with a negative attitude, particularly concerning its feasibility.[38] Consequently, Backer sought a method that was more meaningful than conventional practice, yet was practicable and relatively free of bias. He classified, then examined, five basic models: Historical cost, replacement cost, market value, price-level-adjusted-historical cost, and Chamber's COCOA. Each was found wanting in various respects.

The model developed by Backer was a hybrid form combining the effects of changes in general price-levels and in values. It was eclectic in that various valuation bases and reportings were applied dependent upon the item concerned (Figure 7–9).

The relevant features of Backer's model were:

- Monetary items should be measured in dollars of general purchasing power. Gains and losses from holding monetary items should be included in current income.
- Marketable securities should be reported at market values with changes in these values reflected in income.
- Other nonmonetary items were to be valued and reported in various ways, depending upon the nature of the item, whether it was severable or nonseverable, and the availability of a bias-free measure.
- Items for which reasonably objective values could not be determined were to be addressed by management in a supplemental, informal report.

Severable assets were defined by Backer as those that may be sold or used in the near future, such as inventories or land not in use. Nonseverable items were those not normally held for sale, such as land in use, plant, equipment, and the like. Each type was further segregated into two categories for which, in Backer's opinion, external values were or were not objectively determinable.

In general, current replacement costs (entry prices) were to be

Proposed Value Reporting Model

	Formal Reporting (Balance Sheet and Income Statement)					Informal Reporting (Management Provided Supplemental Information)
	Severable Assets			Nonseverable Assets		
	Objectively Determinable		Not objectively Determinable	Objectively Determinable	Not objectively Determinable	
	Relatively Certain — Realization	Relatively Uncertain — Realization				
Inventories		CRC				
Land in use					OC	EMV
Buildings in use				CRC	OC	
Machinery and equipment				ACRC		
Marketable securities	MV					
Real estate not in use			OC			EMV
Natural resources			OC		OC	EMV
Film libraries			OC			EMV
Unconsolidated non-marketable Securities (affiliated Companies)					AOC	EMV
Measurable intangibles					OC	EMV

Key
MV = Market Value
CRC = Current Replacement Cost
ACRC = Current Replacement Cost Adjusted for Changes in Technology
OC = Original Cost Less Depreciation or Amortization
AOC = Original Cost Adjusted for Proportionate Share of Profits or Losses
EMV = Management's Estimate of Market Value

FIGURE 7-9

Source: Morton Backer, *Current Value Accounting* (New York: Financial Executives Institute, 1973), p. 38. Reproduced with permission.

applied to inventories, buildings, as well as machinery and equipment. The costs related to the latter items were to be adjusted to recognize technological changes. Most other nonmonetary items were to be reported *formally* at historical cost bases.

The most unusual aspect of Backer's model is his proposal that managements furnish, in *informal* supplementary disclosures, their estimates of the market values of all assets for which objective valuations were not obtainable. This approach enabled users to be apprised of "soft" data that may be of value without unduly compromising the objectivity of financial statements. Moreover, auditors would be relieved, presumably, of any association with the estimated information.

Backer's effort represents one of the earlier attempts to synthesize reporting of the effects of general and specific price changes in a workable way. He devised a method to relegate subjective value estimates to ancillary reports. How practicable his model would be for use today by conglomerates and multinational enterprises is altogether another question.

"Commonsense" Proposals

Another group of practitioners considered the basic approaches to price-level accounting and reporting to be defective, and the hybrid proposals to be impractical and/or not worth their costs.

Various forms of "commonsense" alternatives were suggested in order to disclose the *approximate* effects of changing price levels at minimum cost, and with little disruption within existing accounting systems. Space permits only a representative few of such proposals to be examined here.

Price Waterhouse "Common-Sense Accounting." Late in 1977, the senior partner of Price Waterhouse & Company called the profession to task for trying to debate the disease of inflation to death, rather than providing practical information that could be understood.[39] To be precise, the PW proposal should have been termed reporting, rather than accounting, because it retained the present accounting system as is.

The impacts of inflation were to be disclosed in streamlined, condensed, supplemental presentations based upon changes in general price-levels and "sensible short-cuts." Simplified presentations in round amounts were stressed to prevent any illusions of competition with the formal statements.

The overall effects, or the "big picture," of inflation should be *explained* since the change in the purchasing power of money was only one facet. The big picture would be depicted in a condensed reconciliation of income in historical dollars with income in dollars of current purchasing power. The "gain" on holding long-term debt would be segregated from the changes in other monetary items but would be reflected in current income.

Perhaps the most relevant portion of the PW proposal called for "an appropriate *explanation* of the GPP information presented and the basis of preparation."[40] (Emphasis added.)

The Ernst and Ernst Proposal. In 1976, the firm of Ernst & Ernst suggested what appeared to be a practical and unique approach to accounting for inflation.[41] Here again, retention of the historical cost system was urged, virtually without change, and the proposal really called for reporting the effects of inflation.

Briefly stated, Ernst & Ernst considered the disease of inflation to infest primarily only two physical parts of an economic organism—inventories and tangible, long-lived assets. Since the well-known prescription of LIFO had corrected (or at least alleviated) the tax pains of the inventory affliction, why not apply a similar remedy to fixed assets? The remedy suggested was similar to that proposed by George O. May some 30 years earlier (see Chapter 3): namely, to use LIFO for inventories and calculate depreciation on current costs of fixed assets (indexed historical costs), *for reporting and tax purposes.*

The proposal was simple and practical. Neither the original acquisition costs of fixed assets nor their accumulated depreciation amounts would be altered on balance sheets. Only one entry was required: a charge to income for the excess of current cost over historical cost depreciation, and an offsetting credit to an equity account, "accumulated current cost depreciation," for the same amount. (Moreover, the company's "usual rates" of depreciation were also to be applied on current costs; presumably accelerated methods would be retained.)

The Ernst & Ernst proposal was designed to recognize the "twofold influence of inflation on accounting"—upon measurement *and* taxation of income.[42] However, the proposed recognition of current-cost depreciation for tax purposes was considered essential since "any inflation accounting proposal that does not provide for tax relief is unrealistic and inequitable."[43]

Unfortunately, the many desirable features of the Ernst & Ernst proposal became obscured by the insistence upon tax recognition. Many individuals, including the author, considered it primarily another plea for tax relief for business—a separate issue entirely. Realism and equity are relative. It would be difficult to support taxing businesses on so-called real income, if other economic entities, such as households and individuals, remain taxed on nominal-dollar incomes.

TOWARD A CONSENSUS?

Inflation was described earlier as an international disease. Consequently, the impacts of inflation cannot be accounted for or reported— or arrested, for the matter—by a single nation or a small group of countries acting in isolation.

Given the magnitude and increasing trend of international operations, piecemeal approaches to accounting for, or reporting the effects of inflation upon business enterprises can only further impede the interpretability of financial information that travels across national boundaries. A harmonized effort, at least by the world's major trading partners, appears to be necessary. Whether or not the FASB is as yet willing to accept this reality is open to conjecture, but the future does hold promise. (See Appendix 9A.)

The hybrid proposals mentioned in this chapter were developed in response to the shortcomings of the basic proposals. Their publication and the actions taken in other countries have interacted to at least persuade the FASB to do two things:

● Retain the historical-cost framework, and
● Experiment with condensed, supplementary disclosures.

Over time, it is reasonable to assume that the FASB disclosures will gravitate toward the three- or four-line items of data common to the Hyde guidelines, the German Institute's proposal, and the

Fourth Directive of the EEC reviewed in Chapter 4. Some believe that exclusion of the gearing provision, at least initially, would expedite international cooperation.[44] If such a compromise is necessary to promote progress, then well and good. However, any ultimate explanation of inflation that ignores the benefit of gearing ignores the reality it purports to represent.

The inflation debates within the international accounting community appear to have produced a majority that considers inflation *reporting* to be more practicable and realistic than inflation *accounting*. However, reporting the effects of inflation will have no direct impact upon the disease itself. Those who directly or indirectly allocate resources—politicians, policymakers, businessmen, and union leaders—must affect the cure. Meaningful data, fairly and understandably explained, should help diagnosis and treatment.

CHAPTER 7. NOTES

1. The report of the field test was made available for purchase ($12.50; $10 to members) by the AICPA in 1979—*The Accounting Responses to Changing Prices: Experimentation With Four Models.*

2. Philip L. Defliese, "Inflation Accounting: Pursuing the Elusive," *Journal of Accountancy,* May 1979, p. 54.

3. S. Basu, *Inflation Accounting, Capital Market Efficiency and Security Prices* (Hamilton, Ont.: Society of Management Accountants of Canada, September 1977), pp. 31–32.

4. Ibid, p. vi.

5. S. Basu and J. R. Hanna, *Inflation Accounting: Alternatives, Implementation Issues and Some Empirical Evidence* (Hamilton, Ont.: Society of Management Accountants of Canada, 1975), p. 55.

6. Philip L. Defliese, "The Search for a New Conceptual Framework of Accounting," *Journal of Accountancy,* July 1977, p. 60.

7. Warren Chippendale and Philip L. Defliese (eds.), *Current Value Accounting* (New York: AMACOM, a Division of American Management Associations, 1977).

8. Securities and Exchange Commission, *Accounting Series Release No. 190,* "Notice of Adoption of Amendments to Regulation S-X Requiring Disclosure of Certain Replacement Cost Data," March 23, 1976.

9. Sidney Davidson and Roman L. Weil, "Inflation Accounting: The SEC Proposal for Replacement Cost Disclosures," *Financial Analysts Journal,* Vol 32, No. 2, March-April 1976, pp. 57–66.

10. Ibid., p. 66.

11. J. W. Frank, T. F. Kealey, and G. W. Silverman, *Effects and Significance of Replacement Cost Disclosure* (New York: Financial Executives Research Foundation, 1978), pp. 26–28.

12. Ibid., p. 2.

13. Ibid., p. 2; pp. 48–50.

14. Ibid., p. 50.

15. Arthur Andersen & Co., *Disclosure of Replacement Cost Data—Illustrations and Analysis,* May 1977.

16. Arthur Young and Company, *Disclosing Replacement-Cost Data,* 1977.

17. Frank, Kealey, and Silverman, op cit., pp. 46–47.

18. Defliese, "Inflation accounting," op cit., p. 61.

19. D. R. Carmichael, "Standards for Financial Reporting," *Journal of Accountancy,* May 1979, p. 76.

20. Ibid., p. 80.

21. Ibid., p. 78.

22. The Commission on Auditors' Responsibilities, *Report, Conclusions, and Recommendations,* New York, 1978, p. xxvi.

23. For examples, see Edgar O. Edwards and Philip W. Bell, *The Theory and Measurement of Business Income* (Los Angeles: University of California Press, 1961); Robert R. Sterling, *Theory of the Measurement of Enterprise Income* (Lawrence, Kansas: University Press of Kansas, 1970); and Lawrence Revsine, *Replacement Cost Accounting* (Englewood Cliffs, N.J.: Prentice-Hall, 1973).

24. Lawrence Revsine and Jerry J. Weygandt, "Accounting for Inflation: The Controversy," *Journal of Accountancy,* October 1974, pp. 72–78.

25. Lawrence Revsine and James B. Thies, "Price Level Adjusted Replacement Cost Data," *Journal of Accountancy,* May 1977, pp. 71–75.

26. Robert R. Sterling, "Relevant Financial Reporting in an Age of Price Changes," *Journal of Accountancy,* February 1975, pp. 42–51.

27. Richard F. Vancil, "Inflation Accounting—the Great Controversy," *Harvard Business Review,* March-April 1976, p. 61.

28. Raymond J. Chambers, *Accounting, Evaluation and Economic Behavior* (Englewood Cliffs, N.J.: Prentice-Hall, 1966). Also see his article, "NOD, COG, PuPu: See How Inflation Teases?", *Journal of Accountancy,* September 1975, pp. 56–62.

29. Anthony W. King, "Fair Value Accounting," *Management Accounting,* October 1975, pp. 24–26.

30. Arthur Andersen & Co., *Accounting Standards for Business Enterprises Throughout the World,* 1974, 168 pages.

31. Ibid., p. 13.

32. Ibid., p. 22.

33. Ibid., p. 37.

34. Ibid., p. 57.

35. Ibid., p. 8.

36. Touche Ross & Co., *Economic Reality in Financial Reporting,* 1975, 29 pages.

37. Ibid., p. 11.

38. Morton Backer, *Current Value Accounting* (New York: Financial Executives Institute, 1973), 326 pages.

39. John C. Biegler, "Common-Sense Accounting for Inflation," *Financial Executive,* December 1977, pp. 32–38.

40. Ibid., p. 38

41. Ernst & Ernst, *Accounting Under Inflationary Conditions,* 1976, 28 pages. Retrieval No. 38474.

42. Ibid., p. 3.

43. Comment by William G. Anderson, partner, Ernst & Ernst in "Ernst & Ernst Calls for Accounting Method Changes," *St. Louis Post-Dispatch,* February 25, 1977, p. 14C.

44. Charles W. Gill and S. Thomas Moser, "Inflation Accounting at the Crossroads," *Journal of Accountancy,* January 1979, p. 77.

8
Inflation Explanation

The material in the preceding chapters has been presented in order to establish a context for the topics of inflation and accounting. At the risk of redundancy, a brief synopsis will be attempted in order to provide a foundation upon which the recommendations (if not the plea) of this work—*inflation explanation*—can be assessed. Upon that groundwork, the concept of inflation explanation will be offered as a practical means of charting the effects of inflation while moving toward the real challenge—a cure for the disease itself.

INFLATION AND ACCOUNTING

The disease of inflation was depicted as having many causes, each feeding upon the other. It is a complex malady, affecting some, but not all, and in various ways and degrees. Different parts of any economy, and of a diverse enterprise, are affected in different ways. Some parts benefit, and some parts suffer. Small wonder, then, that proposals to account for or report the effects of changing price-levels have been found wanting.

An Intractable Disease

Inflation can no longer be viewed myopically as a national or temporary phenomenon. It is a pernicious, international disease.

Textbook solutions, patent medicine cures, and naive reliances upon unemployment and the "free" market have been ineffectual.

Inflation is caused by people, not by inanimate things such as goods or monies. Human greed and expectations have institutionalized inflation, at least in the United States. The vagaries of human behavior, together with the complexities of the disease itself, render inflation intractable to model-building and the normative approaches of charting its effects.

Faulty Frameworks

Overall, the frameworks examined were found to be inappropriate or, at best, not very useful.

Mathematical models were of little value since their assumptions were either oversimplified or ignored the important variables of human behavior. Accounting models also suffered from many of the same faults. Simplex approaches and normative measures have been applied to complex problems. Economic nonsense was produced, more often than not, and uneconomic actions were encouraged on the parts of managements and investors alike. (*FASB-8* reportings were cited as prime examples.)

Economic frameworks were helpful in that they illuminated the problem. The macroeconomic and uniform systems were depicted as limited-purpose means serving the special needs of certain countries. The microeconomic framework produced multiple languages of business (possibly a different language for each business), and was best suited for economies in which "stakeholders" were primarily governments, large banks, and similar institutions, rather than individual investors.

In the United States (at least to date) accountancy was portrayed as functioning within the framework of an independent profession rather than microeconomics. The foundation of the profession was the public interest, defined as the investing public. Financial reporting was based upon fairness, a concept difficult to define, yet readily adaptable to changing circumstances. This adaptability enabled accounting (and private investment) to grow and prosper. However, this very adaptability generated charges that the profession applied "brush-fire" approaches to problem solving. Double-digit inflation sent the FASB scurrying in search of a conceptual framework—a panacea for present and future problems.

The framework of enterprise theory was useful in problem definition. General-purpose statements could no longer serve the needs of a wide variety of stakeholders without treating alike that which was unlike. Special purpose reports were called for. Accounting necessarily had to change from its reliance upon normative (simplex) modes of thought (appropriate for closed systems), to the use of situational (complex) frameworks suitable for open systems. Financial and managerial accounting approaches were necessary in combination, in order to segment and explain economic events that appeared to be similar, yet occurred in different situations producing different results.

The presence of accounting alternatives mandates that the FASB describe the situations and the preferred methods to be applied. Like things must first be determined, then treated alike. This process requires consideration, judgment, and time. (It is also probable that the process would result in a reduction in the number of accounting alternatives.)

There is no holy grail containing immutable accounting truths. There is no monolithic structure suitable for accounting. The conceptual framework project is an exercise in futility that buys some time from the SEC. The time should be spent in more fruitful endeavors.

Poor Theory, Ill Applied

Price-level accounting and reporting methods have been debated intermittently in the United States for over a half-century. The basic proposals attempted to do the impossible with bad (or at best, poor) theory, ill applied. Small wonder, then, that the profession has been unsuccessful in identifying a comprehensive solution that was generally satisfactory. There is no such normative solution.

General-Purchasing-Power Reporting. Advocates suggested changing only the unit of measure, while retaining the basis of measurement.

Methods were found to be based upon textbook and dictionary definitions of inflation. Consequently, the effects of changes in the levels of general prices were the sole objectives. GPP methods applied macromeasures to microunits by assuming that inflation affected all businesses and economic organisms in the same way. Monetary gains and losses confused profitability and liquidity. Firms that were ill financially were reported not only as healthy, but as steadily improving. The general purchasing-power of equity was to be maintained, although the firm could not and would not every buy anything with it.

When compared with the criteria established, good marks were assigned GPP methods for uniformity and objectivity. Poor marks were given for fairness (not misleading), usefulness (worth the costs), and economic sense.

GPP methods were considered as attempts to do the impossible with bad theory ill applied.

Value Accounting. Proponents argued for retention of money as the unit of measure and as the common denominator. The basis of measurement was to be changed from cost to value. Historical cost systems would be scrapped.

Changes in price levels were considered to affect different economic units and their components in different ways. The focus upon changes in specific prices applied microconcepts to microunits.

However, the proposals ignored changes in the value of money and the effects of gearing. The maintenance of physical capital was considered to be essential to survival of the firm, and survival was taken as a given in competitive environments. Finally, value was not recognized as being more elusive than beauty.

Value accounting earned good marks for fairness and economic sense. Poor marks were assigned for uniformity, objectivity, and usefulness.

Overall, the basic value accounting proposals attempted to do the impossible with somewhat better theory than GPP methods, but were simply not practicable.

Hybrid Proposals. The theoretical and practical objections to the basic proposals spawned myriad hybrid methods. Some of those reviewed were found to be comprehensive combinations of the general and specific price-level methods. Others were condensed, stop-gap measures. Still others were considered to be maverick approaches.

The comprehensive methods attempted to eliminate the conceptual objections to the basic proposals but multiplied their practical hurdles. Most of the abbreviated reporting mechanisms were marred by the defects common to applications of normative measures to unlike situations—only implementation costs were reduced. The maverick proposals actually represented pleas for corporate tax relief.

Reproach is neither intended nor should be implied here. The point is that accounting for inflation or changing price levels is intractable by any reasonable means. Methods that are logically consistent are not worth their costs; those that are practical are primarily pain relievers, not accounting methods.

INFLATION EXPLANATION

The effects of changing price levels can be *explained*. Inflation explanation is the only logical alternative that is relevant and understandable without further interpretation.

Little, if anything, presented hereinafter is new. There are no laudable conceptual breakthroughs, nor any innovative measures that would enable normative approaches to accomplish what they simply cannot do. What follows is merely a call for:

- The recognition of a consensus that has long existed,
- The use of common sense, and
- The end of divisiveness, and the beginning of a united attack against a common enemy.

A Consensus Exists

The need for inflation explanation has been cited in virtually all the major pronouncements, studies, and symposia concerning inflation. In some the recommendations were at the periphery, almost resembling afterthoughts. In others the need was stated clearly, but managements and accountants became so engrossed in (or incensed over) their objections to the mechanics of the pronouncements that the provisions calling for explanation were ignored.

In 1948, *ARB No. 33* charged management with the responsibility for coping with rising costs as well as *reporting to stockholders the perceived effects and the actions taken.*[1] Updating to assist contemporary users of financial reports would require only the addition of management's perceptions of the future and the actions planned.

In the much despised *ASR-190,* supplemental information was *encouraged* to be provided by management in order to prevent the data from misleading users, and to help them *understand* the effects (good and bad) of changing price-levels upon the particular firm.[2] Most managements openly stressed the inadequacies in the normative data required by *ASR-190* but few elected to furnish information they considered to be more relevant and appropriate.

A major study of *ASR-190* published by the Financial Executives Institute reported that 45% of the respondents expressed a preference for inflation disclosures to be contained in *commentaries by management.*[3]

The Arthur Andersen proposal called for several management disclosures and explanations. Segmented reportings were recommended by diverse companies, including the segregation of expenses into variable and fixed categories. Expenses that would require arbitrary allocations were to be treated as common expenses without allocation. Managements were also called upon to *disclose* and *comment* upon commitments of resources, projected capital needs, and the sources of financing available.[4]

In the Touche Ross model, managements were to furnish *explanations* of the reasons for the differences between the historical cost and current value results.[5]

A prominent feature of the Price-Waterhouse proposal was the recommendation that the overall effects of changing price-levels should be *explained* by management.[6]

The Morton Backer model for current-value reporting called for management disclosures and *explanations* of the estimated market values of those assets not objectively determinable.[7]

Even the hastily constructed *Exposure Draft* on changing prices, issued by the FASB in December 1978, stipulated that "there is a need to *explain* the financial affairs of business enterprises to the general public and to those in government who make decisions on various aspects of economic policy."[8] Unfortunately, the FASB clung to its belief that the effects of changing prices could be explained by normative measures.

Outside the United States, the German Institute has perennially championed inflation explanation. The Institute's most recent proposal (HFA 2/1975) require management to *stipulate the mea-*

sures taken and/or planned to maintain the substance of the company's capital.[9]

The SEC has been moving inexorably toward inflation explanation in line with its increasing emphasis upon "soft data."

The Advisory Committee on Corporate Disclosure of the SEC recommended, in its final report, that the SEC should, "Encourage issuers to publish forward-looking *and* analytical information, with appropriate monitoring by the SEC for the purpose of determining the usefulness of the information to investors, the costs to issuers, and the responsiveness of issuers to user needs."[10] (Emphasis added.)

Harold M. Williams, Chairman of the SEC, in an address before the Financial Executives Institute, ". . . warned the financial executives that they must provide *'meaningful' analytic disclosure* information with operating summaries or invite further, more specific and detailed government regulations."[11] (Emphasis added.)

John C. Burton, former Chief Accountant of the SEC, summarized the "new insights" generated during the November 1977 Seaview Symposium as follows: "The most significant issue on which there was a substantial agreement was the need to develop a dual reporting system. . . " based upon historical cost statements, and ". . . a separate set of future-oriented, subjective data *mandated by the FASB* that would *include analytical material prepared by management."*[12] (Emphasis added.)

Finally, two statements relating to the FASB are clear indications that the time has come for inflation and other explanations by management. Donald J. Kirk, Chairman of the FASB, stated that

. . . for approximately 50 years, while the social and economic role of accounting has grown geometrically, an intense debate has raged among businessmen and accountants as to whether financial accounting and reporting should be responsive primarily to the internal needs of a business or to the needs of external users of financial information such as investors and creditors.[13]

According to Kirk, the FASB's work on aspects of the conceptual framework project had settled the issue in favor of external users. However, in the author's opinion, it seems incredulous to suggest that such a debate could have been entertained where the objectives of *external* financial reports were concerned. Nonetheless, user needs have prevailed officially and the FASB has left little doubt remaining for the need of inflation explanation:

Enterprise successes and failures are the result of the interaction of numerous factors. Management ability and performance are contributing factors, but so are events and circumstances that are often beyond the control of management, such as general economic conditions, supply and demand characteristics of enterprise inputs and outputs, price changes, and fortuitous events and circumstances. . . . neither accounting nor other statistical analysis can discern with reasonable accuracy the degree to which management, or any other factor, affected the joint result. . . .

Financial reporting *should include explanations and interpretations* to help users understand financial information provided. . . . usefulness . . . may be enhanced by management's explanations of the information. *Management knows more about the enterprise and its affairs than investors, creditors, or other "outsiders" and can often increase the usefulness of financial information by identifying certain transactions, other events, and circumstances that affect the enterprise and explaining their financial impact on it.*[14] (Emphasis added.)

The Means Exist

Accountants can record, report, and interpret economic events in any way so long as someone is willing to pay the attendant costs. Inflation explanation is no exception.

Managements have been willing to pay the costs of information needed to cope with rising prices on a day-to-day basis. Management accounting (sometimes referred to as management information) has become sophisticated and widely employed since World War II. Standard cost systems probably led the way, followed closely by forecasting methods based upon standards and adjusted for future expectations. Subsequently, the roller-coaster availability and cost of external financing further honed the cash forecasting systems of most well-managed companies.

The information systems needed to explain the effects of inflation are already in place in large companies. Perhaps few American companies employ managerial accounting systems that are as future oriented as those of the publicized Philips Company of the Netherlands, yet Philips has been at it longer. Although further substantiation of management's ability to explain inflation should not be necessary, the findings of a 1978 study for the Financial Executives Institute should put the subject to rest and are worth repeating:

Current management information systems are now well developed in all corporations affected by *ASR-190*. These systems typically portray the impact of inflation in great specificity—in some cases, down to the detail of an individual piece part.

Top management reporting as well as profit and cash forecasting systems are also well developed in major corporations. The information generated through these systems assists management in dealing with the impact of inflation.[15]

The means exist. The business community and the accounting profession need only be convinced of the desirability of applying the means at their command. The alternative to voluntary, common-sense explanation of inflation is SEC direction using normative measures that cannot be as meaningful and, because of redundancy, can only further increase the costs of reporting. Business and the accounting profession have perennially complained about increasing government interference and reporting costs—now is the time for each sector to cooperate and help the other.

Suggestions for a Beginning

Inflation explanation, as suggested here, consists of a multilevel discussion by management within a meaningful annual report. Such an approach represents the only practical way that the effects of changing price levels can be presented and reflect economic sense. At the same time, management would fulfill its obligation to communicate adequate information for use by third parties in an understandable fashion at least cost. Moreover, management is afforded a valuable opportunity to tell the company's story effectively to a diverse group of stakeholders.

Inflation explanation is, at once, both a *responsibility* and an *opportunity*. All too often the former has been overemphasized and the latter overlooked. Accountants suffering from the green eye-shade syndrome have been as much to blame as management. As a result, financial reports have become inadequate, if not sterile. Managements have not really communicated with anyone, and the SEC has been forced to dictate normative disclosures that cannot be expected to fill the void. Each participant readily finds something to complain about. Only the negative aspects are addressed. The perspective and the opportunity are lost.

A responsible explanation of the effects of inflation is one facet of a multidimensional annual reporting system. Three parts addressed to three audiences are recommended:

- Financial Statements—oriented primarily toward sophisticated users.
- Supplemental Data Section—information relevant to all stakeholders (analysts, investors, and the general public).
- President's Message—a report on the past year's events and the company's prospects understandable by all users.

The Financial Statement Package. This section of the annual report would continue to present the traditional financial statements, explanatory footnotes, and the other hard data required by the FASB and the SEC. All the reports and supportive information should continue to be based upon historical cost.

Little change is possible or recommended here. Over the years, required disclosures have been added, layer upon layer, until the customary general-purpose statements have become useful and understandable only to the relatively sophisticated user and professional analyst. Additional layers of data and explanations would only serve to further complicate the financial package. Also, important results could be buried among normative disclosures.

One suggestion can be made, however, and it concerns a change in basic attitude. Managements (and accountants) must adopt a policy of full and fair disclosure. For example, information that the SEC considers to be relevant for inclusion in the 10K report should be included in the formal, financial section of the annual report. Management might also find that time and expense can be saved by making one effort serve two purposes. Statement users should never be required to request and refer to Form 10K for financial information. Users naturally are led to believe that important, confidential (therefore, unfavorable) data have purposely not been disclosed to the general public. The credibility of financial reporting suffers unnecessarily.

The Supplemental Data Section. Information depicting the nature of the firm, how it has developed, where it is, and some idea of where it is headed should be supplied in a section composed of a variety of supplemental disclosures.

Structure of the firm. Some combination of narrative and graphical means should be used to present a concise, clear view of the structure of the company. Names of subsidiaries and affiliates, both foreign and domestic, as well as the extents of ownership should be disclosed. Where relevant, the company's evolution should also be depicted.

Individual investors who have held shares for some time will probably be aware of most of these facts. However, new investors (present and potential) as well as professional analysts may find this information helpful. All users will be in position to assess the relative dispersion of ownership and risk.

Explanation of policies. A section addressing company policies and philosophies can serve as the foundation upon which the effects of changing price levels can be explained.

Where appropriate, the following matters should be addressed concisely. Company policies and goals regarding growth in sales, market shares, productivity, and earnings should be stated. Where foreign operations exist, are they temporary excursions, or parts of a long-term plan for worldwide expansion? The desired capital structure (debt-equity ratio) should be specified. If technology is an important ingredient, a description of policies regarding the levels and targets of research and development would be desirable.

Several other broad questions may be relevant insofar as inflation is concerned. What acquisition and divestiture criteria are employed in domestic and foreign environments? What approach to capital maintenance is followed—physical capital (for single-line companies) or financial capital (for conglomerates and multinationals)? What policies and strategies are used to "keep the stockholder whole," now and in future times of rising prices?

Policy statements such as, but not limited to, the above can establish the goals considered to be important by management, as well as the standards by which past performance and future prospects may be evaluated. All users of the financial reports would be interested and concerned.

Supplemental disclosures. The section of the annual report containing supplemental data should be considered equally as important as the package of formal financial statements. Here is where the company's evolution and position are described.

The profitability of the company should be depicted in macro-terms using historical data. Long-term trends (over 10 years or more) will often be found most useful to illustrate growth and stability. Graphs and charts can provide clear, concise pictures of growths in sales, market shares, productivity, and earnings. Similar methods can compare the company's progress with that of the industry or the national economy, as appropriate. Shareholders would be interested in a chart comparing nominal trends in sales, dividends, and the GNP deflator or consumer price index. Comparisons of actual performances and management goals also lend themselves readily to graphic presentation; operating incomes, returns on assets employed, and earnings-per-share data are examples.

The operations of the company must also be explained in microterms by means of relevant segmentations. What were the sources of earnings by significant lines of business and geographic areas? What is the extent of diversification? Where foreign operations exist, what have their relative profitabilities been, both in terms of: (1) Local currencies and accounting conventions, and (2) U.S. dollars and GAAP? Some diversified companies have introduced variety into their reports by having managers develop the data to depict their segments. Better understandings have accrued to managers and users alike. How do the foreign and domestic sectors compare insofar as sales and earnings generations on assets employed are concerned? In general, the need for presentation of data in microterms should be considered for each aspect depicted in macroterms. The consolidated veil must be lifted if financial reports of diverse enterprises are to regain some semblance of usefulness.

Data reporting the effects of changing prices should be presented in macro and micro forms. Charts can compare succinctly trends in growths of sales, productivity, and earnings for the company and its major segments with movements in appropriate national norms, such as nominal GNP, real GNP, and selected price indexes. For some companies, selected methods of price-level accounting and reporting might be applied to construct "layered" income statements, if and only if the results depicted were fair representations—such cases should be few indeed. Graphic approaches, augmented by brief narrative comments were appropriate, can do much to tell a complicated story in a meaningful way.

An effective and important disclosure of the effects of price-level changes would involve data separating changes in sales due to increases in price and real increases in quantity. The data should be presented for the entity as a whole and for its various segments. Such disclosures would isolate real growth as well as provide some insight into past price elasticities.

Data should also be furnished to indicate the effects of changing price levels upon the economic resources of the entity and the claims to these resources. Comparisons of historical and replacement costs of assets, as well as the related depreciation amounts, should be made if relevant. To minimize subjectivity and/or "forked-tongue" restatements, use could be made of the data on the replacement costs of some 20 categories of assets maintained and updated annually by the BEA. Depreciation allowances on the BEA current costs, using straight-line methods, and based upon 85% of the service lives, could also be compared with the total, *actual* capital consumption allowances afforded the company for tax purposes; that is, accelerated depreciation and additional incentives, such as the depreciation equivalents of investment tax credits and other first-year allowances. Users of reports should be given some insight into the relative quality (age and condition) of assets as well as a *real* indication of the adequacy of actual capital consumption allowances. The effects of changes in debt structures and in the costs of the debt over time should also be reflected for the benefit of creditors and shareholders alike. In this respect, the effects of gearing should also be disclosed to indicate the impacts of changes in the costs and values of money.

Where foreign operations are significant, the exposure to changes in the relative inflation rates among countries should be indicated. This could be accomplished by depicting the dependence of the parent upon short-term repatriations of foreign earnings in the past. Presumably, companies that would report regular repatriations of foreign earnings would be more vulnerable to short-term fluctuations in exchange rates than would companies that reinvest the majority or whole of such earnings in foreign growth.

A reconciliation of statutory and effective tax rates for the current and previous 5 years or so would also be beneficial. Here again, the effective tax rates must recognize the benefits of all capital consumption allowances claimed and, of course, all deferrals of concurrent taxation, domestic as well as foreign.

The supplemental disclosures mentioned above are examples, certainly not all-inclusive, of data routinely collected and *used* internally on a regular basis by the officers of all well-managed companies.

The President's Message. The capstone section of the annual report and the explanation of inflation should be the president's message.

The two previous sections containing the financial statements and supplementary disclosures dealt with historical data and hard information. The president's letter represents a challenge (and an opportunity) to present the company's performance and position to a variety of stakeholders. Historical data and considered opinions should be drawn upon in order to:

- Analyze the important events of the past year,
- Examine existing problems, opportunities, plans, and
- Discuss the future prospects of the firm.

Some cautions must be mentioned. First, credibility requires that problems and failures be discussed with the same candor as prospects and achievements. Second, the message should be as candid as possible and understandable by the average reader. Last, but not least, the company's future prospects should be discussed fairly and without exaggeration. This last factor is extremely important since, although the president's message is presented last in this book, it is the first section of the financial report. A well-crafted message can aid user understanding of all that follows; a poor job may lose the reader's interest altogether.

Past events. All important events of the past year should be discussed. The effects of inflation should be addressed, whether or not they were significant, since the reader will not have that knowledge. In addition to inflation, the effects of specific price changes, both good and bad, should be explained if material. Relaxation by the IRS of its LIFO conformity rule will remove any existing constraints regarding discussions of trends in inventory prices. The impacts on gross margins, supply and demand characteristics, effects of technological advances, and unique circumstances (fortuitous or otherwise) are examples of items to be reviewed. Management actions to minimize the effects of inflation and the constraints encountered should be explained. Naturally, the important past events would be drawn from and supported by data appearing in the financial package and the supplemental disclosure section. Readers could be referred to the supporting data for details.

Present position. Each company usually operates from a unique niche in the larger economic realm. The present position of the firm should be described and discussed.

The circumstances of the industries and the firm's position in these industries should be stated. Important supply, demand, and price elasticity information require explanation. Inflation, alleged oil shortages, and similar economic upheavals have changed the very nature of many industries. These impacts should be addressed. The state of the technological arts, new products, and new markets may also be relevant.

For capital-intensive industries, the ages and natures of physical plants often represent vital information. Are the facilities of adequate size? Does overcapacity exist? Are the plants up-to-date insofar as technology is concerned? What changes, if any, are underway, including contractions and divestments?

Future prospects. Assessing the future involves uncertainty. Inflation tends to increase that uncertainty for most companies. As a consequence, discussions of future prospects cannot draw support from the hard facts underlying the past and present. So called "soft data," or considered opinions, make up the future milieu. The past and present, however, do provide starting points from which reasonable future plans can be discussed.

As with most projections, the underlying assumptions should be presented, including: general economic conditions (domestic and foreign); expected future price elasticities; supply bottlenecks, if any; supply and stability of labor; important legislation pending; and the like.

Areas dealing with technolgy should include the perceived effects upon products and costs, major research and development interests, and planned changes in markets and strategies.

Acquisitions and/or divestments planned should be discussed together with any perceived impacts upon company ownership and structure.

Capital expenditure plans are essential items for explanation. Major expansions, contractions, additions, replacements and similar events need to be addressed insofar as when, where, and how are concerned.

Future plans require capital. The planned sources of the finances needed should be explained. In this regard, management can inform the readers of earnings retentions needed before future dividends can be accommodated. Also, projected needs for new equity or debt capital could be addressed. Should an economic downturn occur, the adequacy of internal financing and the borrowing power of the company should also be discussed.

Upon that foundation, the overall effects of changing prices should be interpreted, and the plans to cope with future inflation discussed.

Auditor Involvement

It has been established that, because they are often intractable to normative accounting or reporting methods, inflation and changing prices can only be explained by those in a position to do so—corporate management. Management accounting has furnished the means necessary. Members of the Financial Executives Institute are beginning to recognize that explanations of the effects of inflation, tailored to the particular firm and its particular circumstances, are preferable to mandated, normative disclosures that make economic sense only by accident. The remaining hurdle appears to be the public accountant.

The Issues. Auditors traditionally become uncomfortable when associated with information that is difficult to verify by objective means. The new kinds of "soft" information being favored by the SEC and suggested in this work are particularly worrisome. Auditors fear that their association with such data would subject them to challenges in the courts by irate stakeholders.

Events that have transpired over the recent past have subjected the auditor's role to reexamination, clarification, and expansion. The most telling blow, of course, involved deficiences in audited financial statements. The "questionable payments" fiascos, involving hundreds of millions of dollars in many cases, led to cries of "where were the auditors?" Studies by the SEC, such as the Wheat Report,[16] found that the most serious types of misleading disclosures in annual reports were found in supplementary charts and in similar condensed highlights of operations. The Cohen Commission determined that auditor responsibility in connection with annual reports was much too vague and often misinterpreted by users. The responsibility for attestation of financial statements was clear; however, the requirement for review of other information in annual reports, with which the auditor was "associated," was varied and unclear. Users tended to assume that auditor association meant that the information was audited.[17]

Considered Opinions. As a result, the Cohen Commission recommended that the FASB "broaden its reach" to cover the annual report, not only the financial statements, and to require auditors to stipulate the extent of examination and review to which the various parts of the report were subjected.

The Commission recommends the auditor read all of the information accompanying audited financial statements and compare it to the information in the financial statements and his workpapers to assure himself that it is not inconsistent with anything he knows as the result of his audit. When necessary, he should recompute information stated in percentages or combined in a manner different from that in the financial statements. His report should include a description of the work performed and his conclusions. . . ."[18]

The Commission further suggested that the auditor's report be expanded to clarify the extent of involvement and review. The following excerpt related to other financial information:

We reviewed the information appearing in the annual report [or other document] in addition to the financial statements, and found nothing inconsistent in such other information with the statements or the knowledge obtained in the course of our audits. [Any other information reviewed, such as replacement cost data, would be identified.] [19] (Bracketed material appeared as shown in the source quoted.)

In addition to suggesting how auditors should approach and stipulate review procedures, the Commission made it quite clear that users of financial reports were entitled to something other than vague assurances by auditors:

The reporting requirements should be made consistent, by requiring the auditor to report on all unaudited financial information with which he is associated, including that appearing in a document containing audited financial statements. Furthermore, it is unreasonable to expect users to make distinctions among different kinds of information all simply labeled "unaudited" but on which the auditor performs a wide variety of work. Users should be informed about the work done and the assurances intended rather than merely about the audit that is not done.[20]

Recommendations. The traditional function of the independent auditor has focused upon attestation of financial statements based upon historical costs and similar standards that produce data that are relatively objective and verifiable.

There is no valid reason to preclude the auditor from being required to *review* the financial information contained in the supplemental disclosure section of annual reports. The supplemental disclosures would include graphs, charts, schedules, and condensed financial highlights—one of which would encompass inflation explanation. Such disclosures would be based upon historical, rather than future-oriented, information which the auditor could review for reasonableness and consistency with the contents of the financial statements and his knowledge of the company.

The third part of the annual report—the president's message—would require a different approach and structure. Preferably, the message should be subdivided into two parts: (1) Interpretations of important *past* events, and (2) *future* expectations—plans, budgets, forecasts, and the like. The auditor should be expected to read the entire message and stipulate: (1) That he has done so; (2) that the explanations of past events are consistent with the supporting facts, although differences may be reflected in interpretations; and (3) that the future projections are entirely the opinions of management.

Accounting students are generally told early in their studies that the expertise and judgment needed to *interpret* accounting information separates the accountant from the bookkeeper. It seems incongruous, then, that accountants have perennially resisted any requirements that they practice their interpretive skills. The profession has preferred to rely upon rigid, normative standards that tend to serve as a safe haven yet mislead users of annual reports. It is high time that public accountants recognize that the heart of the profession is not a set of normative standards, but rather the ability to provide judgment and an independent perspective to financial information.

OVERVIEW

Inflation is intractable to explanation by any normative means. Not all companies are adversely affected by rising prices; it is often forgotten that many firms are in a position to raise prices and increase margins. Other firms can be affected in various ways and degrees.

What is needed is the expertise and judgment of those in the only positions to assess and *explain* the effects of inflation upon a specific entity—its management, primarily, and independent auditors, secondarily.

Managements, aided by their internal accountants and information systems, can make the necessary analyses and assessments. Independent auditors are in position, and qualified to evaluate the fairness of management's explanations of past effects. Presentations of future prospects should be labeled what they are—management plans, strategies, and opinions.

The component factors of inflation explanation were merely examples of the spectrum available. Specific rules cannot be suggested here, nor can they be furnished by the FASB. Instead, the FASB should develop guidelines to assist companies to determine those most appropriate for their unique niches in the economy.

The recommendations made are not held out to be novel. Agreements have existed on most major proposals for some time but have been overlooked or simply ignored. What is required is acceptance of the fact that accounting or reporting for changes in price levels, using any normative means, can make economic sense only by accident. The effects of inflation can only be explained by managements and reviewed for common sense by independent auditors. Cooperation by both groups concerned would not only produce results that make economic sense, but would do much to prevent the imposition of mandated disclosures by SEC regulations.

The means exist. Only changes in attitudes are required. Managements of well-run companies are involved with diagnosing and coping with changing prices on a day-to-day basis. They need only to share their findings and interpretations with their stakeholders. Independent auditors, on the other hand, need to shed their propensity to merely attest to the vague fairness of financial statements (that are becoming less and less useful) while leaving the interpretation and understanding to others—poor hallmarks for a profession.

Users of financial reports would, at long last, be furnished reasoned explanations in addition to a maze of raw data and footnotes.

Furthermore, since inflation is an international disease, inflation explanation would be, at once, practicable internationally. Managements and auditors in all countries can explain the effects of inflation regardless of existing differences in languages, whether written (the language of people) or accounting (the language of business).

CHAPTER 8. NOTES

1. See p. 59.
2. See p. 144.
3. See p. 146.
4. See p. 163.
5. See p. 166.
6. See p. 173.
7. See p. 172.
8. *Exposure Draft,* "Financial Reporting and Changing Prices" (Stamford, Conn.: Financial Accounting Standards Board, December 28, 1978), p. i.
9. See p. 80.
10. Synopsis of recommendations in the *Report of the Advisory Committee on Corporate Disclosure to the Securities and Exchange Commission,* A. A. Sommer, Chmn., November 3, 1977, appearing in *Management Accounting,* January 1978. p. 10.
11. "SEC Chairman Speaks Out on Reporting, Internal Controls," *Management Accounting,* December 1978, p. 7.
12. John C. Burton, "A Symposium on the Conceptual Framework," *Journal of Accountancy,* January 1978, p. 58.
13. Comments of Donald J. Kirk, appearing in "Status Report," Financial Accounting Standards Board, No. 77, December 6, 1978, p. 1.
14. Financial Accounting Standards Board, *Statement of Financial Accounting Concepts No. 1,* "Objectives of Financial Reporting by Business Enterprises" (Stamford, Conn.: FASB, November 1978), pp. 26–27.
15. J. W. Frank, T. F. Kealey, and G. W. Silverman, *Effects and Significance of Replacement Cost Disclosure* (New York: Financial Executives Research Foundation, 1978), pp. 46–47.
16. Securities and Exchange Commission, *Disclosure to Investors: A Reappraisal of Federal Administrative Policies under the '33 and '34 Acts* (Chicago: Commerce Clearing House, 1969), p. 369.
17. The Commission on Auditors' Responsibilities, *Report, Conclusions, and Recommendations,* New York, 1978, p. 66.
18. Ibid., p. 69.
19. Ibid., p. 78.
20. Ibid., p. 84.

9
The Future

Problems have been defined, alternatives have been examined, and some interim solutions have been proposed.

What follows are the actions recommended to be taken by those most directly involved and in position to influence outcomes. Whether or not these suggestions are employed by business and the accounting profession will determine if inflation will continue as a threat, or be transformed into an opportunity to regain credibility—not only in the United States, but in the international sphere as well.

BUSINESS INITIATIVES

The business community would be well-advised to recognize realities and consider some changes in attitude.

The credibility gap between the business sector and the public has widened rather than diminished. Business, in general, has chosen to play the game of "practical politics and tax relief". Myopic pursuits of short-term benefits have obscured realities, and have caused the business community to take actions that are not in its best long-run interests.

Some Myths Revisited

Business has argued that inflation affects profitability, comparability, investment, and corporate taxation. The first two items are really nonissues. Business has evidenced little genuine concern over the fairness of financial reporting, even less over inflation reporting. How to retain a larger portion of current earnings is a real business objective; corporate tax relief has been the means selected.

Reported profits are not illusory. They are quite real. What the profits in nominal dollars will buy in the form of goods and services does vary over time. For what it is worth, this effect can be reported by the addition of a single line item at the bottom of income statements. The business attitude has been ambivalent—management wants high profits on financial reports, yet low profits on tax returns.

Comparability is impaired, whether for one company over time, or among companies at a point in time. The one-liner adjustment mentioned above would help. However, the real impairment results as much, if not more, from the fact that inflation affects different firms (and their segments) in various ways, rather than from inflation, per se. Here again, business has grumbled somewhat, yet clearly prefers favorable comparisons in published statements.

Capital investment suffers, to be sure. The culprit, however, is inflation and the future uncertainties it produces, *not* the absence of inflation accounting. In fact, business should consider the possibility that lower profits produced using inflation accounting might tend to further discourage potential external investors. Many observers (including the author) believe that any contrived method of inflation accounting would only further exacerbate inflation, curtail external saving and investment, and deflate securities markets.

Apparently the business community has elected to lobby for corporate tax relief. Every dollar of earnings retained internally is a dollar that does not have to be cajoled from investors. Lower tax bites would improve the attractiveness of internal investments considered by management. However, some new problems would be created and the two existing ones would remain unaddressed.

To the extent that the government's appetite for tax revenues was not reduced proportionately, corporate tax relief would merely switch more of the incidence of taxation upon individuals. The massive redistribution of resources that would result is one thing, in itself. More importantly, it would represent a *legislated* investment in the business sector by individuals, without offering them the potential dividends or stock appreciation normally afforded investors. Also, it would effectively circumvent operations of the free markets so staunchly supported by the business sector. It should also be remembered that governments do not tax the inflated incomes of companies (or individuals) unwittingly. Governments know what they are about.

Finally, tax relief for business would neither cure the disease of inflation nor provide a way to account for it.

Business Responsibilities and Actions

The business community must act to close the credibility gap that has been created by the pursuit of self-interest. It must reestablish its legitimacy in the eyes of the public—both the stockholder and the average citizen.

The public confidence can only be restored by words and deeds that convince the public that the business community will no longer tolerate inflation, nor continue to act as a carrier of the disease. The political clout developed by the corporate community should be applied resolutely and forcefully to cure the disease of inflation. Such actions would serve the best interests of all while restoring much of the public confidence. The imperatives for the business community are:

- To demand that the Congress index income taxes, both corporate and individual. Only one legislative move would be required. No special interest charges could be levied. This action would remove the textbook effects of inflation. It would also do much to prevent tax considerations from determining accounting practices.
- To also demand that the Congress index government borrowings and obligations. This would close the loop. The great government inflation dynamo would be slowed. Government would be transformed into an affected, interested party instead of a bystanding beneficiary of inflation. Instead of the dependence upon political rhetoric that seldom has any actual effect, checkreins would be imposed upon government spending.
- To insist that the government face up to its responsibilities under the Employment Act of 1946 to avoid depressions and inflations, as well as promote the full employment of resources. This is a gargantuan task and business would have to be willing

to contribute its analytical resources and its full cooperation. Examples of critical considerations are:

—Adoption of a tripartite (government, business, and labor) program of indicative planning or commonsense steering of the economy. Many markets are not free. Others face, or will encounter, major roadblocks—critical shortages of materials; greedy unions; disruptive competitors, trading partners, and host governments. Foresight and oversight, exercised co-operatively by government, business, and labor, can do much to assure that free enterprise and open markets prevail.

—Implementation of effective zero-base budgeting and consolidated, accrual reporting systems by the government. To be effective, the former must limit narrative justifications to two pages. The latter program, while still experimental, has benefited from 3 years' cooperation by government, accounting, business, and academic specialists. Such programs can assist government in managing and accounting for the stable or decreasing revenues to be received and expended.

• To call for the creation of an Organization of Petroleum *Importing* Countries (OPIC). Now more than ever before, the international community is economically interdependent. A nation, or group of nations, must be impressed with the realization that disruption of the world economy can only be pursued at the risk of self peril. Since oil exporters are sovereign nations, oil importers must also be sovereign nations if bargaining strengths are to be equalized.

• To call upon the accounting profession, and the SEC, to cease and desist from inane efforts to report the effects of changing price levels by any normative means. In lieu, a business-FASB-AICPA-SEC roundtable should be established. Business should assert its willingness to:

—Lift the consolidated veil,

—Explain the effects of changing price levels, as well as the actions taken and/or planned to cope with them.

—Participate with the profession and the SEC in devising guidelines (rather than rigid rules) for inflation explanation, review by auditors, and oversight by the SEC.

The foregoing are examples of actions that the business community should consider. The suggestions are certainly not all-inclusive and many spin-offs would result. Collectively, these and similar efforts would do much to restore public confidence in the business community, address the only real threat to capitalism and free enterprise, and prevent the imposition of SEC-directed reporting mechanisms. Business leadership would demonstrate the willingness and ability to set its own house in order. Business would be serving the public interest and, at the same time, its own highest self-interest.

PROFESSIONAL INITIATIVES

The relatively young profession of accountancy must recognize squarely its responsibilities to its several publics and itself.

The Broad Perspective

As a whole, the profession has been urged to recognize the responsibilities it has accepted to assure that the information furnished to business and investors is understandable. It has also been charged with doing "a far better job of explaining to everyone—business, government, and the investor—...."[1]

Participation in the roundtable mentioned earlier would do much to keep the language of business understandable and under the supervision of the private sector. Participation would also serve to eradicate the "insular attitude" that some segments of the profession have developed; that is, the assertion that accountants should concern themselves with the attestation of statements, not with the problems of controlling inflation.[2]

The Role of the FASB

The function of the FASB is clear. It should reaffirm clearly that the historical cost basis of accounting will be retained. Concurrently, it should acknowledge that normative approaches to price-level reporting cannot produce economic sense.

The FASB should accept and acknowledge management's responsibility to explain significant effects on business operations; inflation, of course, would be an important item. Since it has accepted the responsibility to furnish standards for financial reports as well as financial statements, the FASB should reaffirm the SEC requirement that condensed highlights and summaries of operations be neither more or less favorable than depicted by the basic financial statements.

Participation in the roundtable discussions mentioned earlier should result in the publication of *guidelines* to explain the effects of changing price-levels. Last, but not least, indexation of income taxes would require the FASB to reexamine the desirability of LIFO costing, accelerated depreciation, and similar tax-based schemes for use in financial statements. Collaboration with the IRS, and the Congress, ultimately, would be necessary but well worth the effort. The FASB cannot divorce itself from politics. It can, however, separate itself from the taxation arena and, effectively, remove much of the politicization.

The Part of the AICPA

The AICPA would have to implement the FASB standards and charge auditors with recognizing their responsibilities to review, for fairness and reasonableness, all disclosures and explanations of past events appearing in annual reports that contain audited financial statements. The guidelines mentioned previously would assist the reviews; however, auditors would still be called upon to exercise judgment—the real hallmark of the profession.

The major public accounting firms would certainly be called upon to lend their expertise and resources and, just as certainly, would continue to participate willingly.

GOVERNMENT INITIATIVES

Some wise observer has quipped that leadership, commonsense, and determination are qualities not often found in combination in the political arena. To the extent that these qualities are absent today they should be supplemented externally, as suggested, until the political process can identify (or regenerate) the abilities needed.

SEC Oversight

On balance, the SEC has been a welcome exception to the above observation. Historically, the SEC has proved itself to be cooperative and patient. The SEC has demonstrated its willingness to permit accounting standards to be established by the private sector, and has confined itself to the role of oversight primarily. However, the SEC has not hesitated to flex its muscles whenever it believed that the public had lost confidence in the ability or the desire of the private sector to keep its house in order.

In the recent past, the public confidence was eroded—and the SEC's wrists were slapped—as a result of a series of fiascos: Watergate, Koreagate, clandestine payments, and influence peddling. The reluctance of the private sector to disclose and explain the effects of rising prices forced the SEC to resort to its *ASR-190* experiment, probably more as a warning to the private sector to move off dead-center than anything else. That purpose has evidently been accomplished.

The SEC should (and most likely will) pursue its oversight role—prodding, cooperating, and waiting. Should the private sector fail to recognize and adopt inflation explanation, the SEC would have little recourse other than to mandate the implementation of some alternative. Voluntary adoption, as suggested, would appear to be preferable and should produce more meaningful results.

Government Hindsight

According to the adage, hindsight is more accurate than foresight. If so, those who profess to steer the national economy have the opportunity to discontinue the de facto program aimed at reducing the purchasing power of money.[3] The indexation methods suggested represent an initial, critical step toward the de-institutionalizing of inflation. Responsive accounting and budgeting systems can help a stable or declining number of revenue dollars work more efficiently and effectively.

Indicative planning can restore foresight. The explanation of inflation in financial reports would help isolate those areas that suffer and those that benefit—the carriers of the disease. Problem sectors of the economy could be identified and dealt with before they become crises. Selective uses of excess profits taxes and guided investment incentives would enable economic resources to be directed where they are believed necessary in order to remove the imperfections that crop up in the national economy.

Concurrently, the governments of the developed countries must recognize that the international disease of inflation can be checked and controlled, if not eliminated, only by united and concerted efforts on an ongoing basis. No nation or group of nations can consider itself independent.

EPILOGUE

This examination of inflation accounting has touched upon the past, present, and the future.

Inflation was reviewed in order to establish the nature of the disease for which accountants attempted to maintain charts. The methods of chart-keeping proposed over the past 60-odd years were examined as objectively as possible for someone who has a considered opinion. Methods that were logically consistent were not worth their costs. Those that were practical were either illogical or were overtures for tax relief rather than accounting methods. Inflation was found to be a disease intractable to charting by any normative means.

The present was found to be, in the main, an extension of the past. The accounting profession and the business community have not learned much from the lessons of the past. Or, they have permitted their perceived, short-run self-interests to obscure the public interest *and* their own best interests. Present searchings for conceptual frameworks and experiments with normative disclosures can lead only to the recognition that the effects of inflation must be explained by those in the positions to do so—managements, primarily, and accountants, secondarily.

The future can hold promise. Inflation explanation will put many myths to rest. New relationships will be found. One fact should become clear—inflation is caused by people and their greed, whether they be individuals, businesses, or governments. Inanimate goods and monies are merely pawns that obscure the real causes. The business and accounting communities must recognize that the disease of inflation, aggravated by the lack of credibility in financial reporting, represents the only *real* threat to capitalism, free enterprise, and the other institutions that Americans value.

Collectively, the business and accounting sectors have considerable influence. They must be willing to bring this influence to bear constructively upon those who are in position to affect a cure—the government. Constructive efforts also call for the business community to enlist the support of labor to help heal themselves, police themselves, and regain their credibility. Each sector will not only serve the public interest but their own highest self-interests as well.

It should be obvious that curing the disease of inflation would eliminate the dilemmas of accounting or reporting its effects. In the interim, the most reasonable medication is inflation explanation. The approach suggested can be applied today, not only in the United States, but in all the several languages of business and people. We should get on with it.

CHAPTER 9. NOTES

1. William S. Kanaga, managing partner of Arthur Young & Co., "Inflation, Instability, and Accounting," *Management Accounting*, March 1977, p. 68.

2. Ibid., p. 15.

3. Paul Grady, "Purchasing Power Accounting," Price Waterhouse & Co., *Review*, 1975, No. 3, p. 3.

Appendix 9A

FASB Statement of Financial Accounting Standards No.33

Under a virtual ultimatum from the SEC, the Financial Accounting Standards Board reluctantly (yet hastily) issued its *Statement of Financial Accounting Standards No. 33,* "Financial Reporting and Changing Prices." Although dated September 1979, the *Statement* was actually published on or about October 5, 1979. Paragraph references cited hereinafter are keyed to paragraph numbers in *Statement No. 33.*

GENERAL REQUIREMENTS

The *Statement* applies, with some exceptions, to large public companies having either (1) total assets of more than $1 billion (net of depreciation), *or* (2) inventories, property, plant, and equipment (before deducting depreciation) of more than $125 million at the beginning of fiscal years ended on or after December 25, 1979.

Applicable companies are required to provide, as supplementary information in annual reports:

1. Historical-cost income from continuing operations, adjusted for the effects of changes in *both* general price levels (paragraphs 39–46) *and* specific price levels (paragraphs 51–64).
2. The gain or loss in purchasing power on net monetary items (paragraphs 47–50).
3. Current costs of inventory, property, plant, and equipment at year end (paragraph 51).
4. Changes during the year in the above current costs attributed to changes in general and specific price levels (paragraphs 55–56).

5. A five-year comparison of revenues, incomes, earnings per share, and net assets adjusted for changes in price levels. Also, the effects of holding net monetary assets, dividends and market prices per share, and the average consumer price indexes for each of the 5 years are required (paragraphs 65-66).

6. *Explanations* of the data presented, as well as *discussions* of their significance for the reporting firm (paragraph 37).

In addition to item (6), above, which is *required,* the provision of additional information to assist user understanding is encouraged.

The disclosures in items (1) through (4), above, *may* be presented using a format similar to Figure 9-1 *or* the more detailed format in Figure 9-2. The suggested format for the comparative data in item (5), above, is illustrated in Figure 9-3. (For continuity, the figures cited have been furnished at the end of this Appendix.) It should be noted that disclosures of the information are required; the means or schedular forms selected are optional and experimentation is encouraged.

Since most affected firms must also report the replacement cost data required by *ASR-190* for 1979, the FASB has waived the specific price-level portion of (1), above, and the current-cost data, in (3) and (4), above, for years ended before December 25, 1980. The FASB is hopeful that the SEC will withdraw or postone *ASR-190* during the interim period.

Certain combinations by poolings of interest are exempted. Also, the information is to be presented in consolidated format by companies presenting consolidated statements. Segmented presentations are also encouraged, but not required.

During the public hearings preceding the *Statement,* several industry sectors pleaded for and received special consideration: oil and gas, mining, forest products, real estate, banking, insurance, and regulated industries (e.g., utilities). Special task groups were established for all but the regulated industries. As a result, the current-cost data have been waived indefinitely, pending further examinations, for the oil and gas, mining, forest products, and real estate sectors. The problem areas cited by the other sectors were recognized by the FASB, but considered to be workable within the framework of the *Statement.*

CRITIQUE

The FASB has decided not to decide. Instead, since both GPP (constant dollar) and current-cost disclosures were considered to have merit, both will be required while experimentation is continued for as much as five more years. By electing to sit on the fence, the FASB did not win many friends nor did it favorably influence many people. It did buy the FASB some valuable time. How wisely the time is used may well determine the fate of the FASB.

Under conflicting political pressures, the FASB made a political "decision." Hearings and comments reflected an even division of opinion. The SEC, sophisticated users, and half the influential accounting firms demanded replacement-cost or current-cost information. The majority of issuers and half the accounting firms favored GPP (constant dollar) disclosures. The majority of the FASB (judging from outputs of the conceptual framework project to date) clearly preferred current-cost disclosures; however, that decision would have alienated half the Board's constituency at the worst of all possible times. Also, the Board's ongoing battle with the SEC concerning reserve-recognition accounting for the oil and gas industry had to be circumvented (accomplished by exemption of the industry from the current-cost disclosures). Consequently, *Statement No. 33* was structured to appease rather than decide.

Defects. The disclosures required by *Statement No. 33* suffer from all the deficiencies of GPP and current-cost reporting cited previously in this book. The quantity of data to be reported has been reduced to minimize complexity; the quality of the information, however, has not been improved.

The FASB admits that the price-level jargon amassed and used in the *Statement* calls for a "mammoth educational effort." Most readers will agree that the requirements are not simple, cost-effective, or understandable—the avowed objectives.

Two telling faults exist. Most important, the disclosures address only the adverse effects of changing prices. The beneficial aspects are commingled or ignored entirely—such as increases in selling prices, gearing, and others cited earlier in this book. Second, the FASB has belatedly recognized that the macro-statistics in consolidated statements conceal more than they reveal, and has required segmented reportings via *FASB-14*. The consolidated disclosures *required* by *Statement No. 33* are even more aggregative in character—segmented presentations are merely *encouraged.*

Potential Benefits. The aggregative disclosures are, in themselves, sufficiently innocuous that little harm should result. Moreover, the fact that the FASB reneged on making a decision, and the relegation of the disclosures to supplementary sections of financial reports have, at least for the present, protected the historical cost framework.

Another benefit, certainly, is FASB recognition (although belated) that changing price-levels affect different firms in different ways. Normative disclosure methods are finally being recognized as suspect. It remains to be seen, however, whether the advisory group established to develop additional modes of explanatory disclosures (paragraph 70) will address the problems of all firms, or only those industries having the greatest clout (such as the 7 sectors given special consideration by the FASB prior to issuance of the *Statement*).

The benefit possessing the greatest *potential* value concerns the FASB's emphasis upon *explanations* of the real effects of changing price-levels upon reporting firms (paragraphs 2, 3, 14, 15, 27, 31, 34, 37, 38, and 70). On the surface, these calls for explanations finally represent movements in the direction suggested within this book. However, it remains to be seen whether the FASB really means what it has said (and the author has grave doubts), or if the FASB's words prove to be mere window-dressings offered as appeasements.

A SUGGESTION FOR THE BUSINESS COMMUNITY

The business community should consider itself fortunate—it has really been given two choices.

On the one hand, the business community, as issuers of financial reports, can choose to ridicule *Statement No. 33* as useless without furnishing alternative information considered to be more meaningful—as happened with *ASR-190*. In that case, we accountants (manifested by the FASB) will gladly fill the void and foul up the language of business with more normative measures that produce economic nonsense.

Or, the business sectors can realize that the language of business is *their* language. As such, it is much too important to be left to the fiat of accountants alone. Business can force the FASB to stand behind the rhetoric dealing with alternative explanations. Businessmen can develop and report explanations of the effects of changing prices that are meaningful for their particular firms and segments thereof.

The business community can pick up the gauntlet presented by *Statement No. 33*. It may well be the only such opportunity offered in the foreseeable future.

STATEMENT OF INCOME FROM CONTINUING
OPERATIONS ADJUSTED FOR CHANGING PRICES

For the Year Ended December 31, 1980

(In (000s) of Average 1980 Dollars)

Income from continuing operations, as reported in the income statement		$ 9,000
Adjustments to restate costs for the effect of general inflation		
Cost of goods sold	(7,384)	
Depreciation and amortization expense	(4,130)	(11,514)
Loss from continuing operations adjusted for general inflation		(2,514)
Adjustments to reflect the difference between general inflation and changes in specific prices (current costs)		
Cost of goods sold	(1,024)	
Depreciation and amortization expense	(5,370)	(6,394)
Loss from continuing operations adjusted for changes in specific prices		$(8,908)
Gain from decline in purchasing power of net amounts owed		$ 7,729
Increase in specific prices (current cost) of inventories and property, plant, and equipment held during the year*		$ 24,608
Effect of increase in general price level		18,959
Excess of increase in specific prices over increase in the general price level		$ 5,649

* At December 31, 1980 current cost of inventory was $65,700 and current cost of property, plant, and equipment, net of accumulated depreciation was $85,100.

Source: *Statement of Financial Accounting Standards No. 33,* "Financial Reporting and Changing Prices," September 1979, p. 32. Copyright by Financial Accounting Standards Board, High Ridge Park, Stamford, Connecticut 06905, U.S A. Reprinted with permission. Copies of the complete document are available from the FASB.

FIGURE 9-1

STATEMENT OF INCOME FROM CONTINUING OPERATIONS ADJUSTED FOR CHANGING PRICES
For the Year Ended December 31, 1980
(In (000s) of Dollars)

	As Reported in the Primary Statements	Adjusted for General Inflation	Adjusted for Changes in Specific Prices (Current Costs)
Net sales and other operating revenues	$253,000	$253,000	$253,000
Cost of goods sold	197,000	204,384	205,408
Depreciation and amortization expense	10,000	14,130	19,500
Other operating expense	20,835	20,835	20,835
Interest expense	7,165	7,165	7,165
Provision for income taxes	9,000	9,000	9,000
	244,000	255,514	261,908
Income (loss) from continuing operations	$ 9,000	$(2,514)	$(8,908)
Gain from decline in purchasing power of net amounts owed		$ 7,729	$ 7,729
Increase in specific prices (current cost) of inventories and property, plant, and equipment held during the year*			$ 24,608
Effect of increase in general price level			18,959
Excess of increase in specific prices over increase in the general price level			$ 5,649

* At December 31, 1980 current cost of inventory was $65,700 and current cost of property, plant, and equipment, net of accumulated depreciation was $85,100.

Source: *Statement of Financial Accounting Standards No. 33,* "Financial Reporting and Changing Prices," September 1979, p. 33. Copyright by Financial Accounting Standards Board, High Ridge Park, Stamford, Connecticut 06905, U.S.A. Reprinted with permission. Copies of the completed document are available from the FASB.

FIGURE 9-2

FIVE-YEAR COMPARISON OF SELECTED
SUPPLEMENTARY FINANCIAL DATA ADJUSTED FOR EFFECTS OF CHANGING PRICES

(In (000s) of Average 1980 Dollars)

	Years Ended December 31,				
	1976	1977	1978	1979	1980
Net sales and other operating revenues	265,000	235,000	240,000	237,063	253,000
Historical cost information adjusted for general inflation					
Income (loss) from continuing operations				(2,761)	(2,514)
Income (loss) from continuing operations per common share				$ (1.91)	$ (1.68)
Net assets at year-end				55,518	57,733
Current cost information					
Income (loss) from continuing operations				(4,125)	(8,908)
Income (loss) from continuing operations per common share				$ (2.75)	$ (5.94)
Excess of increase in specific prices over increase in the general price level				2,292	5,649
Net assets at year-end				79,996	81,466
Gain from decline in purchasing power of net amounts owed				7,027	7,729
Cash dividends declared per common share	$ 2.59	$ 2.43	$ 2.26	$ 2.16	$ 2.00
Market price per common share at year-end	$ 32	$ 31	$ 43	$ 39	$ 35
Average consumer price index	170.5	181.5	195.4	205.0	220.9

FIGURE 9-3

Source: *Statement of Financial Accounting Standards No. 33,* "Financial Reporting and Changing Prices," September 1979, p. 34. Copyright by Financial Accounting Standards Board, High Ridge Park, Stamford, Connecticut 06905, U.S.A. Reprinted with permission. Copies of the completed document are available from the FASB.

GENERAL BIBLIOGRAPHY

Accounting Research Division. *Accounting Research Study No. 6.*: "Reporting the Financial Effects of Price-Level Changes." New York: American Institute of Certified Public Accountants, 1963.

Accounting Standards Committee. *Inflation Accounting–An Interim Recommendation by the Accounting Standards Committee.* London: Institute of Chartered Accountants in England and Wales, 1977.

American Institute of Certified Public Accountants. *Accounting Research and Terminology Bulletins,* Final Edition. New York: AICPA, 1961.

——. *The Accounting Responses to Changing Prices: Experimentation with Four Models.* New York: AICPA, 1979

Arthur Andersen & Co. *Accounting Standards for Business Enterprises Throughout the World.* Chicago: 1974.

——. *The Brazilian Method of Indexing and Accounting for Inflation.* May 1975.

——. *Client Inflation Clinic.* A Report on Inflation and Accounting for Inflation in Europe. September 1975.

——. *Disclosure of Replacement Cost Data–Illustrations and Analysis.* May 1977.

Andrews, Wesley T., and Smith, Charles A. "A Role for Financial Accounting in National Economic Planning in the United States." *International Journal of Accounting,* Fall 1976, pp. 133–145.

Anthony, Robert N. "A Case for Historical Costs." *Harvard Business Review,* November-December 1976, pp. 69–79.

Arrow, Kenneth J. "Limited Knowledge and Economic Analysis." *American Economic Review,* March 1974, pp. 1-10.

Auditing Standards Board. *Statement on Auditing Standards No. 23*: "Analytical Review Procedures." New York: American Institue of Certified Public Accountants, October 1978.

Backer, Morton. *Current Value Accounting.* New York: Financial Executives Institute, 1973.

——. "A Model for Current Value Reporting," *The CPA Journal,* February 1974, pp. 27–33.

——. "Valuation Reporting in the Netherlands: A Real-Life Example." *Financial Executive,* January 1973, pp. 40–42, *passim.*

Basu, S. *Inflation Accounting, Capital Market Efficiency and Security Prices.* Hamilton, Ontario: Society of Management Accountants of Canada, September, 1977.

——, and Hanna, J. R. *Inflation Accounting: Alternatives, Implementation Issues and Some Empirical Evidence.* Hamilton, Ontario: Society of Management Accountants of Canada, 1975.

Bauer, John. "Renewal Costs and Business Profits in Relation to Rising Costs." *Journal of Accountancy,* December 1919, pp. 413–419.

Biegler, John C. "Common Sense Accounting for Inflation." *Financial Executive,* December 1977, pp. 32–38.

Black, Stephen F., and Koch, Albert A. "Replacement Cost–Charting the Uncharted Sea." *Journal of Accountancy,* November 1976, pp. 72–76.

Burton, John C. "Financial Reporting in an Age of Inflation." *Journal of Accountancy,* February 1975, pp. 68–71.

Canadian Institute of Chartered Accountants. Accounting Research Committee, Discussion Paper. *Current Value Accounting.* Toronto: 1976.

Chambers, Raymond J. *Accounting, Evaluation and Economic Behavior.* Englewood Cliffs, N.J.: Prentice-Hall, 1966.

——. "NOD, COG, PuPu: See How Inflation Teases?" *Journal of Accountancy,* September 1975, pp. 56–62.

Chippendale, Warren, and Defliese, Philip L. (eds.). *Current Value Accounting.* New York: AMACOM, A Division of American Management Association, 1977.

Commission on Auditors' Responsibilities. *Report, Conclusions, and Recommendations.* New York: 1978.

Cowan, Tom K. "Current Replacement Value Accounting: Not a Dead End." *Journal of Accountancy,* June 1976, pp. 83–86.

Current Replacement Cost: An International Perspective. A Symposium Presented by the Department of Accounting, Oklahoma State University (Stillwater). Lecture by Jan Klaasen (Netherlands) and panel discussion of CRVA methods of the U.K., Netherlands, and Germany. Stillwater, Okla.: undtd., 21 pp.

Davidson, Sidney, and Weil, Roman L. "Inflation Accounting: The SEC Proposal for Replacement Cost Disclosures." *Financial Analysts Journal,* March-April 1976, pp. 57–66.

Defliese, Philip L. "Inflation Accounting: Pursuing the Elusive." *Journal of Accountancy,* May 1979, pp. 50, 52, 54, 58–63.

——. "The Search for a New Conceptual Framework of Accounting." *Journal of Accountancy,* July 1977, pp. 59–67.

Edwards, Edgar O. "The State of Current Value Accounting." *Accounting Review,* April 1975, pp. 235–245.

——, and Bell, Philip W. *The Theory and Measurement of Business Income.* Los Angeles: University of California Press, 1961.

Ernst & Ernst. *Accounting Under Inflationary Conditions.* Cleveland: 1976, Retrieval No. 38474.

——. *Conceptual Framework–Our Analysis and Response.* June 1977. Retrieval No. 38608.

——. *SEC Replacement Cost—Requirements and Implementation Guidance.* January 1977. Retrieval No. 38555.

Fabricant, Solomon. "Inflation and Current Accounting Practice: An Economist's View." *Journal of Accountancy,* December 1971, pp. 39–44.

Financial Accounting Standards Board. *Conceptual Framework for Financial Accounting and Reporting.* Discussion Memorandum. Stamford, Conn.: FASB, December 2, 1976.

——. *Constant Dollar Accounting.* Exposure Draft. March 2, 1979.

——. *Field Tests of Financial Reporting in Units of General Purchasing Power.* Research Report. May 1977.

——. *Financial Reporting and Changing Prices.* Exposure Draft. December 28, 1978.

——. *Financial Reporting in Units of General Purchasing Power.* Exposure Draft, December 31, 1974.

——. *Statement of Financial Accounting Concepts No. 1.* "Objectives of Financial Reporting by Business Enterprises." November 1978.

——. *Statement of Financial Accounting Standards No. 14.* "Financial Reporting for Segments of a Business Enterprise." December 1976.

Flynn, Thomas D. "Why We Should Account for Inflation." *Harvard Business Review,* September-October 1977, pp. 145–157.

Frank, J. W.; Kealey, T. F., and Silverman, G. W. *Effects and Significance of Replacement Cost Disclosure.* New York: Financial Executives Research Foundation, 1978.

Friedman, Irving S. *Inflation: A World-Wide Disaster.* Boston: Houghton Mifflin, 1973.

Friedman, Milton. "Monetary Correction," in Herbert Giersch, et al. *Essays on Inflation and Indexation.* Washington, D.C.: American Enterprise Institute for Public Policy Research, 1974, pp. 25–61.

Gay, William C., Jr. "Inflation, Indexation, and the Violation of Human Rights." Price Waterhouse *Review,* 1978, No. 2, pp. 20, 22–29.

Giersch, Herbert. "Index Clauses and the Fight Against Inflation," in Herbert Giersch, et al., *Essays on Inflation and Indexation.* Washington D.C.: American Enterprise Institute for Public Policy Research, 1974, pp. 1–23.

Gill, Charles W., and Moser, S. Thomas. "Inflation Accounting at the Crossroads." *Journal of Accountancy,* January 1979, pp. 70–78.

Goudeket, A. "An Application of Replacement Value Theory," *Journal of Accountancy,* July 1960, pp. 37–47.

——. "How Inflation is Being Recognized in Financial Statements in the Netherlands." *Journal of Accountancy,* October 1952, pp. 448–452.

Grady, Paul. "Purchasing Power Accounting." Price Waterhouse *Review,* 1975, No. 3., pp. 2–4.

Hayes, Samuel L., III. "Capital Commitments and the High Cost of Money." *Harvard Business Review,* May-June 1977, pp. 155-161.

"How Expectations Defeat Economic Policy." *Business Week,* November 8, 1976, pp. 74, 76.

Inflation Accounting: Report of the Inflation Accounting Committee. F.E.P. Sandilands, chairman. London: Her Majesty's Stationery Office, September 1975.

Johnson, L. Todd, and Bell, Philip W. "Current Replacement Costs: A Qualified Opinion." *Journal of Accountancy,* November 1976, pp. 63-70.

Johnson, R. M. "Why a Tax-Based Incomes Policy Won't Work." *Challenge,* January 1978, pp. 3-4.

Kafka, Alexandre. "Indexing for Inflation in Brazil," in Herbert Giersch, et al. *Essays on Inflation and Indexation.* Washington, D.C.: American Enterprise Institute for Public Policy Research, 1974, pp. 87-98.

Kanaga, William S. "Inflation, Instability and Accounting." *Management Accounting,* March 1977, pp. 15-18, 68.

Large, Arlen J. "U.S. Debt Costs Now Bigger than GM's Sales." *Wall Street Journal,* January 21, 1977, p. 8.

Lavely, Joseph A. "Inflation: Does the Firm Benefit?" *Management Accounting,* June 1975, pp. 16-18.

Leontief, Wassily W. *National Economic Planning.* Second Annual Distinguished Guest Lecture Program. Saint Louis: Saint Louis University School of Business and Administration, April 23, 1976.

——. "What an Economic Planning Board Should Do." *Challenge,* July-August 1974, pp. 35-40.

Macharzina, Klaus R. "The Impact of Inflation on German Accounting: Theoretical Background and Professional Issues," in V. K. Zimmerman (ed.) *The Impact of Inflation on Accounting: A Global View.* Urbana, Ill.: University of Illinois, 1979, pp. 225-240.

May, George O. *Business Income and Price Levels.* New York: American Institute of Accountants, 1949.

McCosh, Andrew M. "Implications of Sandilands for non-U.K. Accountants." *Journal of Accountancy,* March 1976, pp. 42-50.

McDougall, Duncan C. "The Corporate 'Ratchet Effect' on Spiraling Inflation." *Harvard Business Review,* November-December 1978, pp. 12, 16, 20.

Meltzer, Allan. "It Takes Long-Range Planning to Whip Inflation." *Fortune,* December 1977, pp. 96-100, 104, 106.

Middleditch, Livingston, Jr. "Should Accounts Reflect the Changing Value of the Dollar?" *Journal of Accountancy,* February 1918, pp. 114-120.

Miller, Elwood L. "What's Wrong with Price-Level Accounting." *Harvard Business Review,* November-December 1978, pp. 111-118.

Neal, Alfred C. "The Immolation of Business Capital." *Harvard Business Review,* March-April 1978, pp. 75–82.

Oppenheimer, Ernest J. *The Inflation Swindle.* Englewood Cliffs, N.J.: Prentice-Hall, 1977.

Paton, W. A. "Depreciation, Appreciation, and Productive Capacity." *Journal of Accountancy,* July 1920, pp. 1–11.

Pechman, Joseph A. "Can Tax-Based Incomes Policies Work?" *Challenge,* November-December 1978, pp. 51–52.

Pyhrr, Peter A. "Zero-Base Budgeting." *Harvard Business Review,* November-December 1970, pp. 111–121.

Raymond, Jack. "Growing Threat of Our Military-Industrial Complex." *Harvard Business Review,* May-June 1968, pp. 53–64.

Revsine, Lawrence. *Replacement Cost Accounting.* Englewood Cliffs, N.J.: Prentice-Hall, 1973.

——, and Thies, James B. "Price Level Adjusted Replacement Cost Data." *Journal of Accountancy,* May 1977, pp. 71–75.

——, and Weygandt, Jerry J. "Accounting for Inflation: the Controversy." *Journal of Accountancy,* October 1974, pp. 72–78.

Rosenfield, Paul. "The Confusion Between General Price-Level Restatement and Current Value Accounting." *Journal of Accountancy,* October 1972, pp. 63–68.

——. "Current Replacement Value Accounting–A Dead End." *Journal of Accountancy,* September 1975, pp. 63–73.

——. "GPP Accounting–Relevance and Interpretability." *Journal of Accountancy,* August 1975, pp. 52–59.

Savoie, Leonard M. "Price Level Accounting, Practical Politics, and Tax Relief." *Management Accounting,* January 1977, pp. 15–18.

Schiff, Michael. "Depreciation Short Fall: Fact or Fiction?" *Journal of Accountancy,* March 1977, pp. 40–42.

Scott, George M. *Research Study on Current-Value Accounting Measurements and Utility.* New York: Touche Ross Foundation, 1978.

Securities and Exchange Commission. *Accounting Series Release No. 190:* "Notice of Adoption of Amendments to Regulation S-X Requiring Disclosure of Certain Replacement Cost Data." March 23, 1976.

Seed, Allen H., III. *Inflation: Its Impact on Financial Reporting and Decision Making.* New York: Financial Executive Research Foundation, 1978.

Solow, Robert M. "The Economics of Resources or the Resources of Economics." *American Economic Review,* May 1974, pp. 1–14.

Sprouse, Robert T. "Inflation: Symptom or Disease?" in V. K. Zimmerman (ed.) *The Impact of Inflation on Accounting: A Global View.* Urbana, Ill.: University of Illinois, 1979, pp. 1–19.

Stamp, Edward, and Mason, Alister K. "Current Cost Accounting: British Panacea or Quagmire?" *Journal of Accountancy,* April 1977, pp. 66–73.

Sterling, Robert R. "Relevant Financial Reporting in an Age of Price Changes." *Journal of Accountancy,* February 1975, pp. 42–51.

——. *Theory of the Measurement of Enterprise Income.* Lawrence, Kans.: University Press of Kansas, 1970.

Sweeney, Henry W. *Stabilized Accounting.* New York: Harper & Brothers, 1936.

Terborgh, George. *Memorandum,* Machinery and Allied Products Institute: "Inflation and Profits." Washington, D.C.: January, 1974. Revised seven times, latest revision, April 1979.

Touche Ross & Co. *Economic Reality in Financial Reporting.* New York: 1975.

Unger, Frank J. "Indexing the Progressive Tax System." *Management Accounting,* October 1978, pp. 55–57.

Vancil, Richard F. "Inflation Accounting–The Great Controversy." *Harvard Business Review,* March-April 1976, pp. 58–67.

Williams, Harold M. "Inflation, Corporate Financial Reporting and Economic Reality." *Journal of Accountancy,* March 1978, pp. 79–85.

Arthur Young and Company. *Disclosing Replacement Cost Data.* New York: 1977.

Zimmerman, V. K. (ed). *The Impact of Inflation on Accounting: A Global View.* Urbana, Ill.: Center for International Education and Research in Accounting, Department of Accountancy, University of Illinois, 1979.

Index

Index

accountancy, profession of, 30, 35, 179
  as business advocate, 35, 41, 139
  as independent discipline, 30, 65
  insular attitude of, 202
  as a political arena, 41
  maturity of, 64, 154–155
accounting alternatives, 92
  absence of guidelines, 41, 43, 180
  need for guidelines, 196
  reduction of, 77
accounting constraints, 38–39, 40, 92
accounting frameworks, 24
  common body of knowledge, 31, 45n
  eclectic nature of, 40
  harmonization of, 77, 180
  legal influences on, 25–26
  monolithic structure of, 42
  as ways of thinking, 24
accounting models, field tests of, 140
Accounting Principles Board (APB), 41, 59, 62
  faults of, 41
  Statement No. 3, 62
Accounting Research Bulletins (AICPA):
  No. 33, 59, 182
  No. 43, 60
Accounting Research Study No. 6, 60–62
accounting roles, 25
  as language of business, 25, 179
  in social reform, 139
Accounting Series Release No. 190 (SEC),

62, 86, 120. *See also* Securities and Exchange Commission
  auditor association, 145, 153
  compared with FASB requirements, 148–149
  disclosures required, 144
  as experiment, 63, 132, 144, 204
  and FASB *Statement No. 33*, 207
  management explanations, 147, 183
  straight-line depreciation use, 144
accounting standard-setting, 42–43
  harmonization of, 76
Accounting Standards Committee (UK), 84, 86
  composition of, 84, 96n
  Hyde proposals, 86, 100–107
Accounting Standards Steering Committee (UK), 84, 86
  Exposure Drafts of:
    ED-8, 84
    ED-18, 86
  Provisional Statement of Standard Accounting Practice No. 7, 85, 88
accounting systems, types of, 92
American Accounting Association (AAA), 60
American Institute of Accountants (AIA), 59
American Institute of Certified Public Accountants (AICPA), 140, 201, 203
  and auditor attestations, 153–154, 203

223